IT'S NOT ROCKET
SCIENCE
It's All about Faith

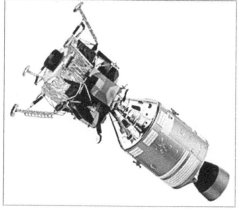

Robert Nance

ISBN 978-1-64140-255-2 (paperback)
ISBN 978-1-64140-257-6 (hardcover)
ISBN 978-1-64140-256-9 (digital)

Christian Faith Publishing, Inc.
832 Park Avenue
Meadville, PA 16335
www.christianfaithpublishing.com

Printed in the United States of America

CONTENTS

FOREWORD

The Lord has blessed me my entire life even though I haven't always been faithful. This book was written to help the reader realize that trusting in our ways will never work out well without the Lord guiding us through life. We tend to tell the Lord how to help us. We are telling the Creator of the Universe what our needs are when He already knows those needs. The Lord wants us to turn our situations over to Him.

When I heard President John Kennedy challenge the nation in 1962 to land a man on the moon and return him safely before the end of the decade, I knew that I wanted to be a part of that mission. I remember that when President Kennedy made that speech, we hadn't even put the first man in orbit yet. At age sixteen, I set my sights on sitting on the console in Mission Control when man first set foot on the moon. My journey was totally improbable, but for the Lord, it was all about whether I was going to give my dreams to Him or whether I was going to try to "do it my way". The journey was just as amazing for our country as it was for me.

During my days at NASA, it was inspirational to see how the Lord was working through faithful men to turn difficult situations into successes. I am honored to be able to share the details of that first landing on the moon and the inside story within Mission Control. Our flight director, Gene Kranz, famously said that getting the Apollo 13 astronauts back safely was "our finest hour." Many people don't realize just how close we came to losing the crew. Time after time, not only did the flight controllers pray but the whole world prayed for the crew as well. It was a time when the whole world came together like no other time in human history.

Sharing my experiences is designed to help the reader realize that we should not take so long to turn to the Lord with every challenge that they have in their lives. After the space program and as an owner of a business, I was constantly making decisions without asking the Lord for guidance. So very often, I trusted suppliers and others to guide me. I learned a big lesson that business people are going to look out for themselves. They might tell you they want to help you, but when the chips are down, the only question they will ask is, "What have you done for me lately?" It doesn't matter how many years you have been their biggest customer; if you don't do what they want you to do, they turn on you. They will push you to over expand and make promises that they can't or won't keep. Way too many times, I listened to suppliers without asking the Lord for guidance. It is amazing if you give your situation to the Lord, he will answer. Sometimes it does take time and sometimes the answer is "no." Sometimes just waiting for an answer is the right thing to do so you don't jump into something that you shouldn't be doing in the first place.

Trusting in the Lord to help you through tough business decisions is one thing, but what do you do when one of your children faces a life critical disease that can only be cured by having a liver transplant? Our son, Rob, contracted a rare autoimmune disease while serving at the Pentagon when he was in the Air Force. We prayed year after year for specific things to happen. We prayed for this test to be good, or this medicine to do better than the last one, but we failed to do what Jesus told us to do. Remember the Lord's Prayer: "Thy will be done." The Creator of the Universe does not need instructions from us. Things had to get bad to the point that Rob got so sick that they took him off the transplant list, for us to give the entire situation to the Lord. Once we gave it to the Lord, things happened that could only be described as miraculous. Share our journey of how the Lord wove people and events together in a way only the Lord could do.

We are totally blessed. Too many people miss the beauty that the Lord puts right in front of them. Try just sitting out in a park, looking at a tree and the small animals going about their business.

The simplest things that God has given us are the most enchanting. Think of flowers, snow, ocean waves, and green grass. There is nothing like them in the universe. Go outside on a clear night away from city lights and spend thirty minutes staring at the stars in the sky. It will put your troubles into perspective.

It was amazing to see all the beauty that the Lord had made for us to enjoy. It makes no sense for trees to turn into beautiful colors in the fall. There is seemingly no advantage to the trees to produce beautiful leaves. They exist to show God's glory, and He clearly put them here for us to enjoy. Because we spend so much time thinking about material things, we can miss all the divinely created beauty that surrounds us.

The Creator of the Universe wants to bless you, but you have to realize that He loves you. The Lord blesses us each day, and most of the time, we totally miss it. We are too busy trying to do things our way.

Please share my journey as we unlock the plan that God has for you. Use my mistakes and victories to help you mold your life to put your faith in the Lord.

Prayer to the Rescue!

Growing up near Richmond, Virginia, was as normal as life could be. Normal during my childhood was like the old TV series, *Father Knows Best*. My parents worked hard to instill a great work ethic and a life based on a relationship with a loving God. Neither of them finished high school, and they wanted my brother and me to not only finish High School but also to be able to get a college education. They were devoted to making this a reality. I am eternally grateful for that. I am sure my brother feels the same.

Thanks to my parents, I got to live my life as a true Rocket Scientist for NASA. I will get to that later, but let me tell you exactly where the journey with my Lord really began in earnest.

Growing up in Bon Air, Virginia, a quaint little town southwest of Richmond, we attended the local Baptist Church. My father had attended the first worship service ever held for what would become Bon Air Baptist Church. When you are young, you learn that since your parents believe in Jesus, that you should also. During Vacation Bible School at age eleven, I realized that I wanted to have the same relationship that my parents had with the Lord.

A couple of years later, we moved to Southampton, a little closer to Richmond, and we joined Southampton Baptist Church. My relationship began to grow with the Lord, but it was a process. When a person becomes a Christian, they are not instantaneously changed, but it is the beginning of a process that lasts one's whole life. As a teenager, I really didn't understand that, but the Lord was working on me just the same. I learned that I wanted God in my life, but I had not learned to lean on Him. That is something that takes time and the Holy Spirit working in our lives.

I had heard President Kennedy give his famous speech in which he said he wanted us to land a man on the moon by the end of the decade of the 1960s. From the moment that I heard that speech, I knew that I wanted to a part of that. What I didn't know was that the Lord was already working to make that happen. I worked hard and made good grades in school, worked part time from the time I was sixteen years old, and with the help of friends, started the Huguenot Rocket Society. I thought I was doing all the things necessary to further my dream of being part of landing a man on the moon by the end of the decade. What I didn't realize was that I was going to need the Lord's help to make that a reality.

My first faith lesson occurred when I was about seventeen years old. Southampton Baptist Church had a program to involve the youth in running the church one Sunday a year to help them use their talents to become active in the church. Each major position in the church would have a young person assume the duties for that one day, usually during the month of February. Students would teach Sunday school lessons, count offerings, sing in the choir, and, in general, fill the positions on a typical Sunday. Of course, all of this would be done under the supervision of the normal staff.

I am not sure how it happened, but I was selected to give the worship service message on that Sunday morning. As a young, confident person, it didn't seem to be an extremely hard task. I had several weeks to prepare, so I wasn't that worried that I could do a reasonably good job. With one week to go, I started reading my Bible for ideas on what I was going to talk about. I really looked for something about how youth should honor the Lord. Everything that I found just didn't seem right. My mother started questioning me concerning my topic. I told her that I had several ideas and was trying to decide which I was going to use. I didn't let on that I was clueless.

As the week went on, the message seemed to elude me more and more. Several messages were started and ended up in the trash can.

School and work kept me busy that final week, and then Saturday night arrived and still no message. I had started a message, but nothing was working. My parents went to bed asking how it was going. I said that I was working on it and would have it finished soon. I didn't want them to worry, but I was really worried.

Sometime after midnight, I laid my head on my desk in my room and felt as if I were a total failure and that I would never be able to come up with a message for the service that was less than eleven hours away. I don't remember ever feeling lower than how I felt at that moment. I had tears running down my cheeks. Finally, in total desperation, I walked over to my bed and knelt down beside the bed and prayed to God for help. I outlined how hard I had worked to bring a good message on Sunday and just hadn't been able to come up with anything. I pleaded for the Lord to help me. At that very moment, something astonishing happened and the Lord spoke to me. I can only explain it in these simple terms, the Lord spoke like it was a computer download. It wasn't like spoken words but an instantaneous download. The message was extremely simple. "Finally, you got it." The really strange thing is that with the words came an instantaneous understanding of what the Lord meant. What He wanted me to talk about was that when things get rough in our lives, we need to turn to Him, not to our own understanding.

I thanked the Lord for answered prayers and reached for a three-by-five index card on my desk and outlined the talk I would give in a few hours. There were but five points on the index card. I outlined how I had struggled with preparing for the lesson, how I almost gave up in despair, and then how it was only when I gave my problem to the Lord in knee-bending prayer that the Lord answered. I read several scriptures and shared with the congregation that we all need to give our problems to the Lord in prayer and not try to fix things ourselves. I don't remember the two scriptures that I used that day but two come to mind. "I can do everything through Him who gives me strength" (Phil. 4:13) and "Be joyful always; pray continually; give thanks in all circumstances, for this is God's will for you in Christ Jesus" (1 Thess. 5:16–18). I am fairly certain the second verse is one I used during the message, since I have that verse written on a three-by-five card stuck in my Bible as I write this.

The Lord used this time to show me what kind of relationship He wanted to have with me. He gave me a great blessing. It is a shame that He would have to teach me this lesson over and over again as I have gone through my life. It is obvious that even today, I am a work in progress.

It was the first time in my life that I would realize that what God does in our lives isn't always about us. God uses us to help others. I have told several Bible study classes that if you feel like you are trying to do things right with God and you suddenly find yourself in the hospital, it might not be about you at all. God may have so much faith in you that He wants you to witness to someone, a doctor, a nurse, or someone else. We tend to think everything that happens to us is about us, but the Lord will use you and your experiences to help others.

2

"Father Knows Best"—After Meeting Dean Griffin

On May 25, 1962, President Kennedy delivered a speech before a joint session of Congress and outlined a vision for surpassing the Soviets in space: "First, I believe that this nation should commit itself to achieving the goal, before this decade is out, of landing a man on the moon and returning him safely to earth." He followed it up on September 12, 1962, with a speech to a crowd of 35,000 people in the football stadium at Rice University in Houston, Texas:

> But why, some say, the moon? Why choose this as our goal? And they may well ask, why climb the highest mountain? Why, 35 years ago, fly the Atlantic? Why does Rice play Texas? We choose to go to the moon in this decade and do the other things, not because they are easy, but because they are hard, because the goal will serve to organize and measure the best of our energies and skills, because the challenge is one that we are willing to accept, one we are unwilling to postpone, and one which we intend to win, and the others, too.

In eleventh grade in May 1962, when President Kennedy challenged the country to best the Russians by landing a man on the moon before 1970 and returning him safely to the earth, I immedi-

13

ately knew that I wanted to be a part of that great adventure. Up until then, I wasn't sure about where I wanted to go to school or what degree was in store for me. The speech at Rice University served to solidify my desire to be a "Rocket Scientist." The summer of 1962, a group of friends and I formed the "Huguenot Rocket Society" and started building small rockets; we were reaching for the stars. We would launch our rockets from a dairy farm that was east of Richmond. One of the guys had a relative that owned the farm. The cows stayed away from us for obvious reasons. We got the rockets high enough that we had helicopters come and check us out. It seems that we were a little too close to

President Kennedy announcing that he wanted to set the goal of going to the Moon and returning safely before the end of the decade.

Richmond's main airport. We solved this problem by moving our operations into the country, west of Richmond, in Powhatan County.

It is important to remember that there was no Internet or Google to get our information about space and rocketry. When we were in school, our best source of information was from a set of encyclopedias. The problem with encyclopedias was that they were always "out-of-date" even with annual supplements. Today we just go to free "up-to-date" encyclopedias like Wikipedia online to gather information about a subject. When Wikipedia was formally launched on January 15, 2001, written encyclopedias began to disappear, freeing up lots of space in home bookshelves throughout the world. In 1962, we got our information about space from the newspapers, Popular Science magazine, Popular Mechanics magazine, and what little TV news there was. There was no cable TV, no CNN, or news channel on TV. There was only NBC, ABC, and CBS evening news.

The space race was just beginning. The Soviets had launched Yuri Gagarin on April 12, 1961, in Vostok 1 to be the first man to orbit the earth. He only orbited the earth one time and ejected with a parachute at 23,000 feet to land, separately, from his spacecraft. His flight lasted 1 hour and 48 minutes. The United States answered with Astronaut Alan Shepard's suborbital flight on May 5, 1961, which lasted 15 minutes and 22 seconds and did not orbit the earth. The third space mission was the suborbital flight of Astronaut Gus Grissom on July 21, 1961; that lasted 15 minutes and 37 seconds. Next, the Soviets answered with their second orbital flight of Vostok 2 on August 6, 1961. It carried Cosmonaut Gherman Titov into orbit for a full day for a total mission time of 25 hours and 18 minutes. Six months later, on February 20, 1962, the United States finally sent its first Astronaut into orbit with the flight of Friendship 7, carrying John Glenn around the earth for three orbits totaling 4 hours, 55 minutes, and 23 seconds. This was a tremendous feat considering the fact that the Mercury spacecraft weighed only about 4,000 pounds compared to the Soviet Vostok, which weighed over 10,000 pounds. The day before President Kennedy made his famous speech outlining his goal of landing a man on the moon before 1970 and returning him safely to earth, Astronaut Scott Carpenter was launched into orbit in the Aurora 7 spacecraft and orbited the earth three times for a total time of 4 hours, 56 minutes, and 5 seconds.

This timeline now brings us to President Kennedy's 1962 speech outlining his goal of landing on the moon. When he gave that speech, the Soviets had a total time in space of 1626 minutes compared to a total time in space for the United States of 622 minutes. The Soviets were clearly winning the space race, flying a spacecraft that was two and a half times bigger and flying almost three times longer in space. America needed to hear the president's message of hope and determination; however, just when things started to look up, the space race got a lot tougher. On August 11, 1962, the Russians launched Vostok 3, carrying Cosmonaut Andriyan Nikolayev who would orbit for almost four days. Much to the surprise of everyone, the Russians launched Vostok 4 on August 12 (the next day), carrying Cosmonaut Pavel Popovich who would orbit for almost three days. At one point, they would come within a few kilometers of each other, demonstrating a successful first attempt at rendezvous in orbit. The ability to launch and control two spacecraft in orbit and rendezvous put the Soviets far ahead of the United States.

Little did the Soviets know that their timing was perfect to excite the United States into accepting the challenge! Less than a month later, the president made his famous speech in Houston, and the race to land on the moon was on its way.

With patriotism and determination, I decided that I wanted to be a part of landing man on the moon and returning him safely. At that time, we were only a few months away from the Cuban Missile Crisis in October 1962. It was a difficult time to be a senior in high school, but I had my eyes firmly on my goal. There were times in October 1962 that I wondered whether we would even have a world to leave to go to the moon. Those were really scary times for our nation.

My senior year in high school was filled with a part-time job, rocket society, SAT tests, and trying to figure out where and how I could go to college to achieve my goal of being part of the team that was going to land man on the moon. Mixed in with all of this was church, being editor of the high school newspaper, clubs, and dating. I had a lot on my plate, but that experience would serve me well in the future. I learned how to do a lot of things at one time, not always with the right priorities unfortunately.

My SAT scores came in well enough to get me in to about any engineering school I wanted. Based on what I could read at the time (remember that the sources were somewhat limited), it seemed that MIT was a great school for engineering. It was the first school I applied to in late 1962. When I was assigned to a local preselection advisor, he scheduled a meeting for early 1963. During our meeting, he looked over my grades and SAT scores and said that I would be accepted to MIT, but I would be in the lower third of the class and I would probably flunk out-talk about having your bubble burst. What he said next was clearly God at work in my life, whether I knew it or not. He said that I would be much better going to a great engineering school like Georgia Tech. He said that MIT was very expensive, and that Georgia Tech was a great school and wouldn't cost as much. Other than the football team, I hadn't heard anything about Georgia Tech. I shared my dream of being a part of the space program with him and thought that MIT was the best road to that goal. I clearly remember that he mentioned that several of the astronauts were from Georgia Tech. I should note that at that time, there was actually only one astronaut from Georgia Tech and that was John Young. Little did I know how important John Young would be to my future with NASA.

At that time, the only way to learn about a particular college was to order a book from that school called the catalog that would outline the school, courses, degrees, expenses, and why you should select that school. There was no US News and World Report of best colleges to guide a high school senior to the best college for them. The next day, after meeting the advisor from MIT, I ordered my Georgia Tech Catalog. In the end, I applied to three schools, but only Georgia Tech had a dedicated Aerospace Engineering Department. The more I studied, the more that I knew that Georgia Tech would have been my best choice from the beginning, and the fact that it would cost half of what MIT would cost would turn out to be a blessing. God was at work in my life, but I just didn't realize it at the time.

I was accepted to all three schools at about the same time, so the next step was to convince my parents that I *needed* to go to Georgia Tech. My second choice school was Virginia Polytechnic Institute (known as Virginia Tech today). It was a great engineering school, and since it was an in-state school, it would cost about half of what Georgia Tech would cost. The problem was that there was no Aerospace Engineering Degree at Virginia Tech. The Aerospace Engineering department was a part of the Mechanical Engineering department at Virginia Tech. I felt that without an Aerospace Engineering degree, I would not be able to live my dream. My parents were great hardworking Christians, and they wanted me to be the first of our family to graduate from college. I had never had a good understanding of where our family was financially, but they had taught me that with hard work, anything was possible. I was already working part time while I was going to high school to save money for college. My dad said that they could pay for all my college education if I went to Virginia Tech, but they just couldn't afford the cost of my going to Georgia Tech. I told them that I would work summers and while at school if I could go to Georgia Tech. The deal was that I would work and pay half if I went to Georgia Tech. Student loans and scholarships did not exist at that time as they do today.

My parents were fairly skeptical about my going to Georgia Tech, but agreed to take me to see the campus to determine if I really wanted to go there. In early spring of 1963, we made a trip to Atlanta, Georgia, to see Georgia Tech for the first time. Georgia Tech was on the quarter system at that time, and we were arriving during their spring break, which occurred earlier than most other colleges. Fortunately, I did get to see the Aerospace Engineering department and the wind tunnel. An added bonus was a tour from some graduate students who were doing some testing on the wind tunnel. I remember walking back from the Aerospace Engineering building with my parents and taking a few pictures, when someone shouted, "Hello there." He introduced himself as Dean George Griffin. I did not know it, but Dean Griffin was known as "Mr. Georgia Tech." Dean Griffin went back to the Coach Heisman days (Coach Heisman is the coach that the Heisman Trophy is named for). When he asked how he could help us, my dad told him that I wanted to go to Georgia Tech and that we had come to see the campus, but he didn't know if the extra expense of going out of state was going to be worth it. I didn't know it then, but there wasn't a better person on the planet to answer that question than Dean Griffin.

Dean Griffin asked my dad to come into his office; he said that he would tell him why I should go to Georgia Tech. To this day, I don't know what Dean Griffin

Sitting next to Georgia Tech's Dean Griffin during a visit in 2000

said, but based on years of hearing his stories about Georgia Tech, I can only imagine that he filled my dad's head with wonderful stories about football, education, and successful alumni. All I know is that when my dad came out of Dean Griffin's office, I was going to Georgia Tech. Knowing what I know today, I should have dropped to my knees and thanked the Lord. Remember, we were on campus when the school was closed for spring break; Dean Griffin just happened to stop by his office to pick something up; we were just walking past Dean Griffin's building when he was exiting through the front door, and Dean Griffin was the best person in the world to tell my dad why I should go to Georgia Tech.

My years at Georgia Tech were great years. There was a lot of hard work. Meeting new lifelong friends and working toward my dream of helping land man on the moon were some of the great bonuses of life at Georgia Tech. On the other hand, it was a rough period for our country with President Kennedy being assassinated just three months after I started college. That event hit the country extremely hard and me, in particular, since I thought he was the reason that I was at Georgia Tech. Just like the rest of the country, I had to dig in hard with renewed determination to achieve that goal that he had set to reach the moon before 1970.

I was learning how to be an aerospace engineer with a great bunch of professors, many of whom were working on various aerospace programs at the time. I especially remember "Ace" Harper who taught aerodynamics; he was called away to help the FAA solve the problem involving several Boeing 727s that had been landing short of the runway. Three flights had crashed short in a period of three months in 1965. Professor Harper would come back from his testing and review those cases with us. He was just thinking out loud with us, but it gave a real world situation that helped us understand why we should be aerospace engineers. Even then, I remember thinking that I was glad I was getting this experience that I am not sure I would have gotten at any other school.

The main Aerospace Engineering building at Georgia Tech had a large wind tunnel in the middle of the building. When it was running, the entire building would shake and vibrate. Much of the wind tunnel testing for the Lockheed C5A was going on at the time, so this gave a new meaning to "rocking and rolling." It was clear that I was getting a great education at Georgia Tech even though the rest of the world in the 1960s seemed to be falling apart with the assassinations of Dr. Martin Luther King and Bobby Kennedy, the Vietnam War, riots, and the cold war. However, between school and working to pay my half of the cost of going to Georgia Tech, I didn't have a lot of time to worry about the rest of the world.

As busy as I was, I still felt a need to be involved with something other than school and work, but I didn't find what I was looking for at first. During my sophomore year, I was asked to visit Delta Upsilon Fraternity by a friend, Tommy Burson, whom I had met in my freshman year. I never thought that I would like a fraternity because, as a good Southern Baptist, I did not drink at all, and I thought fraternities were all about wild times and drinking. Tommy showed me that I had the wrong impression about fraternities, in general, and Delta Upsilon in particular. I found that fraternity life was just like a cross section of life. On Saturday nights, there were some students just blowing off steam, but the fraternity in general was about a group of students who were dedicated to helping each other grow. Fraternity students on the Georgia Tech campus had better grades on average than those students not in fraternities. Of course, there are some exceptions, and those are the ones that the public hears about. Brothers would help each other and if one brother was struggling with a class, there were brothers there to help. Being in a fraternity helped me return to going to church on a regular basis. It was only about a four-block walk to First Baptist Church on Peachtree Street.

I didn't know it, but joining Delta Upsilon would be another stepping stone in my quest to help man land on the moon before 1970. The Lord was guiding me toward my destiny.

3

From Race Cars to Planes to Spacecraft

Georgia Teach was challenging, but the work ethic that my parents had painstakingly instilled in me was beginning to pay dividends. Between school and work to pay for my half of school, I was extremely busy. When I entered my junior year, I began having mainly Aerospace Engineering classes, which required a lot more studying and lab time than the first two years. When freshmen start at Georgia Tech, they are told that one out of three would flunk out (where had I heard that before?), 25 percent would bail out, and the rest would take fourteen to fifteen quarters (four and three quarter years) to graduate. I was determined to beat those odds for two reasons. First, the plan to pay half of my college expense depended that I graduate on time—namely, in twelve quarters. More importantly, my dream of sitting on the console when we would land on the moon depended on my graduating on time. I loved my aerospace classes, but I found that I was doing a big juggling act. In spite of all these challenges, I was still able to maintain a B average, landing me in the upper third of my class.

I did a lot of photography work to help supplement my summer jobs to pay my half of college. I was a photo editor of the Georgia Tech Newspaper and did some work for various fraternities to make extra money. As photo editor of the newspaper and helping with the yearbook, I got access to the Georgia Tech darkroom. The darkroom had the latest equipment, and only two of us students got to use it—

the photo editor of the *Technique*, Georgia Tech's newspaper, and the photo editor of the *Blueprint*, Georgia Tech's yearbook. A real bonus was that the publication staff got great class registration time cards, and we could get our pick of classes. While on assignment for the *Technique*, I covered several NASCAR events in Atlanta. As a member of the press, I got a press pass, which was really great, allowing me to visit in the pits with the drivers and talk to the pit crews. Richard Petty was the reigning NASCAR champion at the time, and there was a big dispute about whether the HEMI engine that Chrysler was using in its race cars was legal. NASCAR, under pressure from Ford, outlawed the HEMI engine, so Richard Petty boycotted the NASCAR races for a period. He started running some drag races in his Barracuda HEMI. HEMI referred to the hemispherical heads on the big block engine. The HEMI engine is still sold today in Chrysler vehicles. There was a big local drag race in Dallas, Georgia, in the spring of 1965, and I went and covered the race. With my press pass, I got to talk to Petty's crew and spent a lot of time with Maurice Petty, who was Richard's brother and chief mechanic.

During one of the runs, Richard had a problem with his gears and asked if he could make a test run. It was all for show, since he was clearly faster than the local hero. There were fences on each side of the strip about forty feet from the strip that had two lanes for the two cars that would drag race. Richard was running on the right track, so I positioned myself about ten feet from the side, well inside the fence (thanks to the press pass) and about 150 feet from the start line. Richard started out really well with a lot of burning rubber, and I was taking pictures all

Richard Petty's "Hemi Barracuda" showing the steering link separating from the tie bar and the left wheel bowing out just before the car veered to the left into the crowd.

the time. When Richard got about fifty feet from me, the car swerved to his left (away from me) and then the car made a hard left turn right into the fence and crowd on the side of the track right opposite from my position. I was so shaken that I dropped my Nikon F camera to the ground. I still have that camera and it still has the dent. After the car flipped upside down into the crowd behind the fence, there were people lying all over the place. There was an ambulance and medical staff to help, so when I gathered myself together, I started taking pictures of the scene. I shot a whole roll of film (remember that we were twenty years before any type of digital photography). When I got to back to the darkroom and developed the pictures, I discovered that I had a picture showing the steering link between the steering wheel and the tie rod coming loose when Richard made his run. One photo showed the steering link loose and the left wheel bowing to the left. I have other pictures from the previous run showing it attached as it should be. At first, I was just excited about getting such a great picture, but then I remembered that one person died that day and seven people were seriously injured, including one person who was injured for life and would never walk again. Then it dawned on me that when Richard adjusted his steering to the left the moment after I took the picture, the car then turned into the crowd. If he had made a slight adjustment to the right, he would have run over me and then plowed into the crowd on the right side. The Lord was really keeping me safe that day.

We ran the picture in the next Friday's edition of the *Technique* as an exclusive, since the press was reporting that Richard lost control of the car. Richard had been saying all week that the car just didn't respond. Within a couple hours of the *Technique* hitting the stands, I had a call from the sports editor of *Atlanta Journal* asking if they could run my pictures and reference my story from the *Technique*. I said yes, so long as they gave me the byline. They ran it at the top of the page in the Sports Section of the *Atlanta Journal* that Sunday, and within hours, I began getting lots of phone calls. Chrysler called as well as someone from the Petty organization and lots of lawyers. All the lawyers and Chrysler wanted copies of all the pictures that I took that day. I didn't charge anything different than I ever charged for an eight by ten black and white photo—$10 a photo. With forty pictures taken that day, that means I got about $400 from each of the people wanting copies of all my pictures. I ended up making about $2,500 to $3,000 from that set of pictures. I had really started running way behind on my money for college because Georgia Tech had raised tuition about 35 percent from when I started, and that money was a real blessing. This sudden windfall of cash rescued me; I just wish it had not come at the expense of Richard Petty and those who were injured that day.

Much to my surprise, about two weeks after I sent the pictures to the folks at Chrysler, I got a call from the race division of Chrysler; they said that my pictures were much better than those they had been getting from their photographers, so they wanted me to cover races on the weekends. They would pay my way and pay my expenses, along with $10 a photo, plus I wouldn't even have to print the pictures. It was a rather lucrative offer for a cash-strapped college student, and I was tempted to take Chrysler up on their deal. As I considered if further though, I realize that I had a much bigger dream than growing rich through my photography. The console at NASA continued to beckon me. The moon landing preparations were moving ahead, and my personal mission was to sit at that console at that very moment. I realized that I could not travel to cover races on weekends and still earn high grades. Chrysler sent me a nice letter with sample pictures of what they were looking for, but tempting as it was, I had to decline. Looking back, this was one of the best decisions I made for my future. I can only imagine what a different course my life would have taken had I accepted their offer.

In the following months, I had something else that was competing for my attention. I became engaged to Patricia Dameron during the summer of 1966, between my junior and senior year at Georgia Tech. Pat and I had gone to high school together but had not dated at that time. I was the editor of the high school newspaper, and she was the editor of the yearbook. She was the competition in high school as we competed for money and resources for our publications. Pat was attending Longwood College in Farmville, Virginia, on her way to becoming an English teacher. We had started dating during our sophomore year when I was in Richmond for spring break. From the moment that we began dating, I knew she was the one. Pat was always supportive of my goals and aspirations. When the going got tough, Pat was there to pick me up. We couldn't afford long distance phone calls, so we wrote letters back and forth on a regular basis. I am sure that if I had a sweetheart in Atlanta, I would have never been able to stay on track with my ambitious plan to get to NASA. It was good that we had a long distance relationship. I still have her letters to me, and they are an inspiration to me today as much as they were at the time. I should mention that the cost of the postage on each of the letters at that time was five cents.

The harder I worked, the more I seemed to be able to take on. I was the treasurer of my fraternity, Delta Upsilon, in my junior year during tough financial times for the fraternity, but my experience in squeezing through college on a tight budget gave me insight into balancing the books. My primary objective was to get brothers to fess up and settle their debts because there were many brothers who left after graduation having not paid their room rent and fraternity dues. We planned many special events, including several big dances and other social events that the brothers who had graduated owing money could attend for free if they paid a percentage of their debt. We even rented Stone Mountain for a party on the top of the mountain at night when the only way to get to the party was with a gondola lift. By my senior year, we were on great financial footing, stronger than we had been in a long time.

I landed a great job that summer between my junior and senior years thanks to Mr. Claude P. Talley, my Sunday school teacher at Southampton Baptist Church. I had a summer job as an engineering assistant at Texaco Experiment, Inc. in Richmond. Today, that type of job would be called an Intern Position. I got my first exposure to real engineering work. In 1963, Mr. Talley had created the first use of composite high strength structures and had filed for a patent in 1965. Texaco Experiment had received a contract to produce structures for a tail of one of the Air Force jets. Jet fighters used a lot of fuel, and the Air Force was looking at ways to lighten the aircraft so they could carry more fuel and therefore increase their range. My job at Texaco Experiment was to help in the testing and manufacturing of devices where this type of construction could increase strength and reduce weight. I will quote from the patent (US3491055):

> This invention relates to high strength refractory filaments and composite structures comprising such filaments, and to methods and apparatus for making the filaments and composite structures, the terms filament and fiber being used herein to denote elongated elements of various cross-section shapes including ribbons.

It sounds technical, but the idea was to make ribbons of metal fibers that could be wound or laid in epoxy at different angles to achieve a particular strength. This way, the manufacturer could produce a part or panel that would the strong in the exact areas that they wanted it to be without carrying extra weight. Today, everything from Boeing 787s to baby strollers are made based on these types of composite structures.

Up to that time, the lab had just been producing small rectangular five-inch panels for testing, and Texaco Experiment wanted to produce some products that would demonstrate the possible uses of composite structures. The first assignment I was given was to design a large drum to produce the panels in various shapes in order to produce larger test articles. This process gave me real world experience in dealing with the Texaco Experiment manufacturing shop to go from engineering drawings to a finished product. Here I was in my white short-sleeve dress shirt with a tie on and dealing with the shop guys who were "salt of the earth" type of guys with white T-shirts and their pack of cigarettes rolled up in their shirt sleeves. Thank goodness one of the shop guys adopted me as his personal "project" and was a great help. He said he wanted to introduce me to the real world. With his help, we quickly were able to build the roller drum that would allow us to manufacture panels and articles that were almost three feet long. These panels were made with a combination of high quality resin and metal strands of boron filament. The roller drum would apply thin layer after thin layer of resin as it laid down the boron filaments. Think of it as making a fiberglass structure that is lighter than fiberglass and stronger than steel.

Once we had a way of producing large panels, we had to come up with products that could have practical application. We could program the roller drum to produce various products based on whether we needed something that needed to be strong or just light weight. We had a great brainstorming session and decided to build several products. First, I was to make a hammer out of the composite material. The idea was to show that we could produce a hammer that would be lightweight but would be very strong in bending, thus being able to drive a nail with less force. After manufacturing the hammer handle and attaching it to the hammer head, we learned that you can have too much of a good thing. It worked too well. You could drive a nail much quicker, but the vibration would put your hand to sleep in about six seconds. Our next product, a golf club, was a huge success. It would drive the ball further and was much easier to swing. I should note to all you golfers that we actually manufactured the first composite golf club.

My summertime at Texaco Experiment was running out, and the last item I built was a putter for General Bernard Schriever who was retiring from the Air Force. He had been overseeing the Air Force contract for the experimental composite panels, and Texaco wanted to give him a retirement gift. I had the task of not only manufacturing the putter, but also got to oversee the construction of an impressive green felt-lined wooden display case used in the presentation to the general. The general loved the putter.

The 1960 Cessna 172 I used to Solo in August 1966

During that busy summer of 1966, I also worked a second job at Galeski Photo to earn extra money to pursue my passion of learning how to fly. My parents weren't too keen on my taking flying lessons because of the perceived danger. Thanks to some help from my uncle Joe Nance, who had taken some flying lessons himself, I was allowed to follow that dream. The problem was that all the money from my day job was being saved to pay for half of my last year of college, so the money for flying would have to come from my evening and weekend job. I would work several days and then get in a couple of hours of instructor led flying at Parnell Field in South Richmond. I would then work some more to pay for the next flying lesson. We were flying a 1960 Cessna 172 on a dirt field about a mile and a half west of the large Dupont Plant near Richmond. I really enjoyed it and that flying time really helped me with aeronautics classes during my senior year. It is one thing to read about how something works and something else to experience it in real life. I would be in the middle of taking a quiz with my hand leaning to the right to "feel" how a plane would react to a particular maneuver. I am really glad I had the opportunity at that time to experience flying. Practical experience truly pays off in anything we do in life.

My flying instructor was a very nice lady who was tough as nails and smoked a lot. I was wearing contact lenses by then, and the smoke really bothered me. Thank goodness that the Cessna 172 had windows that would pop open about ten degrees. As we came close to the end of the summer, I was starting to run out of flying money. One evening after work, I was putting in an hour of flying with my instructor and doing a couple of "touch and goes" (take off, circle, land, taxi back, and take off again) when she said, while we were taxiing for the next take off, that she was out of cigarettes. I was thankful for that, but

Georgia Tech "Tech Tower" serves as an Atlanta landmark

she next said that she was going to get some cigarettes and for me to keep practicing. She said that as she was exiting the plane. I asked, "Do you really want me to keep flying without you?" She said that I could practice fine without her. That was just her easy manner of telling me it was time to "solo". When I did the first touch and go without her, I came in about a hundred feet high because I was so nervous. I recovered and did a "go around" nailing the landing on my second attempt. I did several other "touch and go" landings until my time was up.

As I taxied back to the hangar, there she was standing there with a huge pair of scissors (they looked like sheep shears) ready to cut my shirt tail off to put my name and date on it to display on the wall in the office. I pleaded with her not to cut the shirt I had on, since it was brand-new and my mom would kill me since she had just bought it for me so I would look good at work. She agreed to wait, with the understanding that I would come back with another shirt the next day for her to make it "official." I was more than happy to do that. What a day! It is one of those days that I will never forget.

That whole summer of 1966 with my great job at Texaco Experiment, my flying, and planning our wedding for the next summer was a huge blessing. I went back to Georgia Tech in the fall of 1966 ready to continue on my quest of being part of landing man on the moon. Each engineering group has a society that promotes their type of engineering. For mechanical engineers in the automobile business, there is the Society of Automobile Engineers (SAE). For electrical engineers, they have the Institute of Electrical and Electronics Engineers (IEEE). For aerospace engineers, our society is called American Institute of Aeronautics and Astronautics (AIAA, pronounced *A*, *I*, double *A*). I was asked by my propulsion professor, Professor Hubbard, if I would serve as the chairman of the AIAA during my senior year. It was a great honor, but I already had my plate full. He knew my passion and mentioned that it would look good on my resume to NASA. My decision to accept the position would be critical to my living the dream of sitting on the console when we landed on the moon for the first time. The Lord was guiding my life, even though it would be some time before I realized just how much.

John Young during his Gemini 10 mission flown in July 1966

As chairman of the AIAA, I had some great duties. The one that I remember the most involved hosting astronaut John Young for a "John Young Day" at Georgia Tech in the fall of 1966. John had graduated from Georgia Tech in 1952 with the highest honors and had become a Navy test pilot before joining NASA. The current head of NASA, Astronaut Charlie Bolton, said John Young and Astronaut Hoot Gibson were the two best test pilots that he had ever seen. John had just flown on Gemini 10 in July 1966. He was the commander, and he and astronaut Mike Collins would boost themselves higher than man had ever been in space. John had also piloted Gemini 3 (the first flight of the Gemini spacecraft). That's when he got in trouble for smuggling a corned beef sandwich onboard.

As the chairman of the Georgia Tech Chapter of the AIAA, I had the honor of taking John around the campus to various functions to introduce him and represent AIAA, who was sponsoring the event. I was like a sponge listening to John tell of his Gemini experiences. It was the experience of a lifetime. John is fairly quiet, but I quickly learned that he had a photographic memory. He was a member of a fraternity that was right behind the Delta Upsilon fraternity house, so we had a lot in common. John would go on to fly on the Apollo 10 mission as pilot with Tom Stafford who practiced the first lunar landing. He later commanded Apollo 16 during which he and Charlie Duke landed and walked on the moon, and he was also the first astronaut to fly the Space Shuttle. It seemed to me that John Young clearly had "The Right Stuff." When the Space Shuttle flew the first time, it had never flown before, so it was the ultimate test pilot's dream. The mission went off flawlessly.

The process of job interviews and "plant trips" began in earnest with the New Year 1967. A plant trip occurs after an interview when a company expresses an interest to the point that they offer to fly you to their place of business to meet the people you would work for if you accepted their job offer. In most cases, they would give you a job offer first and then try to sell you on the job. The process started by going to the placement center on campus and signing up for job interviews or just applying for a particular job. Each company would show you a job description along with the perks and benefits of working for them. Different companies would come in over several weeks and post job descriptions. It was important to check regularly for new job postings. The first job posting that interested me was working on the propulsion system for the Delta II Rocket. It was being built by the Douglas Aircraft Corp. in California, and it was the first place that I had applied to for an aerospace job. The second place I applied for was working on a follow-on Big Gemini Spacecraft at the McDonnell Aircraft Company in St. Louis. This spacecraft would have had a crew of nine and would be used to resupply a future space station. It would have been launched by a Titan III rocket. I continued to check job postings every day or two. Then it happened—my dream job posting showed up. NASA was looking for a flight control specialist in the field of propulsion for the Apollo Lunar Lander. There it was, right before my eyes. My euphoria was suddenly dashed when at the top of the qualifications, it stated that you had to have an A average. My first thought was that I didn't know two people who had an A average at Georgia Tech. My 2.9 GPA out of 4.0 was a mid B average, and a low A average would be at least a 3.5 grade point average. I also noticed that hundreds of people had signed up for the position. I couldn't believe it. Here was my dream job, and I didn't even qualify; I was obviously heartbroken. I didn't even sign up for an interview. It was a long, slow walk back to the fraternity house, about seven blocks away.

I remember going straight to my room upstairs in the Delta Upsilon fraternity house, closing the door, and having a chat with the Lord. My roommate, Jack Abbott, was not in at the time, so I had my room to myself. I sat on the side of the bottom bunk, held my head in my hands, and gave my situation to the Lord in prayer. I had a lot of time while walking back to the fraternity house to think about what I was going to talk about to the Lord. My first impulse was to complain, but thank goodness, a clearer head prevailed. I told the Lord that He had brought me a long way to this point and even though I didn't understand it, He must have something even better in mind for me. I said that all I could do now was give this to Him and I would wait for Him to show me what to do.

Obviously, I was disappointed, but I decided to apply for as many aerospace engineering jobs as I could and wait for the Lord to show me what was in store for me. I started applying to several companies all around the country and planning a super plant tour of aerospace companies during my spring break. The offers started coming in from all over during January and February 1967. McDonnell Aircraft Corp and Douglas Aircraft Co., who were in the middle of merging into the McDonnell Douglas Corporation, flew a group of us from Atlanta to their plant in St. Louis to meet the engineers who were working on the new Gemini B (known as the Big Gemini). A couple of astronauts were surveying the Gemini B mock-up while we were there. I was most impressed with the line of F4 Phantoms coming off the assembly line because the Vietnam War was just getting started. They seemed to be coming off the assembly line at the rate of one every thirty minutes or so. Next, Lockheed picked us up in a Lockheed Super Constellation (better known as the Connie) and flew us to Marietta, Georgia, where the C5A was going to be built. The Constellation had four radial propeller engines with three vertical tails. I don't remember much of the visit, but we did get to see Howard Hughes's Lockheed Jet Star plane that was kept at the plant as his backup. I thought it was very unusual, because there were guards with rifles stationed all around it. It would eventually be the plane that Hughes would die in, some years later, while flying to Mexico to get medical treatment. I took these plant trips on weekends while I was in school before spring break.

I continued to plan my super cross-country trip during spring break. Pat would still be in class because Longwood was on the semester system. I planned my trip so I would be finished in time to see Pat during the last weekend of my spring break. It was to be an awesome trip. I was going to drive to Richmond, Virginia, on the Saturday after the last exam and fly out of Richmond on my whirlwind trip. I was going to go to West Hartford, Connecticut, to see Pratt & Whitney first, then I would be off to Schenectady, New York, to visit General Electric, a jet engine builder. I would then fly back to St. Louis where I had gotten a different job offer with McDonnell Douglas working on the propulsion for the Gemini B. From St. Louis, I would travel to California where I had received two job offers from the Douglas arm of the about-to-be-formed McDonnell Douglas. One job offer was working on advanced versions of the Delta Rocket (still in production today) in Huntington Beach, California. The second job offer from Douglas involved working for launch preparations at Vandenberg Air Force Base and that plant trip would send me to Sunnydale, California. From California, I would fly back to Richmond in time to see Pat when she got out of school. I secured a series of plane tickets from different companies. It was a masterful plan. From what I could see, it looked as if I was going to go to work for McDonnell Douglas on some sort of space project. I once again shared with the Lord that I was doing everything that I could to give Him the opportunity to show me what was in store for me. I once again gave it to Him.

Time-wise, it was about four weeks before the super plant trip and about six weeks since I had my talk with the Lord after finding out that my grades weren't good enough to get my dream NASA flight control job. One afternoon, while we were playing basketball after class on a pad outback of the fraternity house, one of the brothers stuck his head out of a window and shouted, "Nance, you have a call. NASA is on the phone." Now, I knew that NASA wouldn't be calling me, so I suspected that one of the brothers was playing a trick on me, since they all knew I was very disappointed about not being qualified for my dream job. They knew that I didn't even apply because of the grade requirement. I was hot and sweaty, but I would go along and play their game. When I answered the phone in the hallway of the dorm section of the fraternity house, the voice on the other end of the phone said, "Hi, this is Jim Hannigan with NASA. I was wondering why you didn't apply for the flight control job." I answered, "Okay, who is this? Who put you up to this?" The reply was, "John Young told me that I needed to hire you and when I couldn't find you on the list, I called Georgia Tech and they gave me this number. I want to interview you and hire you. I have three hundred people on this list, and I don't want to interview them. I just want to interview you and then I can go visit my friends here at Tech. When can you get here"? Jim Hannigan was a Georgia Tech graduate who just happened to be John Young's roommate while at Tech. I mentioned that I didn't have an A average, and Mr. Hannigan said that he didn't know anyone at Tech who had an A average. He said they put that stipulation so that they wouldn't have a ton of people apply. When I explained that I was hot and sweaty, Mr. Hannigan said to come as I was and proceeded to give me the address at the Tech Motel near campus. I remember looking up and seeing several brothers who had overheard the conversation. They asked if NASA had really called me and I said yes. They said they thought that I hadn't applied for the job. I explained that the astronaut John Young had told Mr. Hannigan to hire me. Thank goodness for John's photographic memory.

I then took the quickest shower I have ever taken in my life and went to meet Mr. Hannigan. He was super nice and asked a few questions while I filled out my application and gave him permission to obtain my grades and other transcripts. Mr. Hannigan explained that he was hiring two flight controllers for his branch, which was the Lunar Module Systems Branch. He was hiring one for propulsion and one for electrical. The rest of the positions would be filled from within, but they needed someone that had current computer skills since the use of computers was very new and most of the engineers weren't that familiar with the latest generation of computers and computer programming. We must remember that the hand-held calculator still had not been invented. There were no PCs. We were still using slide rules. He just happened to be in a meeting with John at

NASA when he told John that he was going to Georgia Tech to hire some folks for the Lunar Module Systems Branch. That is when John told Jim to hire me. Mr. Hannigan seemed concerned that I might feel that the salary was too low. I said that I didn't care because this was my dream job. Here my heart was racing, while Mr. Hannigan was worried that I might not think the pay offer would be high enough. He explained that after a year of probation, I would move to a different special flight control pay schedule, and he thought I would be very pleased then. I really didn't care!

Less than two weeks later, I had my job offer from NASA. It was for $7,729 a year. It is 1967 and my top job offer was for $9,350 a year from McDonnell Douglas. I really didn't care about the money. It was fine, but I did have a new problem. I wanted to go to see NASA and skip my super plant trip tour. Mr. Hannigan said that he wanted me to come and see the Manned Spacecraft Center (now Johnson Space Center) in Houston as soon as I could. I quickly found out that NASA didn't pay for plant tours, so I had to arrange my own trip. Mr. Hannigan set me up to tour with guides and temporary badges. All I had to do was to get there. I was running out of money during my senior year, so I called Eastern Airlines and booked what was called a "red eye flight" from Atlanta to Houston Hobby Airport at two in the morning. This was a flight to get the plane back to Houston at very cheap fare. I made arrangements to take my last spring break final early so I could travel to Houston on a Thursday morning flight. It is enough to say that it involved sleeping on the wooden bench seats (like in a train station) in Hobby Airport and walking a mile to the rental car company on the Gulf Freeway at 6:00 a.m. What can I say? I forgot about the hour time difference and assumed that the car rental place would be open when the plane arrived. In the end, I got my car, got to my hotel room, took a shower, and made it to NASA for my 9:00 a.m. appointment.

My day at NASA was a big blur. I was like a kid entering a candy store for the first time. They took me to Mission Control and showed me where I would work, showed me the simulators where the crew would train, showed me the centrifuge where they trained the astronauts, and showed me mock-ups for the Lunar Module and

Command Module. By the end of the day, I was in what today we would call HR signing up for my new job. They then took me to their travel office so I could make arrangements to move to Houston for my new NASA flight controller job. It was a glorious day!

I made it back on the red eye flight to Atlanta where I called my parents and Pat to tell them the good news. I know Pat was relieved, since we were going to be married shortly after graduation and she wanted to know where we were going to live. I know that both my parents and hers were worried that we would end up in California. Now, Houston didn't look so far after all.

When I got back from my trip to Houston, I called the other companies and cancelled my plant tours, telling them I had accepted a job as a flight controller with NASA. I had a lot of plane tickets to return. This took a bit of work since all of my tickets were individual paper tickets. I spent spring break planning my new life at NASA and planning our new life together with Pat. I must admit that I did purchase a new 1967 Dodge Charger. It had been the rep's car and I only paid $3,501 for it. My dad helped me get a loan for it because I was just about out of money by this time. I only wish I still had that gold Dodge Charger when I see them going through the auto auctions today for $65,000 to $75,000. Going to Texas, I really needed a car with good air-conditioning, but the question was whether I really needed a new Dodge Charger. I did really, really like that car. Pat liked it, too. During spring break while I was car shopping, Pat was busy planning our wedding coming up in August.

I want to take a moment to review what it took for me to get to this point:

First, the MIT advisor told me I should go to Georgia Tech when I hardly knew anything about the school. Remember that Jim Hannigan only interviewed for the only Lunar Modular Propulsion Flight Controller job at Georgia Tech. They did not look at any other school.

Second, I don't think I would have ever gotten to go to Georgia Tech if, while looking at the campus when it was closed,

Dean Griffin had not "just happened" to come out of his office door and stumble upon my parents and myself touring the campus. Dean Griffin was the best person on the planet to convince my dad that I should go to Georgia Tech.

Third, while at Tech, I decided to join the AIAA society, and then Professor Hubbard asked me to become the chairman during my senior year.

Fourth, the AIAA decided to ask John Young to come to campus for a "John Young Day" and I ended up spending the day with him. Without this connection, I would never have talked to Jim Hannigan.

Fifth, John Young "just happened" to be in a meeting with Jim Hannigan when he found out that Jim was going to Georgia Tech to interview for a propulsion flight control job. At that meeting, John Young told Mr. Hannigan to hire me.

Sixth, Jim Hannigan sought me out even though I had not signed up to interview for the propulsion flight control job. He had to work hard to make that happen. I am grateful for that.

I am going to repeat what I said to the Lord the night after I met with Jim Hannigan. "Lord, there is nothing, absolutely nothing that You cannot do if I give it to You."

On top of all this, in recent years, I have learned that my great, great (nine times) grandfather came to America in 1620 and settled in Jamestown as an indentured servant. An indentured servant was someone (in this case, sixteen-year-old Richard Nance of Cornwall, England) who traded his passage to the new world for seven years of labor. After that, he would be free of his debt and receive twenty acres of land from the Virginia Colony Company. He survived the

Powhatan Indian massacre of Jamestown in 1624 because he was working in the fields of Neck of Land, about three miles from Jamestown, when the massacre occurred. I only exist because Richard was working in the fields on that fateful day.

Getting me to NASA was clearly the work of the Lord. He is in control if we give our problems to Him. There is no way that all this happened by chance. This is just the beginning of this journey. I am convinced that all of this happened so He, not I, would receive the glory.

4

Pinch Me—Am I really at NASA?

I graduated in June 1967 from Georgia Tech. The ceremony took place at the Fox Theatre on Peachtree Street in downtown Atlanta. The Fox Theatre is a landmark in Atlanta where the movie *Gone with the Wind* premiered a very long time ago. My family and I went to graduation separately, because immediately after I graduated in Atlanta, I had to drive directly to Houston to begin my new job at NASA. It was quite an accomplishment for this twenty-two-year-old, the first member of a long line of Nances (dating back to their arrival in Jamestown in 1620) to graduate from college.

The trip was tiring, but with every mile, my excitement and apprehension grew. All I could think about was my new job at NASA and whether I would do a good job and be everything that they expected me to be. I remember two events from my trip that have stuck with me over the years. I pulled up at an ESSO (later to become Exxon) gas station in Mobile, Alabama, to get gas. In those days, there was still full service. I got my gas, had my windows cleaned. I attempted to pay using my shiny new ESSO credit card. A gas credit card was a rite of passage for graduating from college, if you had good credit. When I tried to pay, the attendant looked at me as if I were crazy and asked if this was joke. Sheer panic set in. The first time I am going to use my first credit card, there is a problem? Of course, the name on the card was Robert S Nance Jr. The attendant pointed to the name over the door of the station which read, "Robert

S Nance Jr". Back then, the ESSO gas stations always posted the station owner's name over the door to the station. I showed the attendant my driver's license and assured him that it was my real name. He wasn't convinced. In fact, he kept asking whether we were on *Candid Camera*, a popular TV show at the time. People were often secretly filmed in weird circumstances, and then Allen Funt would pop out and scream, "You are on *Candid Camera*." I don't think the attendant really was sure that we weren't on *Candid Camera* until I left. I am sure I remember that incident because of my panic when the attendant suspiciously asked me if it was a joke when I handed him my credit card.

The second event from that trip that I still remember, as though it happened yesterday, took place along Route 90 in Louisiana. Route 90 followed the railroad from Tallahassee through Baton Rouge to Houston. Today, Interstate 10 provides the same route but is a lot quicker. It was early afternoon, and I was getting hungry. I traveled with the railroad track on my right side and soon, a little diner appeared to my left. It was one of those cute little diners with few booths and a row of red stools around the counter, with a round Coca-Cola sign hanging on the wall. I went in, sat down, and proceeded to order cheeseburger, fries, and Coke. The young waitress then spoke to me in some foreign language that I had never heard before. Today, I know that language to be Cajun French. After a few moments of trying to communicate, I came to understand that the owner had gone to the bank. Not wanting to wait until he returned, I pointed to a picture on the wall of a cheeseburger and a chilled Coca-Cola and she understood. She then prepared an excellent cheeseburger with a Coca-Cola. I never got my french fries since there wasn't a picture of them on the wall. By now, I am wondering, if all this was happening on just my trip to Houston, what more lay ahead?

I had left Atlanta with about $320 in my pocket, two gas credit cards, a nineteen-inch black and white TV, which my parents had given to me as a graduation present, and some sheets and towels. I had located an apartment on the Gulf Freeway between Houston and NASA in Clear Lake from a list provided by NASA. Remember that back then we had no internet, just expensive long distance phone service. I had made tentative arrangements to secure an apartment before I departed for Houston. Pat and I would need a location between Houston and NASA, since Pat had secured a teaching job in Houston.

I made two mistakes right off the bat. The apartment was $125 a month, and they had told me that I would need to make my first month's rent payment when I signed the lease. What I didn't know was that on top of the first month's rent, they also required a $125 last month's deposit. The second mistake was that I had told NASA I would start work on June 19, almost a week after I got to Houston. I thought I would need the time to settle in. NASA had paid to have my meager collection of furniture shipped to Houston. It turns out that it took ten days to get my furniture out of storage in Houston, so there I was with no furniture, a week to kill, and $60 left in my pocket. The problem was that NASA wanted me to start on a Monday and I graduated on a Saturday, so there wouldn't be time to drive to Houston, secure an apartment, and then start work on the next Monday.

To complicate matters even more, what I didn't learn until I started on the nineteenth of June was that NASA paid every two weeks and my start date was in the middle of the pay period. That meant that I was going to get my first paycheck on the tenth of July, and it was going to be for only one week of work. That meant that my $60 was going to have to last for almost a month. Looking back, I think the Lord wanted me to slow down, not be so proud about my great NASA job, and learn to be more frugal. What I learned was that I could buy Morton TV dinners for thirty-nine cents and that peanut butter and jelly sandwiches would work just fine for lunch. I managed to stretch my $60 until July 14 when I got a paycheck, which netted about $128. It was a humbling experience, to say the least!

The Lunar Module Propulsion Section at NASA was a wonderful group. My direct boss was John Wegener, a devout Christian and a great mentor. John served as the section leader. Bob Carlton was his boss who headed up the Propulsion and Guidance and Navigation (GNC) sections of the Lunar Module Systems Branch. Jim Hannigan, who hired me, was the head of the Lunar Module Systems Branch of the Flight Control Division. Flight Control was headed by Chris Kraft, and his number two man was Gene Kranz. I should report that Chris Kraft was a graduate of Virginia Polytechnic Institute (VPI), which would later become Virginia Tech. I will remind the reader that I didn't want to go to VPI because they didn't have an Aerospace Department. Mr. Kraft was a mechanical engineer who had gone to work at Langley Field, which was part of the Air Force at that time. It was from Langley that he ended up at the Manned Spacecraft Center in Houston after Langley became part of NASA in 1958. Chris and Gene had been the flight directors on many of the Mercury and Gemini flights. They were both awesome leaders and the key to so many successful missions. Chris would move to the head of Mission Operations a few years later and then on to Center Director. Gene moved up to the head of Flight Control Division when Chris moved up. No one just out of college could ask for a better set of mentors than I had at this early point in my career.

Shortly after I arrived, Bob Carlton asked me how I was settling in. We had a good discussion and during that conversation, I asked Mr. Carlton what would it take to be the person sitting on the console during the first landing on the moon? Bob candidly said that it was very simple. The person who knew more about the Lunar Module propulsion systems than anyone else, who also possessed the ability to apply that knowledge would be the person who would be part of the shift that landed man on the moon for the first time. I then knew what I needed to do. Whenever there was a test, a meeting, or briefing, I volunteered for

Mission Control Center as it was during the early Apollo Missions. Lunar Module Systems were on the second row from the front on the right side.

it. Everyone in the section was older than me and was involved in a lot more activities, thus they appreciated not having to come in early or stay late for meetings or a test. They were great guys; I just had the advantage of being the new guy without anything to distract me from my mission.

Pat and I got married on August 12, 1967, less than two months after I started work at NASA. Pat had been working at the C&O Railroad and wanted to get some money together to help with the cost of the wedding. Parents who had just sent their children to college in 1967 didn't have a lot of money. Pat had graduated from Longwood College about the same time that I graduated and went to work immediately.

Here is where the lesson in finances popped up again. My second paycheck would arrive on July 28, and it would be for two weeks' pay. My next paycheck was due to arrive on Friday, August 11, the day before we were getting married, and I would be in Richmond by then. The problem back then was that we got a paper check mailed to us at our home. There was no direct deposit at that time, so I would be in Richmond for my wedding and honeymoon, while my paycheck sat in my mailbox in Houston. I went to the NASA Federal Credit Union and they said that they could give me a loan of $250 after I had been employed for sixty days, which would be August 18. That decision to start on June 19 instead of June 12 was still chasing me, but John Wegener came to the rescue. He offered that he would cosign for the $250 loan so I could get married and have enough money to have a honeymoon, which was the leisure drive back to Houston. It was a six-month loan, and I paid it back early, so John didn't have to worry about it. I always said that Pat and I couldn't have gotten married if it hadn't been for John.

I left for Richmond on Wednesday afternoon, August 9, and drove to Atlanta, staying at the Delta Upsilon Fraternity house to see old friends and score on free lodging. On August 10, I drove to Richmond in time to meet with Pat and the minister who was going to marry us on the twelfth. We were married at Jahnke Road Baptist Church, which was about three blocks from Pat's parents' home. Pat's dad, Jimmy Dameron, was a deacon at the church. Jahnke Road

Baptist Church was started by Woodland Heights Baptist Church just as Bon Air Baptist was getting established. At our rehearsal dinner on Friday night, I gave Pat a Bible with her name on it, and Pat gave me a copy of her driver's license. I had told her we weren't going to be married until she got her driver's license, since I couldn't drive her to and from work with my schedule as a flight controller. It is important to note that few families had more than one car at that time. She had been so busy with school and getting ready for the wedding that it was something that she had put off. She had always ridden a bus to work at the C&O railroad and her dad needed the car to drive to his job. The license would come in handy when we got back to Houston.

The wedding was wonderful. We just about filled up the church with both families and friends, and what I remember most about the wedding was the challenge we encountered when we wanted to pray during the service. We had to kneel on a small bench, and with Pat's dress, that was difficult. The dress was beautiful, and Pat was a beautiful bride, but kneeling in the gown was much harder than the day before at rehearsal. I remember the bench rocking back and forth, and I said a little prayer within a prayer that we wouldn't tumble over. I remember the kiss. We were both perspiring since the church wasn't air-conditioned and it was August. In spite of all of that, the feeling that we had as we walked down the aisle has got to be the closest you can get to heaven here on earth.

We held our reception at the church. On our wedding cake, the top layer was designed for us to take on the honeymoon, which we did. They served the normal lime punch, salted peanuts, and white mints. I loved them all. One thing that happened at the wedding was that my State Farm agent from Houston came to the wedding. I had bought a Whole Life Insurance policy from him, and in the discussion at the time, I mentioned that I was getting married in Virginia in August. He had asked where and I told him. He asked me to send him an invitation. I had Pat add him to the invitation list, and much to our surprise, he showed up at the wedding. It turned out that he was in the Army Reserve and had his summer training at Fort Lee, located about twenty miles from Jahnke Road Baptist Church. My dad was very impressed and went around telling people that my State Farm agent had come all the way from Texas but omitted the part about his Army training. My dad's best friend while growing up had become the State Farm agent in the Bon Air area, and I had moved my auto insurance from him to the agent in Texas when I moved to Houston.

Pat and I made our getaway without getting any soap writing on the car, just a lot of balloons and a "Just Married" sign taped to the back of the car. Our friends followed us for about fifteen miles, honking and yelling at us. I don't think Pat thought it was too cool, plus I don't think people do that anymore. Our honeymoon consisted of the drive back to Houston with stops on the way. We did spend a night in Atlanta to visit friends and then drove to Callaway Gardens in Southwest Georgia. I am sure that both Pat's memories of the honeymoon and mine would be similar with us loving Callaway Gardens, especially the chapel at the end of the lake—not loving New Orleans because we thought it was dirty and getting really, really tired of eating the wedding cake. We were saving money where we could, so every snack was wedding cake. We do have fond memories of an ice cream shop in New Orleans where we each ate a banana split.

I will never forget that we stopped at a gas station just after we got to Texas where they were having a gas war, and each station was trying to outdo the other with price and service. They were bound and determined to vacuum the inside of our car. It was littered with rice acquired during our departure from the church, but I had stopped on the way and thought that I had gotten it all. They managed to find some that we missed, and

Beautiful Chapel at Callaway Gardens over-looking a very peaceful lake

they keep asking us if it was rice, but said we didn't know how it got there. Needless to say, we got the royal treatment; full service at gas stations was wonderful, and we only paid about thirty-five cents a gallon for gas!

I think that Pat was less than impressed with our small apartment, and we didn't have much furniture, but we were newlyweds, in love, and everything was good. Pat had about a week to settle in. We had gotten a lot of great wedding gifts, had brought a lot of them with us, and our parents had mailed the rest. The remaining gifts came a couple of days after we arrived in Houston, and they kept Pat occupied until school started. We had silverware, china, and all sorts of cooking appliances, just very little furniture.

Our first major purchase was a car for Pat. We had gotten some money for the wedding, so we paid off the cash loan that John Wegener had helped me with, plus we financed about half the $700 purchase price of a 1964 Chevrolet Corvair. It was white with a stick shift. It was a cool-looking car, and Pat loved it, but there were some maintenance problems to attend to. It had an air-conditioning unit that overheated if it got hot, requiring a lot of service work. It was the perfect car to take Pat to Jackson Junior High School where Pat had her first teaching job. Pat loved teaching, but Jackson Junior High was located in a poor neighborhood and many of the students did not graduate. Pat had wanted to teach in the Clear Creek School District, which covered the NASA area, but they required at least one year of teaching experience for teachers who came from outside of Texas. It was a very tough year for Pat. She was exposed to things that she never thought she would be exposed to like having to sand off obscene drawings on students' desks before a parent–teacher meeting when parents would come to her room. She had students who wouldn't even guess at the answers on a true/false test. Needless to say, Pat earned an education in inner city teaching in a hurry. To top it off, one of her students was arrested at school for killing another student while off school grounds. It turns out that the student killed was the fifteen-year-old donor for the first heart transplant performed in the United States. Dr. Denton Cooley performed the transplant on May 3, 1968, at St. Luke's Hospital in Houston.

The good news is that early in the summer of 1968, Pat received a call from the principal of Seabrook Intermediate asking her to come work in the Clear Creek School District. It was a blessing from God. That call came on a Saturday morning when we were both home, and obviously, it made her day as well as mine. Her perseverance at the inner city school had paid off!

Meanwhile, we faced a lot of challenges at NASA. The Lunar Module was running behind schedule, and there were a lot of meetings to discuss the current status of the various test vehicles. The first Lunar Module to fly was LM-1, an unmanned test vehicle that first flew in January 1968. Without a man onboard, there was a lot of automation and little chance to rapidly change things if a problem occurred. The LM-1 was launched on a Saturn I rocket. Once in orbit, we activated the program to execute the first burn of the descent engine. After the engine first fired, it suddenly shut down. The computer said that there was insufficient thrust, but in fact the limits on the computer had been set too tight and the time

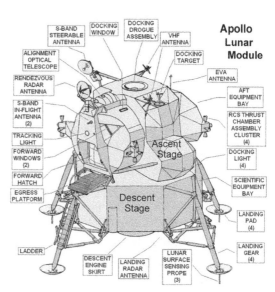

Lunar Module Diagram showing descent stage (lower part with landing gear) and ascent stage (top part of vehicle)

for the engine to come to full thrust was a fraction of a second longer than the time set in the computer. A simple error that had been overlooked in the programming of the onboard computer. The solution was easy. All we had to do was to increase the limit in the computer by one second. In the post mission review, it was discovered that someone had just estimated the time that it should be set at and was never updated to actual test data as the engine was developed. This type of issue is the very reason that test flights of spacecraft are conducted.

Once the engine did not provide the burn that was expected, the entire mission plan had to be changed since the ground coverage (radio reception) was available about 30 percent of the time. Communication with a spacecraft was only possible when it was near a ground station, since there were almost no communication satellites in orbit in 1968. Each mission was planned so we could execute various parts of the mission while in communication with ground stations. When the engine did not fire, the orbit did not change as anticipated and LM-1 did not go over the ground stations needed to send signals to the vehicle or even see what was going on in the various systems of LM-1. This turned out to be a good exercise for the flight planning people and all of us flight controllers because we had to come up with a new plan quickly and manage our systems so they would be ready for the new mission plan. That is what a flight controller does. We had to develop in a few hours what mission planners had taken months to plan. As part of mission planning, there were canned procedures that had been modularized, so we just had to put the blocks together and figure out how to manage the systems.

Our number one objective on the mission was to do what was called an abort stage. This procedure was to test what would happen if during landing on the moon (descent) a problem occurred, forcing us to immediately discard the descent stage (the bottom part that landed the Lunar Module on the moon) and return to lunar orbit by firing the ascent stage (the top part that would normally return the crew back in lunar orbit when the crew was ready to leave the lunar surface). This would be the only time we would ever get to test this procedure, and it was vital to the mission that it was accomplished. We also would need to use the burning of these two stages to put us back on a mission profile that gave us better communication coverage. We only had about three hours to do all this planning and to come up with a command list that would tell the LM-1 what to do and where to point to execute the two burns. It was my first mission and a real "eye opener." The abort stage procedure and the two burns went off flawlessly. The descent engine started and burned the desired time to fully test the engine, and then a command was sent to abort stage. The descent engine started shutting down; the explosive bolts holding the two stages together fired and the stages separated. At that point, the ascent engine started firing and pulled away from the descent stage, and finally the ascent stage turned to a new course as it would do to return to orbit around the moon. It was the first time anything like this had ever been tested. It certainly made us feel better about the mission.

Now that we were in better communication with the LM-1, we were ready to execute our next burn to run the ascent to fuel exhaustion in order to see what would happen if it ever ran out of fuel. Ground testing had shown that when it ran out of fuel, it would cut off without any issues. We wanted to confirm that in space. One of the things we also wanted to test in orbit was to divert fuel to the Reaction Control System (the small jets that control the position of the spacecraft when floating in space and during engine burns) from the Ascent Fuel Tanks during the burn. Without the RCS, the Lunar Module would spin off course and not reach lunar orbit. This would only be needed if the RCS system had a leak or if a lot of RCS fuel was being used. The plan was to burn the ascent engine for about a minute, then open the valves from the ascent fuel tanks and lastly close the valves from the RCS fuel tanks. We would burn in this configuration for about a minute and then reverse the procedure by opening the valves to the RCS fuel tanks, closing the valves from the ascent engine fuel tanks, and then burning the ascent engine to fuel starvation.

All of this was to be done while the spacecraft was over Hawaii where we had good communication with the spacecraft. Everything worked as planned, so we switched to the ascent fuel tank for the RCS and then cut off fuel from the RCS tanks. All of these commands were put on a magnetic tape on the ground that was replayed during the burn and sent to the spacecraft. That is what must be done when there isn't a man onboard. After we burned in this configuration for about a minute, the command was sent to open the valves to the RCS fuel tanks; however, a communication error occurred and the command was never sent. Immediately after that, the command did get through to close the valves from the ascent fuel tanks to the RCS. That meant that there was no fuel to control the spacecraft and after a few seconds, it started spinning wildly. In only a few seconds, we lost the ability to control the spacecraft. When we last got any data from the spacecraft, it was spinning at over one revolution a second. That was the last we saw of LM-1. I will add a note, several years later, somewhere in South America, there was a report of an alien spacecraft crash site and it turned out to be part of the descent stage of LM-1. We were able to confirm a serial number off one of the descent fuel tanks.

I was really upset that we had overcome so many problems only to lose the spacecraft. I will never forget watching the press conference during which NASA said that the mission was a complete success. All the mission objectives of burning of the descent engine, performing an abort stage, and performing a burn of the ascent engine were met. I remember Gene Kranz noting that the reason we lost the Lunar Module after achieving the mission objectives was because there wasn't a man onboard. During a mission, the astronauts would be throwing the switches if we needed to divert from the ascent tanks to the RCS. Communication issues would not be a concern with a crew onboard. This experience taught me a lot about overcoming problems and the importance of having a crew onboard the spacecraft.

The next flight, Apollo 7, in October 1968 would be the Command Module's first test flight with a crew. It was also launched on a Saturn I. Apollo 7 was followed by the flight of the Apollo 8 Command module on the first manned flight of the huge Saturn V rocket. This was the mission that orbited the moon and during which the astronauts read from the book of Genesis on Christmas Eve. The true story as told to me by astronaut Jim Lovell was that each astronaut had a small box in which they could bring personal items on the flight. Astronaut Frank Borman's mother had given him a Bible to take with him on the mission. When Jim Lovell, William Anders, and Frank Borman saw the Earth rise over the moon as they made their first orbit of the moon, they were struck by the beauty of the Earth and knew that God had put it there for them to see. Since all of this occurred on December 24, 1968, they thought it was only fitting that they read from Genesis. Jim said that it was a life-changing moment for all of them. The picture that they took that day is one of the most famous photos ever taken. It is simply called Earthrise.

The next flight, Apollo 9, would test the Command Module and the Lunar Module in earth orbit, together. It would simulate the various maneuvers and burns that both vehicles would perform on a full

"Earthrise" shows the earth rising over the lunar surface as Apollo 8 circles the moon.

lunar mission. It was the first manned flight of the Lunar Module. It occurred in March 1969. Things went a lot smoother for the Lunar Module, and all the mission objectives were achieved, allowing NASA to streamline future missions so they could get two to three attempts at landing a man on the moon before the end of 1969, which was the goal set by President Kennedy.

Between Apollo 9 and the next mission, Apollo 10, the flight control teams were named for Apollo 11. Gene Kranz would be the lead flight director, and his team would be the team that would land man on the moon for the first time. Bob Carlton was named the control flight controller to oversee the two computers and propulsion systems. I was named the Lunar Module Propulsion flight controller for the first landing attempt. My dream of being on the console when man first landed on the man was within my grasp. This was clearly the Lord at work in my life. I am not sure that I recognized it at the time, but in retrospect, it is so obvious that I was being blessed over and over by the Lord. I would have never gotten to this point on my own. I am so very thankful for what God has done in my life.

Apollo 10 was a full dress rehearsal for the first lunar landing mission with the Command Module and Lunar Module in orbit around the moon. The Lunar Module flew close to the lunar surface (about 47,000 feet) and then initiated an abort during which the descent stage was shut off, the ascent stage was separated, and then the ascent engine was used to return to the Command Module. We did not do an abort stage since we had achieved that on the unmanned mission of LM-1. NASA was careful not to tempt astronauts Tom Stafford and Gene Cernan into trying to land by not loading enough propellant to actually land. We suffered a few glitches, but all of the mission objectives were met, and we were certified to attempt the first landing on Apollo 11. The plan was that if there was a problem on Apollo 11 in July 1969, we would fly Apollo 12 in September, and if we were still not successful, we would fly Apollo 13 in November. I should mention that the original schedule had two earth missions with the Command Module and the Lunar Module together and two missions with both spacecraft in orbit around the moon. That would have given us only one attempt to land on the moon before the end of 1969, the Apollo 13 spacecraft in November 1969. We all know what happened to the Apollo 13 mission. Our first attempt to land on the moon would have turned into a rescue mission and who knows when we would have ever landed on the moon. Since Apollo 11 and Apollo 12 Lunar Module spacecraft were to be dress rehearsal spacecraft, they were a little heavier, and that is why there were no lunar rovers on those missions. Apollo 13 carried an early version of the lunar rover, but it never got to land on the moon.

5

Did We Really Land on the Moon?

The Apollo 11 crew – Neil Armstrong, Mike Collins, and Buzz Aldrin

The stage was set. We would try the first lunar landing in July 1969. We started simulations for the Apollo 11 mission before the Apollo 10 mission had even flown. Simulations involved practice flying the mission using computers and simulators to mimic the spacecraft and its reactions to our commands. Since landing on the moon was a totally new procedure, we practiced a lot. The crew would "man" a simulator in another part of the Manned Spacecraft Center, and the flight controllers would "man" their consoles in the Mission Control Center (MCC) and practice landing on the moon. A series of IBM 360 computers were developed for NASA to run the interface between the Lunar Module simulator and the MCC. The Lunar Module simulator looked much like the aircraft simulators we see today. The inside of the Lunar Module simulator looked like the spacecraft, but cameras on the outside projected images on the windows of what the crew would be seeing outside. Just getting all of this to work together was a feat unto itself, considering speed and the size of the computers we used in the 1960s. When we started Apollo 11 simulations, we would come in early in the morning, but it would take hours for the technicians to get all the computers and simulators up and running. The computer programmers did their best to represent what a real mission would look like.

At first, it was all we could do just to fly a normal mission to see how our procedures worked together. There is a fine balance between too much communication and enough communication to know the current status. When a problem came up, it was important to keep flying the profile while we were sorting out the problems, making sure the rest of the parameters were within limits. We were working seventy-five to eighty hours a week by this time with a lot of time spent waiting for the simulation computers to come online.

Lunar Module Simulator in the background and the control consoles in the foreground circa 1969

By the time Apollo 10 was flown, the simulation guys had a better feel for what the actual data would look like and could improve the simulators for Apollo 11. The Powered Descent simulations would last about twelve hours, so if we were lucky, we would be able to complete six to eight landing simulations. Each would start about fifteen minutes before the descent burn to land on the moon and last through the landing and what we called T1. T1 was a preplanned abort that involved the Lunar Module taking off from the moon about ten minutes after landing because of an immediate problem such as a propellant leak or power problem. The simulator guys (SIM) would "program" failures to see how the crew and mission control would react to them. After each simulation, the SIM guys would debrief and tell us what the real problem was and when the problem occurred (propellant leak or other problem). Sometimes, they would give us several problems and that would be a real challenge.

The part of the simulation we feared was the debriefing. During the debriefing, the SIM guys would identify the failure or failures and tell us whether or not we had reacted to it correctly. A bad day is when we would abort the landing only to find that there was a "work around" that would have allowed the landing to continue. Obviously, the simulations were an excellent training tool and a great format to test our descent procedures.

Advances in the computer systems for the Apollo program provided one of the biggest benefits from the space program. The Primary Guidance Computer (PGNS) was an early digital computer.

The Abort Guidance Computer (AGS) was only used for aborts if the PGNS computer malfunctioned. The AGS computer was an analog computer, which was simple, but it only had to get the Lunar Module safely back into orbit in order to rendezvous with the Command module. MSFN (Manned Space Flight Network) should be of interest to everyone. It was the forerunner to what we call GPS today. The way it worked was that a big antenna on the earth would send a signal from earth to the Lunar Module with a time tag on the signal that recorded the time precisely. The Lunar Module would receive the signal and forward it back to the station on the earth. Once the signal was received on the earth, the time was recorded and that information was sent to NASA's Goddard Space Flight center in Greenbelt, Maryland. There, it was processed by dividing the time by two to get the one-way time and dividing it by the speed of light. The result would be the distance from the antenna to the spacecraft. Three antennas were required for lunar landing because each antenna would send its signal at the same time and then Goddard would use the information to triangulate the exact location of the Lunar Module every two seconds. Remember that the exact location of the antenna had to be calculated every two seconds as well as the distance from each antenna to the Lunar Module. It had to be done this way because the size of the computer at Goddard making these calculations every two seconds was larger than the Lunar Module itself. Today your smart phone does this calculation using eight to twelve satellites and is far more accurate than MSFN. I don't think there is a better example of something that we use every day that came from the space program. It takes computers that were developed for the space program, satellites that came from the space program, and the programming that came from the Apollo program to make GPS work today. The PGNS computer was cutting edge technology at the time and it had ten one thousandth (0.01%) of the computing power of my current iPhone.

This discussion of the computers shows the complexity of what we had to do to land on the moon. One other area that was of great concern was fuel management. I mentioned that the Apollo 11 was heavier than the baseline since it wasn't originally scheduled to land on the moon. That meant that we couldn't take a rover, and we would have to use most of the fuel in order to land on the moon. Mission planning said we would have about 5 percent of the fuel remaining at touchdown. To give you an idea how close this was, if you had a fuel tank in your car that got 350 miles per tank and you would get to your destination with 5 percent of your fuel left, you would have seventeen and a half miles to empty. For the Lunar Module, the 5 percent was based on an automatic landing. What we had seen in the simulations was that Neil Armstrong usually took over command when we were at about a thousand feet from the moon and landed the spacecraft manually. First, we realized that this would take more fuel, and, second, we saw a potential problem with fuel slosh in the tank. We first saw the fuel slosh on Apollo 10 when the descent stage was rotated to return to the Command Module without landing. An example of fuel slosh would be if you took a glass and filled it up half full of water, then moved it up and down like the Lunar Module would do during a smooth automated landing. The water would move around a little, but the surface would stay generally flat. Take the same glass and move it right and left and watch the water move up and down the sides of the glass. The more you move it right to left, the higher the water would go up the sides. The problem is that the height of the water in the middle of the glass is going up and down as well. Now think of the Lunar Module during the landing. The moon has one-sixth of the gravity of the earth, so the fuel would go six times higher and lower and do so much more slowly as if in slow motion. To make matters worse, the fuel gauges in the Lunar Module were in the center of each tank, so on the ground and in the spacecraft, we would see the readings going up and down. If the crew looked at the gauge when it was on a high cycle, they would think that they had a lot more fuel than they actually did. Conversely, if the crew saw the gauge at a low point, they might think that they were running out of fuel when they weren't.

All of this meant that our fuel margins were going to be less than we had planned on, and the crew would have a hard time understanding how much fuel they really had. This became a primary concern for the mission. I went to work on the slosh problem by coming up with a program that would take the cycling fuel readings and smooth them out to tell us how much propellant we really had. It was fairly complex since the level was constantly decreasing, while cycling up and down at the same time. We were two months away from the landing attempt, and I had to come with a program that told us how much fuel we had left at any given moment. At the same time, Neil would be increasing and decreasing the throttle settings as he attempted to land. My program took the last twenty seconds of data, got an average amount, determined the slope of the decreasing fuel level and projected the time the crew would have remaining, at an average throttle setting for landing. All of this had to be programmed into the Mission Control computers, and the results would be displayed on my console computer screen during landing. I had a button that I would push to start the calculation when we had about 8 percent of fuel remaining. When testing the program by running Apollo 10 data through the Mission Control computers, the program predicted the actual fuel remaining better than I had hoped. We had an independent contractor verify the results, and I think they were surprised just how accurately the program was able to predict the fuel and burn time remaining. The simulation computers did not simulate this problem because we didn't realize we had an issue until we reviewed the Apollo 10 data and saw how Neil was flying the Lunar Module simulator.

The Propellant Monitoring Program data was displayed as a plot on a separate screen since we didn't have time to reprogram my main screen. It showed the time remaining in seconds until we ran out of fuel. I already had a calculation of the time remaining until we ran out of fuel based on the instantaneous fuel level sent down from the spacecraft every two seconds but because of the slosh, it would fluctuate with big swings of time. It was already on my main screen, and it gave me a good comparison with the time remaining as shown by the Propellant Monitoring Program. The next step was to have a meeting with Gene Kranz, Bob Carlton, and the flight crew to set up procedures for how we were going to handle the fuel callouts for the crew during landing since we knew that their readouts would be inaccurate. We explained the problem to Neil and Buzz along with what we were doing so that we could give them a good handle on how much time they had left. At that meeting, we proposed that we would give a callout at sixty seconds of fuel remaining, thirty seconds of fuel remaining, and a final callout of "Abort" at fifteen seconds. I explained that we were using the fifteen seconds since we could be below the Dead Man Curve when we ran out of fuel. The Dead Man Curve shows that if you run out of fuel at seventy-five feet going down at five feet per second, while taking two seconds to recognize fuel depletion and then taking action, you will be falling at such a rate that you will crash before the ascent stage can pull away safely. Buzz agreed with the fifteen-second final callout. It was a long discussion that lasted over an hour and Neil didn't say anything the whole time. When we asked if there were any questions, Neil said, "Bob, can we rename the Dead Man Curve to something else, and I don't like the Abort callout." Neil explained that if he was fifteen feet above the surface and we called "Abort," he would abort, but if we said fifteen seconds or something else, he would go on and land realizing that the Lunar Module would survive the fall since we had one-sixth gravity on the moon and he knew that we had a few seconds of pad in that fifteen-second number. He said that if we called an abort and he went on and landed, there would be a big discussion on why he didn't abort when we told him to do so. It was decided that the Dead Man Curve would be called the "Abort Curve" and the fifteen-second callout would be "Bingo". The Bingo call came from Buzz who was a Navy Carrier pilot. When landing on a carrier, the flight director on the carrier would call out "Bingo," which meant that unless the pilot diverted his landing right then, he was committed to land. It matched what Neil would do if that situation came up.

One of the things that I learned that day was that Neil Armstrong was an extremely cool pilot who soaked up information like a sponge and had very little to say, but when he did say something, it was profound. For those that remember the movie *The Right Stuff,* I want to say that I have only met two astronauts that I know had the right stuff. They are Neil Armstrong and John Young. I will explain what I consider to be the *Right Stuff.* If headed for a crash landing, pilots with the "Right Stuff" would calmly transmit engineering information on what was happening and what could be done in the future to fix the problem. In addition, both Neil and John had photographic memories and were very quiet. I am so thankful that John Young had a photographic memory; otherwise, I would have never made it to NASA. I don't want to give the impression that there aren't other astronauts that had the "Right Stuff," but those two stand out. I shouldn't forget Jim Lovell. Jim had many of the attributes of Neil and John, but he wasn't as quiet and was more of a leader. That served him well on Apollo 13.

The one thing that I regret about this period of my life was that I was drifting away from church. Pat and I had gone to church a lot during our first year in Houston, but with my work schedule, I didn't go to church as much as I ought. Pat was doing some great work with an ESL (English as Second Language) class at University Baptist Church in Clear Lake while I was working hard to get men to the moon. I realize now that even though the only reason I got to live my dream was because of the Lord; I let my work keep me from being faithful to Him. I think that is a problem for many young people, but considering how blessed I was, I should have given more of my time and resources to the Lord. My entire line of command from John Wegener, to Bob Carlton, to Gene Kranz were all Christian men, and each knew that if we were going to successfully land a man on the moon, we were going to need the Lord. Gene ended each meeting before a major event with a prayer, either said by him or one of the other flight control members.

Things seemed to settle down as we were getting close to launch day. We were working hard on simulations and mission rules. Mission rules are determined by the team sitting down with management and deciding major decisions ahead of time rather than trying to make "on the spot" decisions during the mission. Mission rules were a lot tighter for the Apollo 11 mission since it was the first landing mission, and we didn't want to take risks with a vehicle we had never flown this close to the moon before. There were guidance mission rules that said if we got too far off course, we would have to abort, and those parameters were set out in detail. As we got close to the mission in late June 1969, there was one mission rule that drew a lot of discussion from the crew. The mission rule stated that if we didn't have landing radar data during the last part of the descent or if the distance above the moon diverged from where the computers thought we were, we would abort. The landing radar was an antenna on the spacecraft that told us the distance from the spacecraft to where the Lunar Module was pointed at the time. The burn would initiate with the Lunar Module facing engine first down the orbit around the moon. As the burn progressed, the Lunar Module would start tipping over until it was near vertical the last six hundred feet to the moon. The idea was that the landing radar was the best protection against not landing on the moon at a speed that would damage the Lunar Module. Our computers or MSFN weren't all that accurate and since there were no buildings or landmarks to judge distance to the surface, it was decided that we would need to have the landing radar at least on the first mission so we could gauge the accuracy of the computers better for future missions. Remember that all of this was brand-new, and we would be flying a quarter of a million miles from earth. The crew objected. They said that if all the computers and MSFN all agreed and Neil had a good visual out the window, he should be allowed to land. Management disagreed, so the mission rule stayed in. I am glad that we didn't have to test that mission rule during the actual flight. We almost had to.

We launched on the way to the moon on July 16, 1969. It was a glorious launch, and everything was going as planned. Lunar orbit was achieved on July 19. After the crew got some rest, it was time for them to board the Lunar Module and prepare for Powered Descent. Because we would be out of contact with the Command Module and the Lunar Module while they were behind the moon, we could only talk to them about 55 percent of the time that they were in orbit around the moon. Once the Lunar Module separated from the Command Module, they performed a short burn of the descent engine behind the moon to lower the orbit in order for Powered Descent to start about ten miles above the lunar surface.

During a meeting while the Lunar Module was behind the moon doing its burn, Gene made it clear that he didn't want anyone to feel that we had to press on, no matter what. Gene said that there would be other chances to land on the moon if this one wasn't successful. He reminded us that anyone could call an abort. Gene said he would rather err on the side of caution. We said a prayer. Gene asked us to be the best that we could be and said that if it was the Lord's will that we land on the moon that day, we would land on the moon. Gene asked for safety for the crew. Once the meeting broke up, Gene pulled Bob Carlton and me aside and said that he wanted us to not be afraid to call an abort on fuel if we thought the Lunar Module was running out of fuel. He said that he would back us, no matter what. He reiterated that he would rather we erred on the side of caution.

Since the Command Module remained in a sixty-mile orbit, Mike Collins contacted us first to tell us that the first short burn of the Lunar Module had been successful and everything was going as planned. Shortly after that, we heard from the crew in the Lunar Module as they rounded the moon, saying that the burn was good, and they gave us the information from the PGNS computer. That allowed us to update the PGNS computer with the final targets for the landing. As we prepared for the ignition of the Descent Engine for the Powered Descent, it became obvious that we were having communication problems with the Lunar Module. The signals were coming in and out and the communication (COM) guys were working to fix the problem. Gene announced that he needed the final "GO", "NO GO" for Powered Descent based on the latest data that we had. I never expected to hear that type of call. Everyone gave a "GO" except the COM guys who said they would be "GO" as soon as they got the data back on line. Without good communication (COM) the MSFN ground antennas (the three ground antennas needed to check the position of the Lunar Module), we would not know precisely where the astronauts were, and we couldn't monitor our systems or the fuel levels. Bad COM would end this landing attempt. We started the burn with intermittent COM, but the COM guy got Buzz to move the antenna to a better angle where it could track, and thankfully, communications were restored.

One of my duties was to call out the time since ignition. This was important for the propulsion systems so that we could compare where we were with where we should be on fuel for both the descent engine and the RCS jets. It would be important in the event of a problem; we wouldn't want to miss other important callouts and milestones while we were working the problem. Everything seemed to settle in, and I called out the thrust level of 9820 pounds of thrust. Nominal was 9775. The engine thrust was a little high and we reported it. Using my thrust calculation, the other controllers could calculate when the engine would throttle down from 100 percent thrust to about 50 percent thrust. This normally would occur at about six minutes and thirty seconds into the descent. The RETRO officer announced that throttle down would be about five seconds early at six minutes and twenty-five seconds into the burn. The net result of throttling down early would be that we would be a little long on our landing, which is exactly what happened. Right after I made the thrust call, there was a program alarm of 1202. Steve Bales, the guidance officer, had a few seconds to decide whether we were "GO" or "NO GO" on that error code. Once Steve consulted his software controller, Jack Garman, he realized that the computer was having a hard time keeping up with all its tasks and was saying that it was only going to do those needed for the burn, while ignoring the others. The Lunar Module computer (PGNS) worked on a two-second cycle. What this means is that it would take two seconds to decide where we were and what attitude the Lunar Module needed to be at for the next two seconds. It flew according to those numbers during the next two seconds while it was calculating the following two seconds worth of commands. If it couldn't complete all that it needed to during the two seconds, it would give an error code of 1202.

In post mission analysis, it was determined that there was a checklist error and a piece of equipment was turned on that was not needed for Powered Descent; this was taking away some of the computer power. The other thing that happened was that the crew had turned on the landing radar early because they were worried about it not working and forcing them to abort. The problem with turning it on early is that the Lunar Module was still lying on its back during the early part of the burn to slow it down. As a result, the landing radar was pointing so that it in fact, missed the moon. If you try to calculate a number that is very large, it takes a really long time. That problem resolved itself because while the flight controllers were talking about the 1202 error, the Lunar Module started to tilt over and the landing radar could calculate a number within the two-second cycle. There was some concern about the discrepancy in the difference between the PGNS calculated altitude and the landing radar altitude. This is called Delta H for the difference between the altitude that Landing Radar thinks we are from the surface and the altitude that the PGNS thinks we are above the surface. After about a minute, everything settled down; the two altitudes started to agree, and it seemed that things were going smoothly. We would not violate the mission rule and have to abort. We continued to be a "GO."

The early throttle down occurred just as predicted, and guidance started predicting that we were going to land "long". That meant that we were headed for a spot further down range from the targeted landing site. Everyone seemed to be okay with that, since the area we had picked for the first landing appeared to be relatively smooth. The engine was preforming well, and all the propulsion systems seemed to be tracking close to prediction except that there was a slightly larger difference between the fuel tanks than expected. As the burn progressed, they seemed to come closer together. My next callout other than the once a minute calls was for which tank should be the one for the crew to monitor. They had a switch that they had to rotate to look at each tank gauge and once I gave them the critical tank, they would switch to look at that tank. There were four tanks on the descent stage—two oxidizer and two fuel tanks. The two oxidizer tanks were manifold together and the two fuel tanks were manifold together. There was one on each side for balance, but one always seemed to go down slightly quicker than the other. I made my call as "Descent 2 Fuel Critical," Bob Carlton passed it on to Charlie Duke the CAPCOM (Capsule Communicator), and he passed it on to the crew that they would monitor Descent 2 Fuel. Things were looking good.

At this time, there were a few other alarms about the computer overloading a little, but Steve Bales continued to give "GOs" based on the fact that the calculations needed for Powered Descent were being made, and everything was looking good. Gene made a call at about ten minutes into the descent that the only callouts that he wanted to hear from that point on were the fuel callouts. Gene was saying that once he got a final "GO," "NO GO" for landing, he didn't want anyone giving status updates except fuel callouts. It was crunch time! We were GO for landing!

My computer screen and console showed RCS thruster activity and various engine and throttle settings. It was shortly after Gene got his final "GO" for landing, and it was passed up to the crew that I noticed a lot more thruster activity. In fact, Bill Strum, the AGS computer controller who sat next to me, reported to Bob Carlton that we had a lot of RCS thruster activity. John Nelson, the PGSN systems controller, reported that they were in attitude hold, which meant that the crew had taken over control of the Lunar Module. The Lunar Module was at about seven hundred feet at that time, a little lower for taking over manually, and I remember a sigh of relief that the crew wouldn't use a lot of propellant. What I didn't know is that we were headed for a boulder field, and Neil was having to translate forward to miss the boulder field before he could land. When the fuel level got to 5.6 percent, a low level sensor came on to say that we were low on fuel. Of course, we didn't know if it was reading low or high due to the slosh. It was about ten minutes and thirty seconds into the burn and I started my fuel monitoring program. After about twenty seconds, it settled down. The Propellant Monitoring Program was now predicting 4.5 percent remaining at touchdown. After reviewing all the figures and throttle settings, I made my sixty-second callout. Unfortunately, Neil was using a lot more fuel to get beyond the boulder field.

Normally, the flight director, Gene Kranz, was the only one who had a direct loop to talk to CAPCOM who talks directly to the crew but it was decided that I would get a special loop direct to CAPCOM that would only be used when it was time to make the fuel callouts. We realized that if I said "sixty seconds" to Bob Carlton and each of us passed the call down to the next person, the crew would get the call really late. I was to make the callouts to everyone including Charlie Duke (CAPCOM) two seconds early so that when Charlie said "sixty seconds" and the crew heard it, they would be at sixty

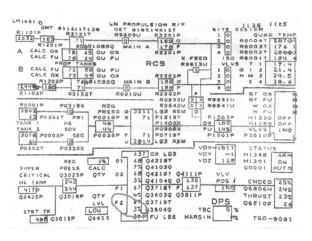

Copy of Lunar Module Propulsion display at landing on the moon. Top part is the RCS system data, the middle part is the ascent propulsion system data, and the bottom is the descent stage data. Note, Descent Fuel 2 was the lowest, as predicted, showing 3 percent at touchdown.

seconds. Remember that the time for the voice signal to the crew took a second. I remember making a strong positive "sixty seconds" call to everyone and Charlie reported it to the crew. The RCS activity continued, indicating that Neil was doing a lot of maneuvering. When the time came for the thirty-second call, there was disbelief in my voice. I never expected to make that callout. Right after I made the thirty-second call, and Charlie passed it on, I heard Buzz say "thirty seconds," acknowledging the call, and then he said, "Kicking up dust." I remember thinking this is going to be really close. I also had the job of announcing when they had landed. It just so happened that my computer display was the only display that showed engine chamber pressure (indicating whether the engine was burning or not), the accelerometer (that said whether the spacecraft was moving), and the engine on command. The screens were hard wired and couldn't be changed, and I was the only person who needed those indications. It was simple. If the engine wasn't burning and the spacecraft wasn't moving, it had landed.

I was hitting a button every second, making a copy of my screen so that I would have a record of all the pressures and temperatures if anything changed after we landed. My fuel program showed twenty-two seconds, which was seven seconds to Bingo when the engine shut off. I checked all the numbers and announced, "Engine off. They are down." Immediately, Charlie Duke announced, "We copy you are down," and then Neil said, "Tranquility Base here, the Eagle has landed."

What came next was Gene Kranz saying, "Settle down, I need everyone to look at their data and give a 'GO,' 'NO GO' for T1 Stay." I immediately checked all my temperatures and pressures. A drop in pressure in one of the ascent fuel tanks would indicate a possible fuel leak, so that was critical. I remember reporting that all my numbers were "steady, steady as a rock." We were GO for T1 Stay! Remember that T1 was a time ten minutes after landing that we could take off and return to the Command Module if we had a serious problem.

The powered descent had been very intense and, to be honest, I could hardly remember any of it at that time. When you are under that much pressure, your mind doesn't think about what has happened, just what you are to do at the moment. It wasn't until years later when I got a copy of the voice loop tapes that it all came back like a DVR playback. I clearly enjoyed hearing the landing more the first time I heard it on tape.

Once we were "stay for T1" and the vehicle got configured for lunar stay, Gene asked how much fuel we had left at landing. I initially told Bob and Gene that we had about 2 to 3 percent fuel remaining at landing. The loss of the "engine on" had locked my fuel monitoring program at twenty-two seconds of burn time. I reviewed the hard copies that I had made and confirmed twenty-two seconds to Gene. Twenty-two seconds is about 2 percent of fuel remaining, and we had 0.6 percent set aside for the slosh. That would mean that we had a total of 2.6 percent fuel remaining at touchdown. Twenty-two seconds was the number that he used at the press

The instruments left on the moon by Apollo 11 are still used to tell us that the moon is moving away from us at the rate of 2 inches per year.

conference a little later. A big study was conducted after the mission by TRW, and they concluded that my twenty-two seconds was well within the margin of error, so there was no reason to change that number. It stands today.

Recalling the earlier example of a car with a 350-mile range, 2.6 percent would equate to nine miles left till empty. But remembering that we could not count on 0.6 percent due to propellant slosh, our example would only have seven miles to empty. It was "scary close." As it turned out, no other mission would come this close. We installed slosh baffles in future Lunar Modules and with the lessons we learned, we never landed with less than 4.5 percent remaining.

As part of the power-down for lunar stay, the remaining helium used to pressurize the descent tanks was to be vented so it wouldn't heat up and possibly cause an automatic venting of propellant while the crew was on the lunar surface. These valves were added before the mission because we noticed during the simulations that Neil did not shut down the engines when he was four feet above the surface like Grumman had planned. They were worried that heat soak back from the lunar surface (think the bottom of the spacecraft overheating do to the exhaust coming back at the time of landing) could overpressurize the descent tanks and cause them to vent helium and fuel vapors on the crew while they were on the lunar surface. This procedure went as planned but created an overpressurization in one of the lines. It took us about two hours to resolve the problem before the crew could go out and walk on the moon.

Gene's shift was over, but we had stayed until the fuel overpressurization issue was resolved. After a lot of backslapping and hugging in the hall beside the Mission Control Room, we headed home to join the other five hundred million people worldwide who were ready to watch Neil and Buzz walk on the moon. What happened next really sticks in my mind. I walked out to my car in the far parking lot. It was very quiet, it was drizzling, and I got wet. It was a stark change from the stress of Mission Control that I had just left. As I drove out of the main road to the front gate at NASA's Manned Spacecraft Center, I turned on my car radio and Peggy Lee was singing, "Is that all there is?" I had a weird feeling that I had just helped land man on the moon at the age of twenty-four, and I had achieved the major life goal I had set for myself. I remember asking God out loud in the car, "Now that we have done this, what is next? Where do we go from here?" I was grateful for the journey that the Lord had provided for me.

I went home, and just as millions of other people did, Pat and I watched Neil and Buzz get out of the Lunar Module and walk around the moon. It was truly a dream come true. I only wish President Kennedy were alive to see it. I hope he was watching from heaven.

The Lord had gotten me to that point through a long list of improbable events. As I write this, I am far more amazed than I was at the time. When you are young, you think anything is possible. When you are older you realize that things like this just don't happen unless the Lord is with you, guiding you step by step. So much had been accomplished in the two short years that I had been at NASA. I give the Lord all the praise and glory.

6

Apollo 13, Failure Is Not an Option!

While the rest of the flight controllers were getting the crew of Apollo 11 safely home, we were already planning for Apollo 12. We had work to do to get the baffles made for Apollo 12 and to use the information that we learned from Apollo 11 to improve our accuracy on the next mission. Baffles are metal panes with holes in them that are unfolded inside the fuel tanks to slow the fuel from moving about. This was going to be really important because one of the goals of Apollo 12 was to perform a precise landing near the Surveyor 3 robotic lander and retrieve a part from it to study the effects of exposure to space. We also had to study our procedures so that we wouldn't have the fuel freezing and fuel line pressure problem we had on Apollo 11.

One of the biggest surprises that I had after the Apollo 11 mission was over was to learn many of the people whom we had worked with at Grumman had announced that they were leaving. It seems that once we landed safely on the moon, their contract for support of mission control would end exactly thirty days after the mission ended and they would lose their jobs. I know that they got nice bonuses and severance packages, but we were shocked that our friends would no longer be there to help us. One in particular, John Salek, was in charge of the Descent and Ascent Engine programs. We had spent hours and hours reviewing engine data, reviewing mission rules, and learning the capabilities of the Lunar Module engines.

John worked hard with us up until he left to help optimize what we had learned from Apollo 11. This knowledge would prove invaluable for Apollo 13.

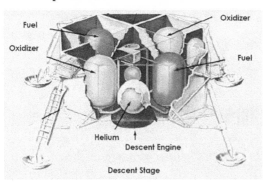

Meanwhile, I got busy working with other Grumman and NASA engineers and NASA Langley to test the new baffles that would be inserted through a service fitting in the bottom of the fuel tanks. The service fitting was a screw-in plug about four inches in diameter that was off center in the bottom of the

Cut-away diagram shows the two Fuel tanks and the two Oxidizer tanks that needed baffles

fuel tanks. The baffles had to be folded up, inserted through the hole, attached, and then unfolded. Grumman did a wonderful job of designing the baffles. I got to go to NASA Langley for testing of the new baffles. A plastic model of the Descent propellant tank was made so we could see the effects of slosh without and with the baffles. An actual fuel gauge assembly was installed in the tank. Each tank was about seven feet tall and four feet wide, a cylinder with domed top and bottom. The baffle would only be needed in the bottom two feet of the tank since that is when the exact amount of fuel remaining is critical. The really hard thing to simulate with the test rig was the one-sixth gravity on the moon. The engineers at Langley came up with a fluid that helped simulate the lunar environment. I was glad to see that the baffles really worked and the slosh problem was minimized. When the Lunar Module was designed, it was assumed that the landing would be automatic. Grumman had built into the software the ability to retarget the landing site from about one thousand to two thousand feet and still make an automatic landing. In the real "moon" world, the size of the boulders and craters would require every crew to take over control below a thousand feet above the lunar surface and manually land.

All aspects of the mission were revised based on the real world data we received on Apollo 11. As a result, all of the rest of the missions made pinpoint landings.

The Apollo 12 flight crew included Pete Conrad as commander, Alan Bean as Lunar Module pilot, and Dick Gordon as Command Module pilot. My mission duties for Apollo 12 were ascent from the lunar surface. Glen Watkins was the Lunar Module Powered Descent flight controller for Apollo 12. It was Glen's job to get them down and my job to get them back. Each team specialized in its part of the mission. There were three shifts, and we sat on the console during our shift whether there was a lot of activity or not. We had to be ready in any emergency to get the crew back on a moment's notice. The flight dynamics officer was constantly calculating times and targets for emergency return to orbit. We really didn't know if the spacecraft would be struck by a micro meteor or not. Today, we know that such things are very rare, but little was known about that sort of risk back in 1969.

Apollo 12 Ascent Stage prepares to re-dock with Command Module with the earth in the background.

Apollo 12 had a very difficult launch. At 36.5 seconds into the launch, there was a lightning strike from the rocket to the launch tower. The fuel cells and many of the systems were knocked off-line, but thanks to the wonderful engineering of Dr. Wernher Von Braun's team at NASA Huntsville, the Saturn V and the spacecraft survived the big jolt, the systems were brought back online, and the mission continued.

The landing on the moon, walking on the moon, and ascent from the moon went very smoothly. There are always small glitches, but that is why flight controllers exist—to solve those issues. It is impossible for the crew to know all the systems as well as dedicated flight controllers who spend every waking moment learning how their system works, what to do when it malfunctions, or how to handle a procedural error. It took three teams of about forty flight controllers on each team to fly each Apollo mission. That does not include the engineers who had particular experiments on the mission. What Apollo 12 taught us was that we could overcome problems and continue the mission. We proved that the lessons learned from Apollo 11 were applied properly on Apollo 12. The Apollo 12 Lunar Module landed about six hundred feet from the Surveyor spacecraft, and Pete and Alan were able to retrieve the part that allowed the engineers to see how spacecraft "weathered" from being exposed to space for two years. It was learned that the number of micro meteors are far less than predicted. That allowed us to dream that a large Space Station like the International Space Station could one day be built without having to worry about constant micro meteorite hits.

One thing that Pete did for his team was to carry about fifty flags in his personal box to the moon and bring them back to earth. Each Astronaut could carry a small box weighing no more than six pounds (including the aluminum box). Each of the small four inch by six inch flags had the edges cut off to save weight. After the mission, Pete had them mounted and gave them to the primary mission flight controllers and his flight support people. My flag from the Apollo 12 crew hangs proudly in our home. The message below the flag reads, "This flag was carried to the moon by the crew of Apollo 12" and below the message was, "November 19, 1969, Ocean of Storms". Ocean of Storms was the area on the moon that Apollo 12 landed. Pete could have taken more personal items, but he chose to honor us this way. He was quite a guy.

By now, everyone had begun to think that landing on the moon was routine. Nothing could have been further from the truth. One thing I have learned in life is that when you say, "Look at what I have done and how good I am," the Lord will send you a wake-up call. It doesn't matter whether you are talking about your job, how much money you make, how great your family is, or how easy it is to land on the moon—Look Out! Apollo 13 was that wake-up call for all of us in the Apollo Program.

The next mission was obviously Apollo 13 that was to land on the moon in April 1970. The missions had been spread out to cut down on overtime and help keep the budget down because we were in the middle of the Vietnam War and budgets were being squeezed. The crew we trained with included Jim Lovell as commander, Fred Haise as Lunar Module pilot, and Ken Mattingly as the Command Module pilot. Ken Mattingly was exposed to measles close to launch, so John Swigert from the backup crew took Ken's place on the mission.

My job on Apollo 13 involved contingencies. Apollo 11 and Apollo 12 were both planned to be on free return trajectories when launched from the earth to the moon. That means that once launched, you don't have to do anything if you want to return to the earth but swing around the moon and you will come back to earth. Apollo 13's weight and trajectory meant that it would not be on a free return flight path. If there was a problem, the spacecraft would arch around the moon and fly off into space. It would not head back to earth. The plan was that if there was a problem, the crew could fire up the Service Module Engine (that was normally used to put the spacecraft in orbit around the moon) for a short burn that would put the spacecraft on a free return trajectory.

Someone asked the question as to what we would do if a problem with the Service Module engine was the reason we were aborting the mission. We announced that we could use the Lunar Module Descent Engine to get the spacecraft back on a free return trajectory. With that in mind, a small group of five people (part of our shift from Apollo 11 Descent) were appointed to come up with procedures for doing a docked burn with the Descent Engine on the Lunar Module if it was needed.

At first, that may sound simple, but not only were there no procedures in place but, in addition, the Lunar Module weighed about 33,500 pounds, and the Command and Service Module weighed about 63,500 pounds. It would be similar to trying to drive your car with a dump truck attached to the front of the car. Your steering wouldn't work very well, the brakes wouldn't work right, and you couldn't see where you were going. We tried some simulations and found that the Lunar Module Computer couldn't control the vehicles docked together. Our team set out to come up with procedures on how to do that burn and how to control the burn once the engine lit. Without getting into all the details, we learned how to trick the Lunar Module Computer into thinking that the Lunar Module weighed over 97,000 pounds. There was a limit in the software to never accept a weight over 36,000 pounds, so we had to learn how to go into the software and trick the Lunar Module PGNS computer into thinking that we had a very heavy Lunar Module. In order to steer the spacecraft during the burn, we had to figure out how to get the engine gimbal to move to follow the docked center of gravity. We discovered that the Lunar Module just wouldn't control a 97,000 plus spacecraft. What we did learn is that if we rotated the Lunar Module about 75 degrees, the Lunar Module Descent engine would pass very close to the center of gravity of the two docked vehicles. We worked up a procedure to go to a soft dock position and then rotate the Lunar Module relative to the Command/Service Module. This wasn't easy because the coordinate systems were totally different in the Command/Service Module and the Lunar Module. We presented all this to the crew people and our flight control team. All they said was that they hoped we would not have to ever use our procedures. We never expected to use any of these procedures, but it was an interesting exercise and I learned a lot more about the abilities and limitations of the Lunar Module.

The Apollo 13 Saturn V launched at 13 minutes after 1:00 p.m. on April 11, 1970. Many people have noted that 1:00 p.m. is thirteen hours Military time. There had been a problem with what is called POGO during the launch of several of the previous Saturn V vehicles. It is a condition where an engine pulses and can cause a serious instability. One of the engines on the second stage had such a problem and the on board computer shut the engine down. The other engines burned longer to make up the difference in velocity.

Once in orbit everything checked out and Apollo was given the GO to do their burn to put them on the way to the moon. The S IV B (the third stage) was used for this burn.

Everything appeared very routine. My shift on the way to the moon was to watch a few temperature and pressure readouts on our propellant tanks to be sure we didn't have any issues with the Lunar Module. I got off shift at about fifty-four hours into the mission and headed

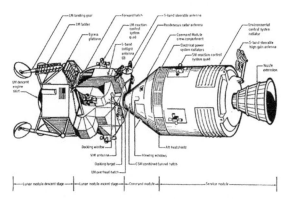

Apollo 13 diagram showing the command module, service module, and the lunar module (ascent and descent stages) at the time of the Apollo 13 explosion. Lunar Module landing gear has not been extended yet.

home. I remember it very clearly. I had changed into my pajamas and Pat brought me my dinner on a TV tray (for those that remember TV trays). It was just after 10:30 p.m. CT and Johnny Carson was starting his monolog. I had a Salisbury steak, mashed potatoes, and green peas. I had just started to eat my dinner when we got a phone call. Pat took the call and said NASA was on the phone. I was told that there had been an accident, to go to my office and get all the contingency studies and procedures, and get to Mission Control as soon as possible. Needless to say, I never ate that dinner. The news did not break on the radio until I was on the way to NASA. I only lived about ten minutes from the Manned Spacecraft Center.

When I got to Mission Control, there was a lot of confusion. The shift on duty was just trying to figure out what was working and what wasn't working. Moments after I got to Mission Control, it was decided that the Lunar Module would have to be a lifeboat to get the crew back to the earth safely. The Service Module had some sort of event at about fifty-six hours into the mission when they were about three quarters of the way to the moon. The fuel cells that provided power to the Service Module and the Command Module stopped working, and the oxygen that the crew needed was going down. The Command Module had limited battery power and oxygen for only about six hours of operation, and it would take days to get back to earth.

Gene did what Gene did best. He took control and announced that he was forming a "Tiger Team" that would work on the procedures for getting the crew back to earth using the Lunar Module, so the controllers that were scheduled to fly the mission would concentrate on flying the procedures that the "Tiger Team" came up with. The "Tiger Team" was mainly his team that performed powered descent on Apollo 11. For your information, "Tiger Team" represents a team that comes together to solve a particular problem.

Gene announced that he would have a meeting every two hours with the Tiger Team to see where we were and what needed to be done during the next two hours. During Gene's first meeting with the Tiger Team, he announced that "failure is not an option." Gene outlined the plan. He wanted everyone to tell him where they were with their consumables—oxygen, fuel, battery power, computers, etc. right then and to predict where they would be in two hours. It was obvious from the early two-hour meetings that we were not going to have enough consumables to make it back to earth. The Lunar Module was only designed to keep two astronauts alive for about two days on the moon. We had three astronauts to keep alive for five days. The numbers did not compute. The good news was that the Lunar Module had oxygen to pressurize itself twice after the crew returned from their space walks. That oxygen could help keep the crew alive while on the trip back to earth.

We had two things to do immediately. First, we had to do a burn to get us on a free return trajectory. In our meetings with the crew about our contingency procedures, Jim Lovell, the commander of the mission, said that whatever we did please do not let them miss the moon and zoom out into space where they would die a slow death with their families watching. He said he would rather crash into the back side of the moon than fly off into space. Not only did we have to figure out when and how to perform that burn, but we had to figure out what systems would be available to perform the burn. Second, we had to figure out how to stop using so much of our consumables so we would have a shot at getting the crew back safely.

When we presented the procedures for doing the rotation with the Command and Service Module, we realized that no one wanted to go to soft undock because it would use a lot of oxygen from the Command Module and that was a precious consumable. All of the oxygen in the Command Module would have to come from the oxygen that was normally used during reentry since the oxygen in the Service Module had been lost during the explosion. Since we had done so much work on the center gravity of the docked vehicle, we came up with an alternate way to do the burn. Since we only needed to do a short burn with the Descent Engine and the stack was so heavy, we could position the stack at a particular point and not try and control the stack while doing the burn. The stack would start to slowly rotate as the burn progressed and would keep rotating while the burn was in progress speeding up all the time. Based on the estimated burn time and thrust, it would only rotate about thirty degrees during the burn. This was based on the work we did premission. After the burn, we would have to use the Lunar Module thrusters to stop the rotation. Gene did not want to bring the PGNS computer online (remember that PGNS was the name of the Lunar Module Primary Computer) because one of the consumables we were really short on was battery power in the Lunar Module. The crew could look out the window after the burn and stop the rotation manually firing the jets. We had to calculate the amount of Lunar Module RCS fuel that would be used to stop the rotation since our RCS fuel would have to last us all the way home to earth. Stopping a rotation of the large stack would use a lot of RCS fuel.

It was decided that this was the best approach. The earlier we did the burn, the better. There was a lot of work to do to translate all of this to procedures for the crew to do a manual burn with an engine that was never intended to do this kind of burn. The good news is the Descent Engine had proven itself in testing at White Sands, New Mexico.

The next big question was how to do the burn and for how long. It turns out that the ground computers were never configured to do this kind of burn and we had to do all the calculations by hand. Remember that even hand-held calculators had not yet been invented. We asked Grumman to give us their best recommendation on what burn profile we should use for the burn. Grumman actually answered that they did not recommend burning the Descent Engine this way since it had never been tested. The problem was that all the people that knew anything about what burn profile to use were no longer working for Grumman.

Red Whitmore, one of the Grumman engineers, got a message to me to call him on the direct phone line. He asked me if I wanted John Salek's home phone. I thanked him for his help and said, "Absolutely." When I called John's home number, his wife answered. She said that John was expecting my call. She said that he was at one of his laundromats. It seems that John took his severance from Grumman and bought a series of laundromats and was managing those. She gave me his phone number, and I gave John a call. I cleared it with my team, and they said it was a great idea, since Grumman was taking the safe road. I brought him up to speed and reviewed the problems with John.

Whenever we did a burn, we fired the RCS engines (one-hundred-pound thrust Reaction Control rockets) for five seconds in the direction of the descent engine in order to push the propellant to the bottom of the tank (remember that propellant floats around in zero gravity). With the weight of the stacked vehicle, we would have to do an RCS burn of forty seconds to get ready to start the descent engine. We just didn't have the RCS propellant to do that. The good news is with the tanks almost full (they were loaded to 96 percent of capacity) there was less chance of this happening. John and I discussed testing that had been done to see how much of this type of abuse the engine could stand. John reminded me that the engine never failed at 10 percent throttle setting no matter how much we abused the engine with alternate fuel and oxidizer. I also remembered that at 40 percent throttle, the engine took a huge amount of abuse before it failed. As far as this situation was concerned, we were the two most knowledgeable people in the world to be having this conversation. From this, we decided that we should do a five-second burn at 10 percent throttle and then have the crew increase the throttle to 40 percent to finish the burn. The five seconds at 10 percent would be more than forty seconds of RCS firing to get the propellant to be bottom of the tank. The remainder of the burn would be done at 40 percent. I presented our plan and our reasoning, and Bob Carlton and Gene Kranz liked it.

Once we knew the velocity we needed to achieve, all we would have to do was to calculate the burn time. The guidance officer (GUIDO) came up with the velocity change he needed and where the velocity vector needed to be pointed.

I had to calculate the burn time by hand, using an Olivetti desk top calculator, and my slide rule. There is a funny story about my slide rule. I was sitting there with my slide rule checking and rechecking the burn profile when Dr. Low, the program manager, came up behind me and said, "Nance, what are you doing using a slide rule?" I responded, "Dr. Low, I have calculated the burn time by hand, by Olivetti Desktop calculator, and now I am confirming my work with my slide rule." Dr. Low said, "Okay, go ahead." I don't think he was as convinced as Gene about our burn. The next time you watch the movie *Apollo 13,* notice there is a quick take of a slide rule sitting on a console. You probably never noticed it before. There is no one in the picture just a two or three-second shot of a slide rule lying on the console. Now you know why it is in the movie.

The burn time I calculated was 41.6 seconds with 5 seconds at 10 percent throttle and between 36 and 37 seconds at 40 percent throttle. The crew did this burn totally by hand. The procedures to make this happen were fairly long since the Lunar Module was never designed to do a manual burn of the descent engine, and the crew was starting to get cold since we weren't heating the Lunar Module to save battery power.

At about six hours after the accident, we performed the get back on free return burn without a hitch. The crew performed flawlessly and the burn went exactly as we intended. GUIDO said that he was happy with the burn. There was so much more to do at this point, but, at least, we were going to get them headed back to earth. They would now continue on to the moon, swing around behind the moon, and head back to earth. Now, the really hard work began.

Gene Kranz continued to have the two-hour meetings with the Tiger Team. The first thing he would do was to ask exactly where we were on consumables. It wasn't until almost twelve hours before we had a good handle on the consumables and how to stretch them out. There were a lot of hard decisions to make. Every area thought they really needed their system to operate; it was evident that battery power was going to be a major limiting factor. Powering up computers and heaters just consumed too much power. We had the crew minimize their movements to save oxygen, another consumable that was in very short supply. We couldn't use the RCS to keep the spacecraft stable because we would need them for any future burns of the Descent Engine. By then, the Tiger Team had come up with a plan to bring Apollo 13 back to the earth safely. We would do another burn with the Descent Engine to speed up the spacecraft to arrive back at the earth ten hours earlier than just continuing on the free return trajectory. That would get us within the limits of the oxygen available and the battery power available if we minimized their use after the burn.

Since the burn was a larger burn than the first burn, we decided to use the horizontal RCS jets to keep the spacecraft pointed in about the same direction during the burn. We had learned from the first burn that we could get a good burn if we could keep them pointed close to the direction we needed. We decided to put the spacecraft in a "barbecue mode" after the burn where we would use the RCS jets to put the spacecraft in a slow roll about its axis so it would stay stable and equalize the temperature inside the Lunar Module. Since we couldn't run the heaters very long due to limited battery power, the Lunar Module was continuing to get colder and colder.

Since the burn profile that John Salek and I had come up with for the first burn worked well, we repeated it for the second burn except the 40 percent throttle part would last about ninety seconds. The burn went well and the crew was able to keep the spacecraft within about five to seven degrees of the direction we needed for the burn. Once again, the variations to the right or left nulled each other out, and the burn did exactly what we needed. In the movie *Apollo 13*, the burn shown was nothing like the actual one performed. The 3800 pounds of thrust from the Descent Engine would not wildly move the vehicle very fast. The two vehicle stack weighed 97,000 pounds at that time. It moved slowly from side to side. We did use a lot of the RCS propellant but we knew we would. The RCS propellant was down to about 38 percent remaining after the burn, and we had days to go. We had just enough propellant left in the RCS to perform the last small course correction.

We still had a lot of work to do, but, for the first time, we really could see that if we didn't have any other issues, we were going to get the crew back safely. Our team had just gotten off shift before the accident, gone home for a few hours, were called back, and had been working for another fifteen hours. In total, we had been working for over twenty-four hours. It seemed like an hour. There was a bunk room behind Mission Control on the same floor, and the cafeteria people had

Deke Slayton shows flight director, Milt Windler (left) and Chris Kraft (on the right with dark glasses) the device to get the carbon dioxide out of the Lunar Module

brought us sandwiches. I remember that John Wegener and I went to the bunk room to try and get some sleep. We each said that we were very thankful that we had gotten as far as we had and needed to thank the Lord for that and asked for His help in getting the crew back. I remember falling asleep praying for help. I awoke about an hour and a half later with my head full of actions we were going to have to take to "safe" the Descent Engine (safe means to keep its pressures within safe limits), since we had pressurized it some fifteen hours earlier. I think that brief hour and a half sleep was the only sleep I got during the rest of the mission. I was worried about the RCS engines not getting enough heat and the possibility of the fuel lines freezing during the barbecue period. We were running on adrenaline.

When I got back from my short rest, the environment guys were discussing the fact they were running out of lithium hydroxide canisters to scrub the carbon dioxide from the air. The third person in the Lunar Module was breathing out more carbon dioxide than the Lunar Module could handle. The Command Module had the same type of system as the Lunar Module, but since they were built by two totally different manufacturers, the lithium hydroxide canisters were totally different. I was working on my RCS profiles to be sure that we were going to have enough RCS to conduct the last burn and have enough to maintain attitude during the final phases of the flight back to earth. The environment controllers assigned to each person various items that were on board the Command and Lunar Modules that they might use. Each person was to go out and get their item or items and come back so the environment controllers could figure out how to make the square Command Module canister work in the round Lunar Module canisters. This is a perfect example of how the

A photograph of the actual emergency Carbon Dioxide Canister was released by NASA in October 2015

Apollo 13 movie deviated from the facts to simplify the events. Instead of one guy coming in and dumping a bunch of items on the table, in fact, it took several hours to locate the pieces from all over the Manned Spacecraft Center Campus and bring them to Mission Control.

Solving the canister issue was a group effort. As I saw them about to carry the contraption to show Gene, I asked one of the environment guys if the crew really had duct tape on the Command Module. One of my first tasks when I first started work in 1967 was to help identify all the things that were in the Lunar Module that could be a fire hazard since the Apollo 1 fire had happened just months before. One of the items our group identified was duct tape. It seems that duct tape has a paper product in it and can ignite in an oxygenated atmosphere. We therefore removed all duct tape from the Lunar Module. I was surprised that there would be duct tape in the Command Module, since I knew we removed it from the Lunar Module. The environment controllers made a quick check and discovered that there was no duct tape in the Command Module. They scrambled around and discovered that there were two rolls of white adhesive tape in the first aid kit onboard. They quickly redid the canister adapter using white adhesive tape that would normally be used for putting a gauze patch over an injury. Since there was such a limited amount, the crew was given detailed instructions on how long each piece of tape had to be so they wouldn't run out. The crew was asking Mission Control to hurry up with the procedure to make the adapted canister, and the environment guys were working feverishly to design a procedure that wouldn't run out of tape.

It is amazing that something that I did during my first days at NASA while I was living on $60 for a month could have had such an impact on helping to get the Apollo 13 crew back safely. Getting the crew back safely involved hundreds of acts like this from hundreds of people all pulling together for a common goal. I call it answered prayer. The Lord had His hand all over this mission. I fully understand now why Gene Kranz called this "Our Finest Hour."

The crew fought cold temperatures as low as forty degrees, but still performed the last burn using the RCS thrusters in the reverse direction to slow the spacecraft down a little. Now the attention turned toward getting the Command Module fired up again as the spacecraft stack approached the earth. The Command Module had about six hours of consumables that would get them safely back to earth once the Lunar Module was jettisoned. The problem was that the Command Module had gotten really cold during all this time.

We had to bring the Command Module computers up again and get them aligned so they knew the exact position of the Command Module. The Command Module flight controllers had been working all the way back from the moon to write procedures that were different from any the crew had ever seen before. The crew performed flawlessly, and the Command Module came back to life. Understand that the systems from the Service Module are dead at this point and the Command Module is independent of the Service Module.

The first order of business was to jettison the Service Module. Since we didn't know how badly it had been damaged, there were fears that it might not jettison properly. The power for this operation normally comes from the Service Module, so the flight controllers had to come up with a backup plan to make this happen. The good news is that they succeeded and the jettisoning of the Service Module was successful. However, the astronauts were in for a big shock when they saw a big hole in the side of the Service Module where a whole panel had been blown off. The immediate concern on the ground was that the heat shield, which is right above where the panel blew off might be damaged. I remember Gene asking whether we could we do anything about it if it was damaged,

Apollo 13 Service Module right after it was jettisoned - showing the damage from the explosion

and the answer was no. Gene said that there was no reason to mention this to the crew; they had enough to worry about.

After the Service Module was jettisoned, the Lunar Module was used to reposition both the Lunar Module and the Command Module for Lunar Module jettisoning. By now the two vehicles were much lighter without the Service Module and the maneuver looked fairly normal. The crew put the Lunar Module in "Attitude Hold" that would hold its position, and the last two crew members left the Lunar Module and closed the hatch, effectively bidding farewell to their lifeboat. By now, the two spacecraft were nearing the earth's atmosphere, and the Lunar Module was jettisoned. A short time later, it burned up in the atmosphere. The Lunar Module flight controller's job was over. As it entered the atmosphere, I noted that only about 5 percent of the propellant remained in the RCS fuel tanks.

I remember walking to the front of the Mission Control Center and standing beside the column on the right side right in front of the big screen to the right of the other screens. The communication flight controllers had told us that since the crew was coming faster than we had ever come before, the blackout was going to last closer to five minutes instead of the normal three minutes. The blackout occurred because the heated atmosphere around the spacecraft during reentry disrupted radio signals. Looking back to the *Apollo 13* movie, this was its greatest flaw. The movie suggests that no one knew that it was going to take extra time. In fact, we had much to worry about without that little Hollywood moment thrown in there. First, we were coming in very "hot" because of the burn we had made to get to the earth earlier. The Command Module had never been tested to this speed before. On paper, it should be able to handle it, but success was not guaranteed. Second, we didn't know whether or not the heat shield had been damaged in the explosion in the Service Module and whether it would hold. Finally, atmosphere modeling at these speeds was an educated guess, making it unknown whether the Command Module would be able to steer the spacecraft close to the landing site.

What I do remember about the blackout period was looking back at Gene Kranz. He had his head bowed in prayer—I mean serious prayer. His fingers were pinching the top of his nose together. I realized that I needed to join him. It was so very good to have a mentor like Gene Kranz in my life. Moreover, I am sure that there were millions of people praying for the Apollo 13 crew at that time.

About ten seconds after we were told that we should hear from the crew, we did hear from them, and seconds later, on the screen right in front of me, we saw the picture of the three chutes opening up. This picture was being shot from one of the helicopters assigned to retrieve the crew, and the crew was returned

President Nixon presents the Presidential Medal of Freedom to the Mission Operations Team represented by the four flight directors including Gene Kranz in the middle in the dark suit

safely. Millions of people had their prayers answered that day. On top of that, Apollo 13 had made the most pinpoint landing to date. I really think that the Lord does things like this just to remind us that there is nothing, absolutely nothing that He cannot do. I think of it as God putting His explanation point on the situation.

A lot of very dedicated people did a wonderful job coming together and doing what needed to be done to get the crew of Apollo 13 back safely with the whole world watching and praying. I played just a small part in achieving that goal. In the space of just a few days, God had reminded us that we are never as good as we think we are, but if we turn to Him in prayer, nothing is impossible. The pride of Apollo 11 changed during those days. The Lord does not want us to say, "Look at what I have done," but rather, "Look at the way the Lord has blessed me." The Lord showed us in Apollo 13 both failure and victory. I just wish that spirit would be applied to our world today. I know the Lord would be a lot happier with us if we did.

I received a crew emblem from one of the spacesuits signed by all three crew members, and President Richard Nixon came to the Manned Spacecraft Center to present the National Medal of Freedom to the Flight Operations Team. I am certainly proud of that; however, those honors were nothing compared to the satisfaction of bringing the crew back safely. It was truly NASA's finest hour as Gene had said.

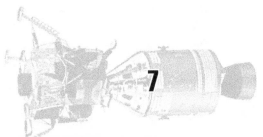

7

All Good Dreams Must Come to an End

Apollo 13 showed just how far the space program had come. Not only could we land on the moon and return the crew safely back to earth, but also we could all pull together to overcome huge problems and get the crew back safely. We also learned that we had made space travel look too easy, and it is hard, really hard, and full of potential disasters. After Apollo 13, we realized it was time to devote more time to learning just how much we could maximize our abilities to overcome problems.

The crew of Apollo 14 was named. Alan Shepard, the first American in space would serve as Commander. Edgar Mitchell was named Lunar Module pilot, and Stuart Roosa, the Command Module pilot. A lot of time elapsed between Apollo 13 and 14 because we needed to conduct a full review of what had gone wrong on Apollo 13. We needed to reassure ourselves that we would not suffer any issues such as those that occurred on Apollo 13. It would be nine months before the next Lunar Landing attempt. We explored the possibilities using alternate procedures to get more out of the Lunar Module, both for operational issues and for emergency situations. We came up with what we called Malfunction Procedures. These procedures amounted to an expansion of our mission rules to include work-arounds that would allow us to continue the normal mission after certain types of failures, using available systems to continue the mission. We were taking what we learned from Apollo 13 and applying that knowledge to future missions.

We passed some of our procedures to the crew division for comments. We had worked with several crew members while devising the various procedures, but we wanted more feedback. Jim Hannigan came to me and said that John Young wanted to know if we would like to use the Lunar Module Simulator to test some of our procedures. John knew from our time together at Georgia Tech that I had flying experience. I jumped at the prospect of spending time in the simulator.

In the lead-up to Apollo 14, the simulator computers would normally get going by 5:30 or 6:00 a.m. They would just sit there idle until the crew came in at 7:00 a.m., so John made arrangements for us to come in at 5:30 a.m. If the computers were ready to go, the simulation guys would let us carry out some test runs. We would come in with scripts of failures and then we would test our workaround procedures to see if they were practical.

It took me quite a few landing attempts to be successful. When the pilot crashed, there was a big bang on the floor to let you know you didn't do so well. By the third session, I was getting the hang of it so we started testing our procedures. First, we tested the procedure to give the crew a second "engine on" command from the computer. Mission rules required that we have two "engine on" signals in order to continue powered descent. If we lost one of the "engine on" signals during landing, we would have to abort and scuttle the landing. Our procedure if we lost one of the two "engine on" signals during descent was to pull the "abort" circuit breaker and then flip the Descent Abort switch. That would give us our second "engine on" signal since it was hard wired into the "abort" button. Since the computer would not see the abort command with the circuit breaker pulled, the crew could keep on landing. If we had to abort, all we had to do was push in the "abort" circuit breaker and the computer would abort. As good as it sounded to us, John Young knew better, and that is why he suggested that we simulate this procedure first.

We were about halfway through our powered descent simulation when the sim guys caused us to lose one of our "engine on" signals. We analyzed the problem but were unable to restore the second "engine on" signal. We carried out our procedure and went to reach for the "abort" circuit breaker only to find that it was located on the back wall of the Lunar Module. The crew was strapped into a standing position during landing, and the switch was about three feet away. Oops—we forgot to take into account the physical aspect of our procedure into account. In our simulation, then, we had to abort the descent. John Young had made his point and we had a lot of fun at the same time. By the way, we changed our procedure to tell the Abort Guidance Computer to ignore the physical "abort" switch unless we gave it a command to proceed with the abort. The good news is that we never had to use the procedure.

View from inside the Lunar Module Simulator. Views outside the windows generated by cameras taking pictures of models and projecting the images on the windows. Computer generated images would be 15 years in the future.

Over the next couple of weeks, we reviewed our malfunction procedures using the Lunar Module simulator and made corrections where needed. I thought that I was quite competent at flying the Lunar Module simulator until the day John Young came in early and decided to have some fun. The game was to see how many failures he could get the sim guys to put in before I could no longer fly. They dealt me leaks, thruster failures, and computer failures. John had a big laugh and I came back to the real world knowing that I wasn't an astronaut after all.

As we got closer to the Apollo 14 flight, we started using some of our Malfunction Procedures and work-arounds during joint crew and flight control simulations. The Grumman guys started getting nervous, since we weren't using the Lunar Module the way it was designed. It was decided that we would go to Grumman on Long Island and review the procedures with Grumman management and the crew. Ed Mitchell came to represent the crew, and several of us went to explain our procedures and why we had come up with them. We spent the better part of a week reviewing the procedures. It was only about five weeks before Apollo 14. Ed Mitchell was a great astronaut to work with. He really wanted us to help him learn more about the systems and how the procedures would increase their chances of landing on the moon. What surprised me was that he was a chain-smoker. I had never met a chain-smoker before. Ed explained that a chain-smoker is a person who finishes one cigarette and lights his next cigarette off the one he is smoking before putting the first one out. I asked Ed what he was going to do during the mission. He said that he was going to go "cold turkey" and that there was some sort of "patch" that was going to help him with that. I guess now we know where the nicotine patch got its start.

I spent a lot of time doing presentations on my Descent Stage Propellant Program because the Apollo 14 Lunar Module was heavier than the previous spacecraft and that meant the fuel margins would be lower on this mission. The slosh baffles were working very well, but there was still some slosh, just not near as much. The rest of the Apollo flights would use a newer version of the Lunar Module that was somewhat lighter. The margins would be much better even though they would carry the Lunar Rover on those missions. Several months before the mission, I was giving a presentation to management in a small auditorium in the Manned Spacecraft Headquarters building (Building 2). During that presentation, I was asked to stop because a test of the Apollo Service Module was being performed at White Sands Missile Range. The Apollo 13 explosion was being duplicated so we would understand what happened on the Apollo 13 mission. We had a video and audio feed from White Sands, so we sat and watched as the test was conducted.

The test of the Apollo Service Module finally went off, and it exploded just as Apollo 13 did. It was amazing how similar the damage was in comparison to the photos the Apollo 13 crew took of the Service Module after it was jettisoned. I finished my presentation realizing just how lucky we had been on Apollo 13. The White Sands test confirmed how very close we came to losing the crew.

Ed Mitchell on the lunar surface during Apollo 14

The Apollo 14 mission went beautifully, and I think most people remember that on that mission, Alan Shepard hit a couple of golf balls on the moon. Shepard said that the golf balls went for miles and miles, a bit of an exaggeration. However, they would go six times as far due to lunar gravity being a sixth of the earth's gravity. Alan, a big-time golfer, now had bragging rights for hitting the longest drive in history.

We were back on track now that Apollo 14 was a great success. Next up was the Apollo 15 mission. This was the first mission using the Lunar Rover, and which meant they could go much farther from the Lunar Module. The missions were becoming a lot more exciting. The first missions were about ensuring that we could land and return safely, and subsequent missions would involve exploring. Altogether, there were three periods of moon walking and rover driving totaling eighteen and a half hours. Other than a few small issues, future missions went smoothly. The cameras were improving, meaning space walks on the surface were especially exciting. Color video from the Lunar Rover was possible because technology was improving at a rapid clip. I am sure that this developing technology quickly advanced our television industry here on earth. It is important to remember that we were doing all of this without communication satellites. It was the space program that pushed communications forward by decades. It is hard to believe that when the attached picture was taken it had been just ten years since President John F. Kennedy challenged us to go to the moon. The difference then was that we were on a mission to land on the moon and politics didn't get in the way. We were all about just getting the job done, and it was an amazing time.

Only six months later, we would take off for the moon again. Apollo 16 was a very special mission for me. John Young served as commander, and Charlie Duke was the Lunar Module pilot. Charlie was the capsule communicator on Apollo 11, and I had worked with him a great deal as we came up with the fuel callouts. In addition, Apollo 16 would be the third time I worked as the prime Lunar Module Propulsion flight controller for powered descent. I felt that I could enjoy it more this time as procedures had gotten more routine. Of course, I learned another life lesson—never think like that. Just when you think you have it made, God will remind you that life is full of surprises, and even road blocks. Those troubles, difficulties, and complications help us grow in our walk with Him.

Everything on the mission went well until the Lunar Module separated from the Command and Service Module. Shortly after undocking, a problem appeared in the Service Module control as Ken Mattingly prepared for a small burn to change the Command and Service Module's orbit. It took about six hours to sort out the problem and come up with a work-around so that the mission rules could be met for the Command and Service Module. If the Command and Service Module flight controllers hadn't come up with a solution, the mission would have been aborted and the Lunar Module would have been used as a back-up much as it had on Apollo 13. The burn was successfully performed by the Command and Service Module, so the mission was ready to proceed.

This mission was a really big test for the flight controllers because the entire burn profile and timeline had changed greatly due to the issue with the Service Module. The issue was that the landing site moved during the time it took to sort out the Service Module problem. The good news is that the moon basically only rotates once every twenty-eight days, so the landing site had not moved too far from the Lunar Module during the extra six and a half hours. This did mean that we were doing a slight out of plane burn that would use more propellant. The computers that we were using on the ground really were challenged to come up with how the burn was going to be done, how the earth ground stations would be used, and a lot of other considerations that we normally would require months to complete ahead of the mission. Recall that there are only three ground antenna that can support the landing. One antenna is in Goldstone, New Mexico; one is in Spain; and one is in Australia. While we were sorting out the problem, the ground stations had moved ninety degrees from where we had expected them to be. Since we had used so many Lunar Module consumables including RCS fuel, oxygen, and power while the problem was being sorted out, we had a very narrow window to make the landing. I must admit that for a while it looked as if we weren't going to land on the moon that mission.

Powered Descent went smoothly with hardly any issues. Since John knew we were going to use more propellant, he didn't deviate much from where the computer was taking him. As it was, we landed only about nine hundred feet down range from the desired landing site and only two hundred feet to one side. Considering that the Lunar Rover would be able to take them miles and miles from the Lunar Lander, the landing was nearly on target. The fact that we were so close was a tribute to the guidance flight controllers who had to make large changes to the guidance targets because Powered Descent started almost a mile higher than the normal ten miles high due to the delay.

Once we were on the moon, the entire timeline had to be changed because of lost time and where the ground stations would be during the moon walks. Without the proper ground stations, we wouldn't be able to get the TV coverage we were becoming accustomed to during these missions. Changes also were needed to be made to conserve battery power. The propulsion side of things weren't affected very much except that our shifts were all out of sync. My landing shift was supposed to be about nine hours long, and it turned out to be over sixteen hours. The next three cycles were all adjusted so that we would match the crew's revised sleep and moon walking schedules.

One thing that Ed Fendell in flight control communications had worked on involved the Lunar Rover camera setup to broadcast a live picture of the liftoff from the Lunar Surface. Success was all about timing, specifically when commands had to be sent to the moon so the camera would move upward to track the Lunar Module. Ed had tried it on Apollo 15 and had gotten the first couple of seconds, but we lost the picture of the Lunar Module after that. He got everything perfect on Apollo 16, and we got a spectacular view of the Lunar Module taking off as a result.

John Young on the lunar surface during Apollo 16

Once again, we had overcome adversity and continued our mission. I was clearly learning that we see what we are made of when the chips are down. I am sure that is why every time we get too proud and think that we have it made, God sends us a wake-up call. Even rocket scientists seem to have very short memories. In our personal lives, we seem to forget that everything we have and are able to do is because the Lord blesses us. NASA, for all its great achievements, is no different. Even with all the lessons learned during and after all the problems and mistakes of the Apollo program, we still suffered the Challenger and Columbia accidents. Both the Challenger and Columbia accidents were preventable and were caused by human failure, not by accident or faulty equipment.

After the Apollo 16 mission, John Young gave me a flag that they had carried to the moon and he wrote on it, "Bob, thanks for all your hard work," along with the signatures of all three crew members. That means more to me than any other keepsake I got during my NASA days.

Due to budget cuts, Apollo 17 turned out to be the last lunar mission for Apollo. The hardware was built and ready to go for Apollo 18, 19, and 20, but they were never flown. The crew for the Lunar Module on Apollo 17 was Gene Cernan as commander and Harrison Schmidt as Lunar Module pilot. Because Harrison was a geologist, the scientific community was excited about having a "real" scientist going to the moon.

The Apollo 17 mission was a textbook flight. There were no major problems, and the crew landed very close to the desired landing site. Gene had let all the other astronauts know that he was going to land closer to his targeted landing spot than anyone else. That was no small task since Apollo 12 had landed quite close to its target. Gene pulled it off and landed right on target.

The thing I remember most from Apollo 17 was the sheer excitement that Harrison Schmidt exhibited while being on the lunar surface. During each moon walk, Harrison would beg for more time. He only received about twenty minutes extra on each moon walk, even though Gene was right there with Harrison asking for more time. Gene loved driving the Lunar Rover, and he made it look as if he were driving a sports car. He didn't drive the wheels off it but did manage to knock off a fender. Other than getting covered in moon dust, this wasn't a big problem. In one-sixth gravity, the Lunar Rover would really "sport around." The astronauts drove a long way out from the Lunar Module and collected some excellent samples, to Harrison's delight. It was a great mission to conclude our

Gene Cernan loved to drive the lunar rover on Apollo 17

exploration of the moon. The 842 pounds of moon rocks brought back from the Apollo missions are still being studied today.

Many years later, after the fall of the Soviet Union, we would learn that Russia had tried to mount a lunar landing program, but it had met with disaster when two of the moon rockets had exploded. The first one exploded while it was being loaded with propellant resulting in many deaths. Their moon rocket never flew. The Soviets did manage to send an unmanned spacecraft to the moon (Luna 16) in September 1970, bringing back about twenty pounds of lunar dust and small rocks for study. We learned that the Soviet Union launched an unmanned lunar spacecraft while Apollo 11 was on the way to the moon, with the objective of retrieving small lunar sample before the United States could. The Soviet spacecraft, much smaller than the Apollo spacecraft, crashed into the moon without landing. It was clear at this point that we had won the space race.

During this time, Pat had been busy teaching seventh grade English at Seabrook Intermediate School. She had a lot of the astronaut kids as students, and it was a lot different from her first year at Jackson Junior High School in Houston where many of the kids weren't motived to even graduate from High School. With the end of the lunar landing missions, I found myself with a lot more time on my hands. Pat and I started planning to build a new home in Clear Lake Forest and start a family. We bought our first boat and had fun boating and fishing. Now it was time to enjoy the fruits of all the hard work and long hours.

After the final Apollo flight, we wrote many reports and papers regarding what we learned from Apollo. One of the reports I was asked to write involved my prediction on the state of future propulsion for future spacecraft. I reviewed all the propulsion studies that were underway at NASA, including Nuclear, and predicted that for long range spaceflight to the planets, we would have to use Ion Propulsion. It seems that my prediction is just now starting to come true. The world thought that Nuclear Propulsion was going to be the answer, but the lead or water shielding for a nuclear engine defeated the efficiency of Nuclear Propulsion. It simply made the spacecraft too large. Another propulsion system that seemed to be promising was a plasma rocket. The problem at that time was the solar cells simply couldn't produce enough power to make them work with anything but a very small spacecraft. Thanks to much better solar cells, plasma rockets are now being deployed on some interplanetary spacecraft.

NASA started trying to decide what was to come next for manned space flight. We had a lot of hardware left over from the Apollo program and there was talk about building a Space Transportation System in the future. The idea of a space station based on an empty S-IV B Saturn rocket third stage was born. The plan was to launch the space station on a Saturn V rocket and then have astronauts visit the lab in three visits, all launched by Saturn IB rockets. All of the main hardware would come from the leftovers of the Apollo lunar landing program. Part of this mission was to build a series of telescopes that the crew would operate during their one month stays on the Skylab. This would be a totally new project called the Apollo Telescope Mount or ATM. Since the Lunar Module would not be used for this mission, our group was assigned to be the flight control team to "fly" the Apollo Telescope Mount. It would replace the Lunar Module during launch and then swing down and attach to the S-IV B Skylab during the mission. Two large solar panels were added to the S-IV B to provide power to the mission. An unusual detail was that the telescopes on the ATM used film canisters since digital photography didn't exist then. This meant that there were going to be a lot of Extra Vehicular Activities (EVA) to change out the film canisters on the ATM. It would be like taking twenty rolls of film during your vacation, hoping that they would all come out.

As part of the ATM program, I was promoted to be one of the lead flight controllers on the ATM part of Skylab. This meant that I got a raise in pay. I had started as a GS 7 in 1967 and now was a GS 11 making about five times as much as when I started at NASA. It was only a short wait to make the next grade which was a GS 12. I did not know it, but John Wegener, Bob Carlton, and Jim Hannigan had been working so I would get my raise in the minimum time. In the middle of this, we suddenly heard that we were about to undergo a Reduction in Force (called a RIF). Because

NASA had never previously gone through a RIF, no one had any idea how it would work. Budgets had been tight and many of the contractors had left. We never thought that we would be caught up in a layoff. Engineers at NASA at that time made about 80 percent of what they would be paid working for a contractor. Government benefits and job security were supposed to make up the 20 percent difference in pay. Nonetheless, we were very concerned about what it would mean for us. Each division was given a certain number of jobs to eliminate and Gene Kranz, who by then was the head of the Flight Control Division, would be the one making the decisions. We were all assured that we would be okay.

When the date of the RIF was announced, it was also announced that on the day of the RIF, all pay grade raises would be frozen. As it turned out, my first day of eligibility for my pay upgrade was three days before the RIF. I didn't know anything about what was going on so it didn't matter to me. John Wegener, Bob Carlton, and Jim Hannigan had devised a plan to get my pay grade processed in three days instead of the normal three or four weeks. The paperwork was literally sitting on Gene Kranz's desk waiting for his signature on the first day that I was eligible. Gene signed the papers and sent them to the center director, who by that time just happened to be Chris Kraft who once held Gene's job. Chris signed the papers, and since John Young was flying to Headquarters in Washington, DC, the next day for a meeting, Jim got John to hand carry the papers and take them to the proper person at NASA Headquarters. John was able to get them signed the day before the RIF, which was on a Friday.

The guys called me into Jim Hannigan's office, told me what they had done, and congratulated me on my promotion. I was very proud, not so much about the promotion, but the fact that these guys would work so hard against all the odds—we are talking about the US government here. I was still worried about the RIF but was feeling a little bullet proof since I had just gotten a promotion.

The next day, it was announced that there were two people affected in the Flight Control Division. One had already volunteered to leave and the other gentleman was Gary Watros who had a staff position in Gene Kranz's office. Our office had missed the layoff!

Not only was I safe, but I also had just gotten a promotion, thanks to the guys' hard work. I was feeling especially blessed and proud. Remember, I have said over and over again that as soon as we get too proud, watch out. What happened next, no one expected or could have predicted.

About a week later, John Wegener called me into a small conference room located beside our offices. I will never forget seeing John sitting at the end of the conference table with his face flush and telling me that they had screwed up big time! Since no one had any idea how the RIF actually worked, there was a procedure called "bumping" that would come into play. The oldest GS 13 could "bump" the newest GS 12, and the newest GS 12 could "bump" the newest GS 11 and so forth until there were no more people to "bump" in the Flight Control Division. Gary Watros was the oldest GS 13, and I was the newest GS 12 in all of NASA so he would automatically "bump" me and I would "bump" one of the guys in Guidance, and he would "bump" someone else, and that person would be laid off. All of this meant that the salary saved would only be half of Gary Watros's so someone else in the lower ranks would have to be laid off too. I wouldn't be out of a job but I would go back to being a GS 11, which to me wasn't a big deal. The issue was that Gary was not an active flight controller and knew nothing about my job. Likewise, I knew very little about the guy's job that I would be taking in Guidance. Only our government could be so stupid to come up with a system like this. This really showed the difference between the way NASA had been run for ten years and how it was going to be run in the future as a government agency. Needless to say, my bubble was burst.

About a week later, Gene announced that with the help of several people at NASA, Gary had found a great job at the new Department of Transportation, so this "bump" crisis was averted. I thanked Gary for his decision, and he explained he didn't really like working for flight control and thought he was going to be happier working in Washington, DC, where the action was. When I spoke to him several years later, he said it was a great move and that he was very happy.

My job would never be the same. I could not believe that after all the hours that I and other flight controllers had worked to advance

NASA's goals, we would be treated like warm bodies filling a quota. This was an insult to us as the dedicated engineers that we were.

Since I didn't feel so secure in my job anymore, I started to consider what I would do if my NASA job disappeared. Not only had we gone through a RIF, but budgets were really tight, and it was starting to look as if the Space Shuttle wasn't going to get off the ground in Congress. I started talking with my neighbor in Clear Lake City, Bob Panneton (who worked for TRW in communications at the time) about our job situations. Bob was worried about TRW's contract with NASA. If there weren't any missions to fly, NASA wouldn't need TRW. We liked living in the area, so we started thinking about business opportunities that we could get into if our NASA jobs folded. We had both invested some in the stock market, yet we weren't getting more than the 5 percent that one could get in passbook savings in those days. We came to the conclusion that we needed to start a business that we could turn to if NASA slowed down.

I went to the NASA library on my day off and began to study books on starting businesses. I was surprised that such books would be on hand at the NASA library, but it was a very good library. The books I read said that in order to support several jobs, a business either needed large contracts or needed to provide big products or services. In other words, we couldn't start a small business at a mall and expect to make a living for a couple of ex-NASA engineers. We outlined several businesses that we thought were needed in and around the Clear Lake area where NASA was located. At that time, there was no McDonalds and that seemed to be a great opportunity—until we found out that it would take about half a million dollars in cash to start a McDonald's in our area. Today, it would take four or five times that to start a McDonald's. Even a Steak and Ale for about $300,000 was out of our reach. We then looked at car dealerships and boat dealerships. What we discovered with the car dealerships and the boat dealerships was that most of the financing was provided by the manufacturers, mainly through floor plan assistance. The problem with the car dealerships was that they wanted people with a lot of experience in the automobile industry. That left us with boat dealerships. Smaller pleasure and ski boats from sixteen to twenty-two feet were very popular in the Clear Lake area near NASA. In addition to these boats, bay and near offshore fishing boats were extremely popular. These ranged from eighteen to twenty-five feet. We felt there was a real market for these types of boats in the Clear Lake area.

Mercury outboards were very popular at the time, but we didn't have a Mercury Outboard dealership in our area. I had to go to Texas City, about twenty miles south of the Clear Lake area, to get my own outboard when we bought our boat. When we talked to the Mercury distributor in Dallas, they said that they planned to put a Mercury dealership in the Clear Lake area. After several months of research, we decided to place a bid for the Mercury Outboard dealership. Thanks to our engineering background, we put together a great business plan. I went to the NASA library for books on marketing and business plans. We learned how to do market research. We found out from available data that in an area like ours about 10 percent of the people owned boats. We found out what percent should be Mercury Outboards based on state averages. We walked our neighborhoods to see if the predictions were true. We added the percent of homes that had a boat on the grounds to the number of boat stalls in the area and compared them to the population in the area. We discovered that about 12 percent of the people in the area owned boats that they kept in the area. We went to the boat dealerships in the area and counted the number of boats in their inventory (undercover type of work). From the national inventory turns (number of boats sold per year divided by the average number of boats in stock) that boat dealers had, we came up with the number of boats that were being sold in the area. We found out that nationally people that owned boats traded them about every four to five years. We went to the state and found the number of new boats registered in our area for each of the preceding five years. From all of this, we arrived at the fact that the market for new boat sales in our area was twice as much as the dealerships were selling in the area. That meant that half of the people were having to go to other areas to purchase new boats. In conclusion, we found that about 35 percent of boats sold in Texas were powered by Mercury Outboards yet there wasn't a Mercury Outboard Dealership in the area.

Bob Panneton and I put our plan together with charts and graphs, budgets, marketing data, and reasons why we were going to be very successful. We set up a meeting with the Mercury representative in the area and made our presentation. His name was Bill Scroggins. Bill said he had been in the boat business for a lot of years and had never seen a presentation like ours. He said that Mercury Marine had been after them to sign up people with great business plans, but he had yet to come across one. We were feeling pretty good by that time. Bill then told us that he had one other person in the running for the franchise. He said the famous oil well firefighter Red Adair wanted the franchise. Red Adair had been made famous when John Wayne played Red in the movie, *Hell Fighters*. Red was a folk hero in Texas. We were talking about getting an SBA loan and Red was flush with cash. We left the meeting thinking that the presentation did go well, but we were concerned that in Red Adair's case, cash would talk.

Much to our surprise, we got a call a few days later and Bill said that when he showed Mercury Marine our business plan, they said that they wanted him to give us the franchise. They said that they felt we would work hard to make the business successful, but it would be like a toy for Red. Bill said that he didn't have to take Mercury's recommendation, but he wanted to give us a chance to prove him wrong. Years later, when Bill retired, he told us that he gave us the franchise so that we would fail and he could tell Mercury that they were wrong. He admitted that he was the one that was wrong, and we were the biggest success story of his career.

We started putting our dealership together over the next six months as we continued to work our jobs at NASA and TRW. We had both been accustomed to working sixty to eighty hours a week during the various missions and working forty hours a week gave us a lot of spare time. John Wegener and Bob Carlton both had boats, so we asked them to join us as minority owners of our dealership. It was John and Bob taking me on fishing trips that had renewed my interest in boating. We took some awesome fishing trips. I have attached a picture from one of our fishing trips when we took Pat's dad, Jimmy Dameron, along. Pat's mom and dad were visiting from Virginia and Jimmy loved to fish. The picture shows him with the largest of many king mackerel we caught that day. Altogether, we caught about thirty kings that day and ran out of places to put them.

Pat's Dad after an awesome fishing trip in Texas

We were in Bob Carlton's nineteen-foot Thunderbird boat fishing offshore from Freeport, Texas. Many years later, as Jimmy was about to go to be with the Lord at age eighty-seven, he told me that was the best fishing trip he had ever been on in his life. Jimmy fished a lot in his lifetime since he was from Weems, Virginia, and his family was always involved in fishing and harvesting oysters. God blessed all of us that day.

We were able to open our business in January 1973, during the Houston Boat Show. We sold forty-two boats during that Boat Show, and we had only budgeted to sell about sixty boats the entire year. Our boat business was off and running. We hired several people to run the store and sell and service the Mercury Outboards. We started with four boat franchises—Wellcraft Boats, Ebbtide Boats, Del Magic Boats, and Monark Aluminum Boats. Bob and I both continued at our day jobs, but the business was growing rapidly. We took turns checking on the store after work and since we lived next door to each other, we were able to compare notes at the end of each day. We had gotten our SBA loan for $17,000 and built a metallic building on NASA Road One in El Lago, just east of the Manned Spacecraft Center.

Back at NASA, I was working on the operational plans for the upcoming Skylab missions. We were devising plans to work with the principal investigators who were in charge of each of the eight instruments on the Apollo Telescope Mount. The problem was that they were scientists and all they were interested in was getting as much operational time as possible on their instrument. There were several telescopes that operated in various wavelengths. It was the forerunner of the Hubble Telescope. We did not have the computer capacity to run their instruments from the ground, so they relied on having the crew onboard operate their instruments. The station was circling the earth every ninety minutes, so a lot of the time it was out of communication with Mission Control. Each one of the principal investigators wanted to be able to tell the astronauts real-time what to do, and that would not be possible. The fact that these were film type of instruments, which did not provide instant results, made it even more difficult. Some of the instruments gave operational data as to the number of pictures taken, exposure times, and other data but not actual results.

We decided to hold a big meeting at the University of Colorado, in Boulder, Colorado with the principal investigators so we could work out the operational considerations for operating their instruments. We met in Boulder since that was the home of Ball Brothers, who made most of the instruments. My plan was to have them help us produce the ATM mission rules so if we had a contingency, we would get the maximum operation of their instruments. I sent out memos to everyone about the meeting and asked them a series of questions concerning their priorities and operational considerations for their instruments. When I started the meeting, I thought that they were going to tear me limb from limb. We had several electric buses in the ATM for them to use as power to their instruments. One of the buses was a DC bus (think power in your car) that was supposed to provide power at 24 volts plus or minus 0.5 volts. I had asked them in my memo if the voltage dropped, at what level would their instrument stop working, or could it operate at a degraded voltage. The idea was to write ATM mission rules that if the voltage dropped due to some sort of malfunction, at what voltage would we not be able to run their instrument? By planning ahead, if there was a problem, we would be able to instruct the crew which instruments would and would not work. When I started explaining this to them, they went ballistic. They said NASA had promised that the voltages would be stable and now NASA was telling them to expect problems.

They were so suspicious of NASA that they couldn't see the forest for the trees. It was a really, really tough week. About half of the PIs got it and worked with me to write ATM mission rules that would help them get the most from their instruments if a problem came up. The other half would only question why we were thinking about such contingencies. They said that if there were problems, we could ask them then and they would tell us how to run their instruments. I tried to rationalize that if they didn't help with the ATM mission rules, their instruments would be turned off and the crew would operate the instruments that we knew would work in the contingency situation. One of the things that become obvious was that they didn't know what would happen if the voltage was lower, and I pointed out that now was the time to test their instruments while they were still on the ground. There were two DC buses and two AC buses and each instrument had different power requirements. As I said, it was a really tough week. I said that I was never coming back to Bounder again. Who was it that said never say never? Many years later, I would go back to that same auditorium for our daughter Christie's graduation from the University of Colorado at Boulder with her master's degree.

While all of this was going on, the boat business was doing great. We did almost four times the business that we had budgeted that first year and doubled that the second year. I sold Jim Lovell a 165 Wellcraft Airslot boat that first year. Jim lived on the water near our store. His kids used that boat more than any boat that we ever sold. Jim said that they were using $200 worth of gas a month and gas was only about 75 cents a gallon then. One Saturday, Jim came in with his mother to pick up something, and Jim's mom started telling me how her Jimmy was supposed to land on the moon but there was a problem and they had to work to get him back. Jim walked up about then and told her that I was one of the guys who helped rescue him. If you remember Jim's mom from the *Apollo 13* movie, she sounded just like the actress who played her in the movie. Several other of the NASA family bought boats from us that first year.

NASA decided to mount a joint mission with the Soviet Union and the Apollo-Soyuz Test Project was born. The mission did not fly until 1975 since an adapter had to be made to connect the two space-craft. I sold a sixteen-foot Del Magic ski boat to Tom Stafford who had been named to head up the joint US and Soviet Union mission. Tom drove his boat like he flew his spacecraft. I will never forget his delivery test drive. Tom raced up to the dock really fast, slammed the boat into reverse, and came to a dead stop at the dock. It was scary, but Tom could really handle a boat. Tom lived across Taylor Lake from Jim Lovell, and their kids could be seen skiing all over Taylor Lake after school. The west side of our dealership bounded a cut between Taylor Lake and Clear Lake. Clear Lake then emptied into Galveston Bay, which then emptied into the Gulf of Mexico near Galveston. One day, early in 1974, Tom brought some Russian cosmonauts to the dealership after work and I just happened to be there. Tom introduced them to me and said that they were going to meet in space the next year. Tom had taken them skiing in his boat earlier, and he had told them about our dealership. There was no way that they were going to believe that anyone could come into our shop and buy a boat. The cosmonauts were convinced that the store was just for the astronauts to come and get their boats. I tried to explain to them that as much as I appreciated the astronauts' business, we would be out of business if I just relied on their business. There was nothing we could do to convince them that regular people could just come in and purchase a boat. It seems that only the "in" people like cosmonauts could own things like boats in the Soviet Union.

Back at NASA, I was making slow but steady progress with the PIs with the help of the guys from Ball Brothers. One of the Ball Brothers' employees had been assigned to our team to help us in pre-paring the Operational Procedures and the Malfunction Procedures that would allow us to operate their instruments and get the most data for the PIs. I think that it helped when the doubtful PIs saw the draft of the procedures and the PIs that were cooperating with NASA had outlined how they would get the most out of their instruments if there was a problem. Many of them said that they couldn't see any reason that NASA wouldn't be able to provide the power that had been promised. I continually told them that our job was to prepare ahead of time to maximize their science. I told them that the Apollo program had taught us to never say never.

When it came time to launch the Saturn V with Skylab and the Apollo Telescope Mount unmanned, everything went wrong. The micro meteor shield fell off during launch and tore one of the two solar panels off of Skylab. There were to be two large solar panels to power the Skylab and four smaller panels to power the Apollo Telescope Mount. The Skylab was a mess by the time it reached orbit. NASA jumped in to solve the problems and devised a plan to rescue Skylab. Power would be diverted from the ATM to help power Skylab while a plan was devised to save the mission. NASA had to build an umbrella-type shield to provide the needed micro meteor shield for the crew. In addition, they needed procedures to allow the one good Skylab Solar Panel to deploy and start producing power. The plan was for the first manned crew to Skylab to make repairs. That was delaying the mission. In addition, the shield had to be produced and tested and procedures for its deployment had to be devised. NASA finally came up with a parasol type of arrangement for the shield, one that could be deployed out an instrument window. The first manned mission to the Skylab was primarily used to repair the station and make it operational. Since most of the power would come from the ATM, the power drain actually caused some of the voltages to go below the desired levels. As it turned out, the very DC voltage that I discussed in Bounder ran between 21 and 22 volts instead of the normal 24 volts. Thanks to the work we did in Boulder, we knew that most of the instruments would work at that level. The PIs satisfied their wish for science. They couldn't operate the instruments as much as they had hoped but using the very procedures that we had produced, they got most of their science. They were more impacted by the fact that the crew on the first mission didn't have much time for science because they spent much of their time just getting Skylab operational in its degraded state. As I said before, "Never say never."

After the first manned mission, most of the PIs called me and thanked me for helping them get their instruments up and running in spite of the problems. I told them that we were just doing our job but that no one would have ever guessed what happened would ever really happen. I even had two of the PIs that were in town come to

Skylab showing the missing solar wing, the added micro-meteorite shield, and the Apollo Telescope at the top.

the boat dealership on a Saturday to thank me in person. They had been the toughest to get on board, but I never gave up on them.

With the boat business booming and the Skylab missions in progress, I was having a hard time balancing my workload. Many things weighed heavily on my mind: the RIF, the fact that I really wasn't doing the propulsion work that I came to NASA to do, the fact that it looked like Congress was going to kill the Shuttle Program which was still seven or eight years away, and finally the fact that the boat business was booming. I decided to leave NASA and run the boat business full time. Bob Panneton and I decided that he would continue to work until TRW lost its contract. This way, I could build up the boat business so that there would be room for both of us in a year or so. Leaving NASA was a hard decision, but the RIF experience made it much easier than one might think.

I had about three months of Comp time accrued, so I told NASA that I would work for two more weeks, take a couple of months off, and then come back for one final week to close out. John Wegener reminded me that under that plan, NASA couldn't fill my position until I officially resigned. That meant there wouldn't be anyone to train for the next mission. I was a team player, so I decided to take two weeks off and come back for one last week to help train my replacement and then officially resign. Thus ended my NASA career.

Of course, there is something missing here. What I did and what I should have done are two different things. What I should have done was to get on my knees and ask the Lord for guidance over what I should do. After all the blessings that the Lord had given me, it seems strange as I reflect back that He wasn't who I turned to first. The God that had gotten me to Georgia Tech when I hardly knew anything about it, the God that, through the Holy Spirit, had guided me to NASA against all odds, the God that provided me a way to be able to marry my mate for life when I didn't have any money, the God that helped me live my dream of being on the console when we landed on the moon the first time, the God that got me through Apollo 13, and the God that had helped me successfully start a business was not the one I turned to when making such an important decision. I should have listened to Paul when he wrote the letter to the Philippians. I quote from Philippians 4:6–7: "Do not be anxious about anything, but in everything, by prayer and petition, with thanksgiving, present your requests to God. And the peace of God which transcends all understanding will guard your hearts and your minds in Christ Jesus."

Now you can see why I am writing this book. Don't make the same mistakes I have made. Go to the Lord in all things in prayer. Paul, in his letter to the Thessalonians, gave us another impactful command in 1 Thessalonians 5:16–18: "Be joyful always; pray continually; give thanks in all circumstances, for this is God's will for you in Christ Jesus."

As I look back, I see that I was letting pride rule my life instead of the Lord. I don't know what path I would have taken if I had gone to the Lord at that time, but I can see that the Lord was working on me and molding me even if I didn't realize it.

8

Let the Good Times Roll

About the same time that I went to work full time in the boat business, Pat and I moved into a new home in Clear Lake Forest. We had done very well on our first house and sold it for over two times what we paid for it. We were able to build a much larger home on a corner lot with a three-car garage (so we could keep our boat at the house). Pat had

Marine Products Clear Lake store in the 1970s

begun working—since she stopped teaching—at the store in the parts department. We had doubled the size of the store after only a year and had added air-conditioning in the showroom. By the end of the second year, we had become Wellcraft Marine's largest dealer in the entire country. We were on a roll. We more than doubled the business in only two years. My ego was being reinforced by the manufacturers telling us how wonderful we were, so we would buy and sell more boats. We were marketing and servicing our products like no other dealer around, and it was paying off. I had a lot of my old friends from NASA stop by and tell me that I made the right decision, since the Shuttle Program was continuing to slip and every

111

few months, there were threats from Congress that the program was going to be cancelled.

Pat and I were feeling much more secure with the boat business going so well, so I was glad that I had left an unsecure job at NASA. I missed my job at NASA, but it didn't really exist anymore. What had been an entrepreneurial spirit during the Apollo Program had turned into big government bureaucracy where employees were spending more time writing memos than accomplishing tasks. We had done a study at NASA, from a flight control perspective, to see whether the plan to make the Shuttle fly like an airliner would ever work. We came to the conclusion that it would take as many or even more flight controllers on the ground to fly the shuttle missions than we had used during the Apollo program. The administration had sold the idea to Congress that it would only take five people in flight control, and the shuttle could be turned around in a couple of days and fly again. We now know that idea was totally wrong. Our study had come to the right conclusion. The model for the shuttle would prove to be totally in error. It would become a wonderful space transportation system, but it would cost double or triple what NASA originally proposed. For NASA, it would be almost ten years before there would be a mission requiring flight control assistance. We were all pushing for a smaller shuttle-type vehicle that would fly on a rocket like the Saturn IB. We could use the Saturn V to lift large items like Space Station parts into orbit. As it turns out, we are now starting to do exactly what we proposed. The new Space Launch System that we are currently working on is a new rocket based on old technology from the Apollo Program.

Pat and I were ready to start our family but were surprised that when Pat stopped taking birth control pills, she didn't get pregnant. After trying for over a year, we decided to get checked out. The doctor said that we were fine, but Pat's fallopian tubes were partially closed. During Pat's examination, he said that he opened them some and told us to keep trying. That is all that it took because forty-five days later, Pat was pregnant with our first child. I would encourage anyone trying to have a child to consult a specialist because it could be something simple like our situation, and trying for years without a doctor visit could cause an unnecessary delay in having a child. We were very excited. At the same time, the boat business continued to grow, and Wellcraft gave me an 18-karat gold Rolex for being their largest dealer. Unfortunately, pride was continuing to creep into my life. A great business, suppliers telling us how terrific we were, living in a beautiful new house, and now we were going to have a baby. The Lord was blessing us and instead of giving Him all the glory, I was getting puffed up with pride.

In November 1974, it was time for our first child to be born. We didn't know whether it would be a boy or a girl, so all the blankets were yellow. At that time, it wasn't easy to know whether the baby was going to be a boy or girl. Pat had a few problems during the pregnancy, but everything seemed to be going fine. We had made arrangements for Pat's mother to come when the baby was born to help out when Pat and the baby got home from the hospital. Because she developed toxemia, Pat was forced to take it easy during her last month of pregnancy. Pat's doctor had her come in just before the baby was due and said that she should give birth sometime that weekend, but if she didn't, he would have her come in on Monday and induce labor. She didn't have the baby over the weekend, so we went in about six on Monday morning. They got Pat ready, gave her some medication, and told us the doctor was going to his office and would be back after his morning appointments. The doctor came in about noon and announced that Pat was ready. Our daughter Christie was born about 1:00 p.m. The doctor delivered Christie and went back to his afternoon office visits. I don't know how he did it, but it certainly wasn't anything like rushing to the hospital and enduring hours of labor like we had seen on TV. I had never heard of such a smooth delivery. Life was good—very good.

A big issue when we got home was that Christie didn't sleep very much, and Pat was up every two hours with Christie wanting attention and to be fed. With help from family, we were starting to get on a regular schedule. I got back to work planning for the boat show in January, and Pat and I were reading everything we could about raising a baby along with taking lots and lots of pictures. About ten days after Pat and Christie got home from the hospital, it seemed that something wonderful happened—Christie slept through the night.

When she awoke in the morning, she seemed a little hot and lethargic, so Pat called the pediatrician who said to bring her in around lunch. Although Pat had an appointment for a two-week check after birth appointment the very next day, the doctor said she should bring Christie in a day early, since there had been such a dramatic change in just one day. I will never forget the phone call I got from Pat. She was crying so much that I could hardly make any sense of what she was saying. It seems that Christie's white blood count was over 200,000, which was extremely high. There were a few cases of spinal meningitis in Texas at that time, and the doctor was afraid that Christie had it. The doctor's office is a block from Clear Lake Hospital where Christie had been born, and the doctor took Christie in his arms and walked her to the hospital, with Pat in tow. By the time I got there, they had done a spinal tap and they were waiting for results. There was our beautiful baby girl lying naked in an Isolette, with orange disinfectant all over her back where the spinal tap had taken place. She was sleeping, but the Isolette totally contains the patient, so we couldn't even touch her. We were terrified. Now we needed the Lord! It is a life lesson that I have had to learn and relearn. When you become too prideful, the Lord will send a major correction into your life. This clearly was ours.

We stayed with Christie day and night, taking shifts. They put her Isolette in a small room with one lounge chair where we could sleep. The good news is that they determined that Christie didn't have spinal meningitis and were running test after test to find out what was making her white blood count so high. We have never prayed so hard. We needed the Lord's help, bigtime! We had lots and lots of people praying for Christie. The doctors were giving Christie antibiotics, and the white blood count had started to go down. We noticed that a red spot on her leg where they had given her injections had started to swell. We asked the doctors and nurses why there was such a lump on her leg, and why it was so red. They said that sometimes the injection site reacts that way. I went to the library to see if I could find out why this was happening. We had no internet back at that time. I got several medical books and discovered that a staph infection mirrored what had happened to Christie. It seems that a staph infection can come from unclean needles from injections, and it takes about ten days to two weeks for the symptoms to appear. That is precisely the time frame for what had happened to Christie. The good news is the antibiotics were having the right effect, and the white blood count was continuing to decrease. We could never get the hospital to admit that her problem had been caused by a bad needle when Christie was born, but we didn't care at that point because she was getting well. Once the white blood count came down, and the antibiotics had run their course, Christie was able to come home from the hospital. Pat also developed a staph infection and would have had to be hospitalized except for a doctor in our neighborhood who was able to give her the regular injections needed to get rid of it. Now the Lord had super blessed us. We were so thankful for what He had done in our lives. God is good! Christie bounced back quickly and has never shown any bad effects from her illness.

We celebrated a very blessed Christmas that year. I decorated with tons of lights and even created a moving deer before you could even buy one in a store. We wanted to share our blessings at Christmas with everyone. To our surprise, there was a neighborhood competition that year, and we won first place. You have to realize that we were living in an area full of NASA types who had time on their hands and were very competitive. I have attached a photograph of our house in Clear Lake Forest that Christmas. I have been going crazy with Christmas lights ever since.

Our home in Clear Lake Forest near NASA the year
we won the Christmas Light Competition.

The next year, we were Wellcraft's largest dealer for the second year, and Bob Panneton received the 18-karat gold Rolex that year for our achievement. Bob was still working at TRW, but his job was about to be eliminated and the boat business had grown enough that we needed him full time. Bob served as the vice president and treasurer. At the urging of Wellcraft, we decided to expand to a second store in Bayou Vista, just north of Galveston. We opened the second store just as Bob Panneton started full time in the business. That store never did as well as the store in Clear Lake, but it did give us a great service location for people in Galveston. That store never lost money, but it never made very much either.

By this time, the country had grown really tired of war in Southeast Asia, and we were winding down our involvement there. The Watergate scandal had just occurred with Nixon resigning in September 1974. Other than the constant threat of gas lines and oil embargos, our country seemed to be headed toward better times. All of this seemed to be working well for the boat business, and we were setting records every year. The Shuttle program had survived the threats from Congress and was getting on track, so NASA was becoming busy again. That also continued to be good for business. Christie was growing up to be a wonderful child, and Pat would help in the parts department when she could. It was a real family affair. We all loved boating but couldn't find enough time to boat as a family, as we should have.

Our second child, Rob, was born in January 1978. Rob's birth went almost exactly like Christie's with no dashing to the hospital, just the doctor telling us when to come in, and somehow working it all out so Rob would be born at about the same time of day as Christie. Rob was healthy and didn't have any problems after coming home like Christie had experienced. Our biggest problem with Rob was getting him to go to sleep. He would fall asleep, though, as soon as we put him in his car seat and the car started moving. We could be seen on many a night driving Rob around the neighborhood. The trick was to get Rob out of the car and into the house without waking him up. We later discovered an indoor swing that would put him to sleep. It was great having two kids in the house. Pat would help out on weekends at the boat store and at boat shows but did not go back to teaching until the kids were in their teens.

Again, Wellcraft pressured us to open another store, on the north side of Houston this time. They threatened to set up another franchise in Houston if we didn't open one on the north side. We found a good real estate agent who helped us put a deal together with a company called Charter Financial Group. CFG wanted to build a store for us, lease it back to us for five years, and then let us buy it from them at a predetermined price. The partnership worked very well, and we opened our third store on Interstate 45 on

Pat would help in the Parts Department at the Clear Lake store.

the north side of Houston in 1978. That store had a lot of potential. We did purchase the store from them after five years, and we got about 20 percent instant equity when we bought it. It was a good deal for everyone.

Just when things started going really well, disaster struck. On May 30, 1978, late in the evening, I had just watched the news and was getting ready to go to bed when I saw a big flash outside of the kitchen window. I went outside and stood in the middle of the road in front of our house and looked south. The whole sky was glowing orange. It was very strange. It looked as if there might be a big fire to the south of us. If you have ever wondered what you would do if an atomic bomb went off, I got the answer that night. Suddenly, the entire sky lit up in a huge flash; it was like total daylight except everything was orange. I could see all the clouds in the sky. They were orange. All the houses around me were orange. I assumed that an atomic bomb had gone off at the refineries in Texas City. The answer to what you would do when you think an atomic bomb has gone off is—you just stand there with your mouth hanging open. All I could think of was those pictures of an atomic bomb test with all the houses being blown away. The color was right, and I was just waiting to be blown away. A few seconds passed and I was still standing. A big boom followed in about fifteen seconds. Finally, the orange sky started to fade some. I ran in and turned on the TV, but there was no report of anything happening. The next day, I would learn that there had been a gas explosion in Texas City, seven people were killed, and there was a huge release of fumes in the air. The first thing I felt and the first glow came from the initial explosion. The gas that was released had risen to about ten thousand feet and then ignited—this accounted for the big lighting up of the sky. About ten minutes later, I got a call from the alarm people saying the alarm had gone off at our Clear Lake store. It immediately sent panic through me because I thought it was our store that had blown up. I awoke Pat and told her what had happened and that I was rushing to the store. While driving there, my engineering mind allowed me to figure out that the explosion must have happened at least fifteen miles away, because of the time delay and the difference between the speed of light and the speed of sound. The store was only two miles from our home in the direction of Texas City.

When I arrived at the store, I saw two police cars, and several of our showroom windows had been blown out. Two of the policemen had gone into the store through the broken plate glass windows and said that there wasn't anyone in the store. About that time, they got word on their radio about the Texas City explosion. It seems that the front of our store exactly faced the Texas City plant, and the explosion had blown our windows out. I was relieved that our store was basically still in one piece. Because of hurricanes, we had fitted the windows with plywood inserts to protect them from storms. The police officers helped me get the coded plywood inserts for the three windows that were broken, and we filled those holes. I got home about 2:00 a.m. It was hard to go to sleep that night.

The next day was Pat's birthday and I had given her some money the day before so she could get herself some clothes. I have never been very good at picking out clothes for her and even though I had gotten her something else, I wanted her to get some things that she really wanted. Pat does love to shop. I love for her to shop too, just not with me.

I called our insurance agent the next morning and told him what had happened. I also reported that when we got to work that morning, there seemed to be much more damage than just the windows. Several of our doors wouldn't close, and we were having some electrical problems. It seemed as if the whole building had shifted due to the explosion. Since the insurance agent lived close to the store, he said that he would stop by on his way home to inspect the damage. About one

The author in his office in 1970s

o'clock, I was in my office and heard someone yell "fire". I went to the door between the showroom and the back where we service new boats and saw people running with fire extinguishers. They said that they had it under control, but I wanted to call the fire department, just in case. I used a phone in the showroom and called the fire department. I was proud of myself for being very calm. I hung up and walked back to the door to the shop and when I opened it, I saw flames shooting out of the rear storage area. Everyone had dropped their fire extinguishers and they were running out of the shop. I ran back to the phone and called that fire department again, and I don't remember being very calm that time. I told them to hurry that the whole place was going up in flames.

I went to my office and gathered up as many important papers as I could. I remember Travis Leach, our sales manager, running in and asking what in the world I was doing in the office. He dragged me out of my office to safety. We did a head count; everyone was accounted for, and we were just waiting for the fire department.

Flames were now shooting from the roof and it was ablaze. The parts department and half of the service area were in a second building attached by a fifteen-foot breezeway. We were hoping that the fire department would get there in time to save the smaller building. Since the Seabrook fire department is a volunteer fire department, they have to wait until the firemen came from their jobs to get on the truck so it can depart. The problem is that the police had closed NASA Road One in front of the store and the firemen couldn't get to Seabrook. I ran across the street and borrowed their phone (remember, no cell phones yet) to see what had happened to the fire truck. The fire department was waiting for people to arrive. I told them that most of the fireman were there waiting for the fire truck. A few minutes later, we heard the fire truck heading toward the store. They had to get through all the traffic to get to the store. Once there, they were having trouble putting the flames out, and I told them to not worry about the main building since it was totally in flames, just put water on the second building to save it.

The fire was being fed by something, and the fire department couldn't figure it out. A few minutes later, the NASA fire department arrived, and they quickly realized that the gas line that fed the heating system had ruptured and was feeding the fire. The NASA fire department put the fire out in about twenty minutes, once they shut the gas off. It is not the thing that you would want the world to see, but since there were so many press people on their way back from Texas City, we made the nightly news on all three channels.

Thankfully, the mayor of our community came to me and asked what we needed. I said that I needed electrical power and phone service to get operating again. He made some phone calls and before the cinders had stopped glowing, the telephone company and the power company were there. The phone repairman went right to work and got one phone on the parts counter operational. The electric power repairman said that he couldn't do anything without a permit, which could take days. The mayor turned to the chief of police and said that he wanted a permit there in thirty minutes. The electric company guy said that he would start working on it, but he couldn't turn on the power until he had the permit. The good news is that parts and service building had a separate panel and all he had to do was to set a new meter. He had his permit before he was finished.

We were surveying the damage about 5:00 p.m., when one of the parts guys came to me and said that Mrs. Nance was on the phone and that she didn't have any idea about the fire. It was one of the first calls that came in on the temporary phone. I asked him if he told her and he said, "Not on your life." He was a good kid, and that was probably the only laugh of the day. Pat asked if she should take back the clothes that she was excited to tell me all about back, and I said, "We will get through this" and told her I would be late for dinner. The police agreed to post people there for the night so I wouldn't have to deal with security until the next day.

About 6:00 p.m., our insurance agent showed up and said he thought I said there were a lot of issues, but he didn't expect what he saw. I told him what had happened and he said he would work really hard to expedite the insurance claim. A few days later, the fire marshal determined that the fire had started in an electrical box above the rear upstairs storage, most likely the result of a short caused by the shifting of the building from the explosion the night before. I asked him why it didn't occur when the explosion happened, and he said that as the building heated up during the day, it must have pinched a wire, which triggered the fire. He pointed out that the lights had been off, and just turning on the lights (for example, when someone went upstairs to get something) probably started the chain reaction. We learned that things like life jackets in cardboard cases burn really, really quickly. So do Outboard Motor boxes. A lesson here is that cardboard dust is really quite flammable.

I finally got home about 10:00 p.m., just in time to relive it all again on the evening news. Pat was more interested in me getting a shower and out of my clothes that smelled burnt.

This was a big hiccup, but we got through it. It cost us a lot of business. If you are going to have a fire in the boat business, the worst day of the year to have one is June 1. Thanks to good insurance and the help of a lot of people, we were back in full business and totally rebuilt by Thanksgiving. We were thankful that no one was hurt. There were a few casualties, though. I had a saltwater aquarium in the wall between my office and the showroom. When I got back in my office at the end of the day, the wall on the shop side of the office was partially open from burning and the thermometer in the fish tank registered 140 degrees. I had some shrimp in the tank for the trout to eat, and they had turned pink, but they were still moving around, but I had bigger problems on my hands. By the next afternoon, the temperature was back to normal, but all the fish had died.

There was a really great lesson to be learned, although I totally missed it at the time. All I asked the Lord for was to help us get through this crisis. I never stopped to consider that He was trying to tell me that we were expanding too fast, and I needed to spend more time with Him and my family instead of growing our business. I think a lot of people make this mistake. We strive for more stuff and think that is the most important thing in our lives. The Lord and our families are the most important things in our lives. The Lord was sending me a wake-up call and I wasn't listening. Instead of asking to get through a crisis, we should ask the Lord what lesson does He want us to get out of a crisis.

We lost a lot of business that year, but by the next boat show, we were booming again. Our store on the north side was opened by late 1978, and it helped with the business lost in the fire. We had a great boat show, and our fire was merely a topic of conversation by then.

Unfortunately, the price of gas went up 250 percent between 1978 and 1980. We had a second gas crisis in 1979, and Iran took a bunch of our people hostage in 1979. Things seemed to keep getting worse and worse. Interest rates started rising like crazy, and inflation was going up equally fast. Tough times had returned for most of the country. One big exception was Houston. Our economy revolved around the oil industry. With oil in short supply and the price of oil soaring, Houston was thriving. The Houston economy started going straight up, unlike the rest of the nation.

Our boat business benefitted greatly from this situation. Dealers in other parts of the country couldn't take boats that they had ordered, so I made deal after deal with our suppliers to take their excess inventory at big discounts. By 1981, interest rates went through the roof, with home mortgages hitting 17 to 18 percent. Auto and boat loans were reaching 20 percent. Some states were passing laws to limit how much lenders could charge, and in those states, lending simply dried up, making business even worse. Houston was booming because of the oil business, and people were spending money.

Many workers were going overseas and working for oil companies that paid all their expenses and gave them their yearly salary all at one time when they came back to the States. Workers would spend it and then sign up for another twelve or eighteen months overseas. Once they came home, they were tired of sand and wanted to do something on the water. Houston had great freshwater lakes to the north, and Galveston Bay, and the Gulf of Mexico to the south to enjoy. All they needed was a boat. Marine Products was there to help them, and help them we did. Credit didn't matter to them because they were paying cash. Some who were in areas overseas that had access to water, even took their boats back with them. One customer who had purchased a thirty-foot Scarab race boat was planning to ship it overseas ahead of his going back. Instead, I got a call from him about lunchtime one day, saying that his company had leased a cargo 747 to take a bunch of equipment to the Persian Gulf. He explained that some of the equipment hadn't arrived, and if we could get his boat to fit a certain container size, they were going to let him put his boat on the cargo plane. We had four hours to get the boat ready. We removed the windshield, the dive platform, the bow rail, and the outdrives. We packed everything inside the cockpit, and took the boat to Houston Intercontinental Airport, only four miles away from the North Houston store. The freight forwarding company only had about an hour and a half to make a cradle for the boat. It was close. The plane was flying to Italy to refuel, and then on to the Persian Gulf. That was the type of craziness we were dealing with.

We had an opportunity in 1980 to purchase another dealership that had a store in Houston and on Interstate 45 in Conroe, near Lake Conroe. They were the exclusive dealership in the Houston area for Chaparral Boats and Cajun Bass Boats. We really wanted both of those lines. Chaparral had been great competition for several years. North of Houston, Lake Conroe was not only a popular place for boating, but bass fishing was very popular. The Cajun line of bass boats would really fit into our long range plans, and they would sell really well at our North Houston store. Wellcraft really pushed us to make the deal, since we had become almost 18 percent of their total business around the country. We were doing well in Houston while the rest of the county was in a big slump. Dealerships were going out of business, but we were growing. For some strange reason, I just assumed that the oil business would be really good for a long time and chose to listen to people like Dick Genth, the president of Wellcraft, instead of going to the Lord. After doing a lot of financial and budget planning, we came to the conclusion that we just didn't have the capital to make the purchase.

Both the seller and Dick Genth wouldn't take no for an answer. The seller agreed to keep ownership of the buildings and leased them to us, and Dick Genth proposed to give us a $300,000 open line of credit with zero interest for ninety days on a perpetual basis. With that line of credit, we could turn our inventory and fully stock the new Houston store with no cost for the inventory. The two deals were just too good to pass up, so we decided to go ahead with the deal. We decided that since the lease would run out on the Conroe store in a year, we could close it and pull that business down to our North Houston store, which was only twelve miles south on Interstate 45. There was only one problem with this deal—when I asked Dick Genth to put it in writing, he said that I could trust him, since his word was his bond. Dick said that the parent company would not want to have it in writing because it would show up as a liability, and the way he was structuring it, the deal would just show up as a receivable. The way this transpired was he initially agreed to put it in writing, and just as the deal was going to close (after he had repeatedly told me that it was coming in writing), he said that the parent company wanted to do it this way. Much later, I found out that he never told the parent company about the deal. At that time, I talked to Mack Spencer, the CFO and comptroller, about the situation, and he said that there wouldn't be any problem. He reviewed exactly how the deal would work, and it was as we had agreed. I got Dick to clarify that as long as we had that store, we would get the deal. Dick needed more wholesale sales right then and would have said almost anything to get the deal done. He was loading trucks while we were talking. We did discuss it with our outside accountant, and he said that the deal was just too good to pass up. Going along with this deal was probably the biggest mistake I ever made in the boat business.

Once we closed on the deal, things began to go well in our opinion. We made lifelong friends with the people at Chaparral Boats. The company had been started about eight or nine years before we acquired the franchise. They were operating out of Nashville, Georgia, near Valdosta in Southern Georgia not too far from Jacksonville, Florida. The company had been started by Buck Pegg, and Jim Lane had join Buck a few years later. They had started in Hollywood, Florida, and when someone needed to purchase their location near the Fort Lauderdale Airport, they moved to Nashville. They got a great deal on the facility, which was at a small industrial park on the Nashville Airport grounds. I will admit that Nashville, Georgia, is really way out in the country. At the time, there were no fast-food restaurants there, so you get the idea just how small Nashville was at the time. The people who worked in the plant had a great work ethic. Buck was the chairman of the board, and Jim Lane served as president. Buck had been around boats all his life, and Jim was an accountant by trade. Together they made a great team. Buck wanted someone to give him ideas on new models. As an engineer, I had helped Wellcraft design several of their runabouts and Buck wanted my help with their runabout line. We really enjoyed our time together.

Business was so good that I was spending a lot of time flying around the country making deal after deal. Our managers, together with Bob Panneton, were running the stores, and I was the deal maker. When we started handling Cajun Boats, the owner came and picked me up in his six-person Piper Cherokee 6 airplane to talk to us about selling more of their boats. When visiting Chaparral, Jim Lane had taken me flying in his 4-place Cessna Cardinal. The airplane bug bit me big time. I "needed" an airplane to fly around the country to make my deals. In 1981, I bought a new 1980 Piper Warrior (four passenger) airplane and started taking lessons, again, to get my pilot's license. Since business around the country was not doing as good as Houston, I was able to get it at a great price. After only a few months, I was ready to take my flight test to get my license. In August 1981, there had been a strike of Air Traffic Controllers, and the time between take offs and landings were being spread out. There a lot of delays across the country. I was thinking just how smart I was to get my own plane so that I wouldn't have to put up with all that mess.

I scheduled my test flight (called a "check ride") with a FAA examiner for the day before Thanksgiving in 1981. I had been taking my lessons out of Hobby Airport, where the plane was based at that time. The examination was at 4:00 p.m. at the West Houston Airport. I got to Hobby at around noon, and my instructor went over all the procedures that he thought the examiner would cover during the exam. I was really nervous. He said that I had better get a reservation to take off, since that was the busiest day of the year, and the tower would be encountering major delays. I decided to go early. I called to make my reservation which was for 3:00 p.m.—two hours away. When I got in my plane and called again, it had been delayed to 3:30 p.m. I finally got off and arrived at the hanger where I was going to take the exam precisely at 4:00 p.m. The examiner was very nice but didn't leave any stone unturned, which was a good thing. After about a thirty-minute oral exam, it was time to fly. We taxied out to the runway, and we sat while plane after plane landed. We saw business jets, small planes, and medium-size planes. He said that a lot of people were coming into West Houston airport because of the strike and Hobby Airport being so crowded.

Finally, it was our turn. I pulled out on the runway and then he handed me a hood and told me to put it on. A hood is a device used to train instrument pilots to fly strictly on instruments, without being able to see out the window. I only had about twenty minutes of hood training during my lessons, which was not very much "time under the hood". He said that since most people haven't had much hood training, one of the things he wanted to do during his exam was to be sure that his pilots had enough hood time to get out of trouble if they flew into a cloud unexpectedly. I told him that sounded good, but I wasn't sure I could take off without being able to see the runway. He said if I flew within three or four degrees of the runway heading, I wouldn't deviate more than a few feet from the center of the runway. He said that he was training me in case I ran into ground fog while taking off. He wanted me to have the confidence to keep going, rather than slam on the brakes, and run off the runway and crash. Once in the air, one would clear the ground fog in a few seconds.

I must admit that I wasn't so sure I could keep in a straight line that well, but just as we were about to lift off, he said it was okay to peek. I took a quick look, and I was dead on the center line. That day, the examiner made me a much better pilot. We flew under the hood for about forty minutes with him giving all kinds of altitude changes, turns, maneuvers, and heading changes. He said I was a little shaky at the start, but then improved as I gained more experience under the hood. He then said getting my license was simple. All I had to do was remove the hood and find my way back to the airport. I found myself a bit disoriented because I did not have a clue as to where I was. It was as if I had just woken up from a dream and didn't know where I was. As a pilot, you plan your flights and review landmarks and beacons, then watch your trip unfold. Once again, the examiner wanted to put me in an uncomfortable situation and see if I could respond. I quickly tuned my radios into the two local radio beacons (VOR) and determined my location. Looking at my maps, I discovered where I was and then plotted a course back to the airport. It was now getting dark. I had to manage the heavy traffic around the airport and land at night. Once on the ground, he said I really did well under what he called some of the worst conditions he had ever seen for a flight exam. It was the best exam I had ever had because I learned so much. This would prove invaluable in my flying career. I am so grateful that the examiner spent the extra time helping me become equipped to pilot my airplane. God had blessed me again.

I would get to test these new flying skills the following spring when Pat and I, and our children would fly to Sarasota to visit Wellcraft and take a little vacation. What I didn't expect was having to use my new skills that the examiner taught me during the exam. We were flying over northern Florida and the ceiling started to lower. It was supposed to have a floor of 1800 feet, but we were flying at 1200 feet and it seemed to be getting lower. It is hard to judge ceiling height when you are in the air with clouds surrounding you. Suddenly, we entered the clouds and the windshield went into total white out. The propeller is going one way and applies torque to the plane. Without the horizon to look at, it is very hard to go in a straight line. Training tells you to go directly to instruments, watch altitude, and make a thirty-degree bank right turn (against the turn of the prop) for 180 degrees. That returns you to where you came from and back in clear air. It seemed like an eternity, but about thirty seconds later, we had completed our 180-degree turn and were headed back from where we had come. I checked my charts, and we were close to Cross City, Florida, where there was a small landing strip there. We landed, got a ride to a motel, stayed the night, and woke the next morning to clear weather. I immediately knew that I had to get my instrument rating so I wouldn't ever again put my family in that kind of danger. I thanked the Lord that night for the examiner whose instruction helped save our lives.

By September, I had sold my plane for a profit since inflation was going up about 8 to 10 percent a year. I purchased a demonstrator 1981 Piper Saratoga six-passenger plane, and within about six weeks had my instrument rating. They told me that they had never had anyone get an instrument rating that fast, and I told them I was on a mission. I was really affected by what had happened in Florida. I only kept the Saratoga for about ten months, but it was a really good airplane. I just had the need for speed! Notice what motivated me at that time. My priorities were really all messed up.

By the model year 1982 (September 1981 to August 1982), we distinguished ourselves as the world's largest dealer for Wellcraft boats, Chaparral boats, and Cobalt boats, plus we were Ranger Bass boat's number two dealer. We would have made it a sweep except that a Ranger dealer in North Carolina bought seven boats on the last day to beat us by two boats. We were flying high. We had taken a fun trip in the summer of 1981 with Buck Pegg and Jim Lane and their wives to Walkers Cay (the northernmost island in the Bahamas). We flew over from Fort Lauderdale in our plane and in

Jim Lane's plane, and we stayed on Buck's large boat he kept in the marina there. We topped that trip with an all-expenses paid trip to Hawaii in 1982, with Jim Lane, his wife, myself, and Pat as a reward for being Chaparral's largest dealer that year. Jim and I even rented a plane and flew around the islands. It was one of my best trips ever.

Back on the work front, I had been running the North Houston store for about two years and I was really getting tired of driving an hour each way, every day. I would spend one day a week at the Clear Lake store, however, to see how things were going. When I took over the North store, we doubled its business the first year and doubled it again the following year. During a trip in our Saratoga back from Florida during the summer of 1982, we were at about ten thousand feet and noticed that we could see Houston because of the smog coming from the petroleum plants around Galveston Bay. The smog appeared orange due to the flares where excess gasses were burned off. It did not look very healthy at all. What was our solution? We needed to build a new home north of the Houston area to get away from the smog. We asked around, and everyone said that we needed to move to The Woodlands, a hot new planned community off Interstate 45 between Houston and Lake Conroe. We visited The Woodlands and loved it. We went through the lengthy process of selecting a lot, an architect, and a builder, and we started building our "dream home" in the spring of 1983. The Woodlands with its parks, bike paths, plenty of trees, and quiet neighborhoods seemed a great area to raise a family. The question is whether we really "needed" to build a 3,800-square-foot home with a circular driveway and an oversized three-car garage, but we were living the dream. The problem was that we weren't consulting the Lord on any of this. It is easy to look back now and see that we were probably moving too fast toward that dream. We were reacting to the great business that we had at the time, but "all" good things would eventually come to an end.

Remember how I said awhile back that the Lord will step in and give us a wake-up call if we needed it. In July of 1983, we sold our house in Clear Lake Forest for over twice what we had paid for it ten years earlier. Our new home in The Woodlands wouldn't be ready until the middle of August, so we rented a fully furnished home in The Woodlands for thirty days. We packed what we could and put the rest of our furniture and belongings in storage with the moving company. The wake-up call came in the form of Hurricane Alicia in mid-August 1983. It unexpectedly raced right up Interstate 45. Alicia was a huge storm and caused so much damage that the National Weather Service retired its name. It directly affected our Galveston store, the Clear Lake store, our North Houston store, and the Woodlands. We boarded everything up at each store and sent everyone home. Pat, the kids, and I were in the rental house in The Woodlands where we rode out the storm. As the storm was coming up I-45, I got a call from the gentleman who was putting in the pool at our new home. He said that I needed to go to the home and fill up the pool. Since it didn't have water in it, it could pop out of the ground once the ground became saturated, he stated. I asked him how long I should let the water run, and he said that with a garden hose, it would take over a day to fill up, but not to worry about it, just get it started.

I remember driving the two miles to our new home and parking in the circular driveway in front of the house. The wind was howling. I went through the house, threw the end of the hose into the pool, and started the water running at full blast. The pool already had a bunch of limbs in it from the trees around the pool. As I was walking through the house, back out front I heard an extremely loud noise, along with lots of other very strange noises. What I remember is how loud the sounds were. When I opened the front door, I saw downed trees everywhere. The rest of our driveway was blocked, and there were two feet in diameter pine trees lying across the road. Since our house was on a corner lot, I was able to back out of our driveway and exit our street. I looked back and saw three large pine trees lying across our street, which was a cul-de-sac. Except for our new home and the home across the street from us, everyone else was blocked in. On the way back to the rental house, I saw people rushing to put tarps on roofs that now had big sections missing, trees sticking through the roofs of multiple homes, and a new Cadillac that was split down the middle by a big tree. The split Cadillac was about five hundred feet from our rental home. I remember thinking, why was I worrying about a silly pool, when I ought to be fearing for my family's lives. When I got to the rental home, there was no power, and since we hadn't planned on needing a portable radio, we really were "in the dark" about what was going on. We later learned that there were twenty-three tornados in the Houston area from Alicia, and one had passed overhead while I was making my trip. Since there were so many trees, the tornados couldn't reach the ground and just had their way with the trees.

When we woke up the next morning, the storm had passed, and we were okay. When I checked on our new house, I found the pool okay and about half full. The new house came through fine, and the new neighbors were out with chainsaws cutting up the trees lying across the road so they could get out. We had no phone service, so I couldn't check on our stores. Of course, the authorities were telling everyone to stay at home (the radio in the car worked), but I needed to check on the stores.

When I got to the North Houston store, I was surprised that it sustained very little damage. The building was tilt wall construction and very sturdy. The only real obvious damage was that our twenty-five-foot tall sign out front had crossed ten lanes of Interstate 45 and was lying on the other side of the freeway in a field beside the Oldsmobile dealership. I was just glad it didn't hit anyone. Since the store had electricity and phone service, I was able to talk to Bob Panneton, and he was going out to check on the Clear Lake store. He had moved to Clear Lake Forest, and the roads had been flooded. He said that there were a lot of trees down but not any big damage that he could see. Bob said that he had walked down the block to check on our old house, since he knew that the people that had bought it had asked if hurricanes ever hit, and I told the owners that we had never had any problems in the ten years that we lived there. Bob Panneton said that other than a few small limbs in the yard, it wasn't hurt at all. I was thankful for that.

I made it to Clear Lake that afternoon and found some damage at our Clear Lake store, but nothing like the damage I had seen in The Woodlands. It seems that most of the damage in The Woodlands had come from tornados. We did some clean up at the Clear Lake store, but it still didn't have power. There had been a lot of rain associated with Alicia, and there was a lot of flooding in the Clear Lake area. We could not find out anything about the Galveston store, since there was no power or phone service. The freeway was closed about halfway to Galveston to prevent looting, and many of the roadways were still underwater. I went back to The Woodlands that night without knowing the status of the Galveston store.

While we were watching the news at 10:00 p.m. to try and get some information on the damage, they broadcasted some footage of the Bayou Vista area where our store was located. We could see a lot of damage but in one picture, we could see our store was still standing. We had good insurance and also had flood insurance, but flood insurance just covers the building, not the inventory. I was feeling better seeing the store still standing, but at the end of the newscast, they said they had just received some footage taken during the storm and it was very dramatic. They had mentioned that several tornados had hit Galveston and then showed a series of videos taken from Interstate 45 where the water was covering the Interstate. While filming the high water, they shouted that there was a tornado and turned the camera toward Bayou Vista. To my horror, they actually caught a tornado roaring over our store. So much for not too much damage. Since the still pictures were taken after the tornado hit, I at least knew that the store was still standing. I could see in the tornado video that a lot of the boats in the yard were being blown around by the tornado.

The news reports said that one had to prove that he owned property in the Galveston area before being allowed to go into the area. I gathered proof that we owned the store and finally got to the Galveston store about 2:00 p.m. the next day. Some of our employees who lived in the area were already there trying to make things safe. One of the designs that we put into the building was two large overhead doors on opposite sides of the store, so if water rose in the store it could flow through the building. It had worked well. We had gotten about five feet of water inside the store. It had broken down the doors and a lot of the contents of the building were missing, probably due to the water rushing through. What we did have was a bunch of refrigerators and freezers in the shop area. The Bayou Vista subdivision is made up of houses that are built on stilts with storage rooms and parking underneath the main floor. Many people put an extra refrigerator or freezer on the ground floor and since they are airtight, they float. We had six or seven of them in our shop area. Boats were everywhere. Many of the boats had floated away even though our staff had taken the drain plugs out of them. The water rose so fast that they floated until the inside of the boat could fill with water. There were

Hurricane wreckage at the exit off I-45 close to our Galveston store. The feeder road is full of water.

boats all over the freeway. What I remember the most was the place stunk terribly. All the sea life in the water died when the water receded, and their rotting bodies left a horrible smell. The ground was about a foot deep in gooey mud.

In the parts department, all the parts on the bottom four shelves were totally gone, and all that remained was a thin layer of mud. From the fifth shelf up, all the parts and the parts bins were totally undisturbed. That was about the only thing that was okay. The water had risen so fast that the boats in the showroom had floated through the plate glass windows and were nowhere to be seen. The boats were on the showroom floor with their drain plugs in them so they wouldn't drip on the floor. The shop had just finished a large job installing two brand-new engines on a large fishing boat, and we had been trying to get the customer to come in and pick up his boat and pay for the job. That boat had been in the shop because we had cleaned it up and had it ready for him. It had vanished. I talked to some of the local police that stopped by to see how we were doing, and they said that they had a report of a large boat with two large outboard engines being stuck under the overpass where Texas Route 6 went under Interstate 45. It was only about a half mile away so I drove over to that area. What I found was two really big guys trying to unbolt the two engines from the boat. They had their pickup backed up to the boat, and they were ready to make off with the engines. In a really stupid move, I jumped out of my car and yelled, "Why are you stealing those engines?" Thankfully, they jumped in their pickup truck and drove away. The good news was the boat had floated out of the shop and got stuck under the bridge so it didn't sink from all the rain, and the engines and the boat were okay. The trailer was still at the dealership, so all we did was to go get the trailer, winch the boat back on the trailer, and return it to the dealership.

In the showroom, we had a row of engines on engine stands, and all but one of the engines were gone. I am not sure whether the tornado got them, or they were stolen before we got there. One of our mechanics lived close by, and he saw the tornado hit the store. He thought that when it hit the store and the two big doors blew out, that is what saved the store. We never really totally reopened that store. For the next month, we did cleanup and moved what inventory was left to the Clear Lake store, mainly for security. Our insurance agent was very helpful, and getting the flood insurance to pay was very quick because the area had been declared a federal disaster area. The wind, storm, and theft adjuster kept saying that most of the damage was due to rising water, not wind and storm. He said that if we could prove that a lot of the damage was from wind, he would pay to the limits of the policy. He thought that he was being really smart. I asked him to put it in writing, and he did. Then he asked me how I was going to prove that it was wind damaged. I asked if he wanted to drive to Channel 2 NBC News and obtain the tape of the store being hit by a tornado with merchandise and parts of the building flying away, or did he want me to get the video and bring it to him instead. The insurance agent was standing there and told the adjuster that everyone in the whole area had seen video of the store being hit by a tornado. That's what happens when an insurance company brings in out-of-the area adjusters when a disaster hits. The adjuster did go to the station the next day, and they showed him the tape. As a result, he paid the claim to the limits of the policy, which covered everything including totaling the building and paying for the inventory that was damaged.

The Galveston store was in a great location right on the freeway, so before we even decided whether to rebuild or not, we started getting offers for the property and the damaged building. The offers were good, and we were going to be able to pay the mortgage and get our equity and then some out of the store. Of course, we had been paying salaries and cleanup costs, but great offers for the property made it easy to decide to sell the store and consolidate the Galveston business into our Clear Lake store. It turns out that the biggest offer was from a strip club that got washed out in Galveston. I didn't want to sell the property to a strip club in that nice neighborhood, so I went to the owner of Bayou Vista and asked if he wanted to buy it. He said that we couldn't sell it to a strip club because of deed restrictions. I told him that there weren't any deed restrictions on our property. He checked and admitted that he had made a big mistake and forgot to include them in the deed of trust when he sold us the property. He offered us $10,000 more than the strip club's offer if we would agree to sell it to him right then. He said that everyone in Bayou Vista had been told that there were deed restrictions on our property when we moved there, and he said half of them would sue him if they found out he had made a mistake. I told him that we had always been good neighbors, we loved the area, and we wouldn't do anything to hurt Bayou Vista or him. We took his offer. Of course, while all of this was going on, I wasn't spending as much time as I should have on the other stores. The Houston store had lots of employee problems, and the North Freeway store wasn't hitting its numbers. There was a lot of business to be had from all the storm damage to boats, but the insurance companies were being very slow to pay customers' claims. Many people waited almost a year to get their claim paid. The insurance companies were busy taking care of home and auto claims first.

By December, we had cashed out of the Galveston store and had moved most of the employees to the Clear Lake store. We were ready to get our business going strong again and prepare for the January boat show where we typically made 35 percent of our yearly sales. We had just come off the best year in our history, and there were a lot of people beginning to receive insurance checks to replace their damaged boats. I was the principal stock holder of the Galveston store and it was a Sub Chapter S Corporation. That meant that the profits from the sale of the property rolled into my personal income so far as the IRS was concerned. Since we had depreciated the Galveston store during the last seven years, I was looking at a fairly large tax bill. Some of the losses had offset the gains, but we also got a fairly large amount of cash as part of closing and selling the store.

I discovered how I could get rid of the tax liability. It was Jim Lane, president of Chaparral Boats, who told me about some really great tax opportunities. Remember, his background was in accounting, and I had mentioned that I was going to have to deal with a large tax issue from the Galveston store. There had been an investment tax credit of 10 percent that was going to run out on December 31, 1983. That meant that 10 percent of the cost of a new airplane for business purposes could be deducted from my tax liability. It came off the

Our home we moved to in The Woodlands in 1983

tax, not the deductible. In addition, there was a 25 percent first year tax deduction if it was purchased before December 31. It was designed to get the aviation business going again after the high interest rates of the early 1980s. I purchased a beautiful new 1982 Beechcraft Baron twin-engine airplane on December 22, 1983, and the $30,000 in tax savings that I got more than made up for my Galveston store liability. It was fast and the engines gave us extra security. I had a passion for our business and everything I did seemed to work out great, even if there were some bumps in the road. I always seemed to be able to overcome the obstacles and charge on.

We had moved into our new home in The Woodlands in late August 1983 and were really enjoying The Woodlands lifestyle. The 1983 January boat show was the best we ever had or would ever have. Business was so good that we chartered a flight from Houston on a new airline called Southwest Airlines that summer and took all of our employees to SeaWorld in San Antonio. As far as I was concerned, all of my decisions seemed to be right on track.

It had only been nine years since I left NASA, and we were rolling with the big boys! At the time it seemed great, but as I look back, I wonder what I was thinking. Hindsight is always a lot better. The good news is that we have someone to go to for advice, our Lord, if we will only stop and let Him guide us through our lives. The problem continued to be that I was not considering what would happen if there came a calamity that would affect our business, the Houston economy, or both. After all, I was in control!

Again, I am reminded that the Lord will step in and give us a wake-up call. I was ripe for a serious dose of reality. The Lord had blessed me and our family over and over again. We were going to church, but that's about as far as it went for me. I put the emphasis on "going to church". Pat had always been better about going to church. Much too often, I had something else going on or had to travel for business. Now that we had kids, we were going to church much more regularly. This being said, "going to church" is not what the Lord wants. He expects us not just to attend church, but to also have a day-to-day relationship with Him. He had blessed me over and over again thinking that I would be grateful and want to have a day-to-day relationship with Him. It is no different than our relationship with our children. We are the Holy Father's children. Sometimes, we have to exercise "tough love". I had become way too dependent on myself and not the Lord. The Lord loves me so much they He had to exercise some "tough love" to get me back on track.

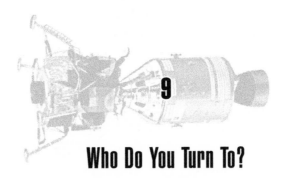

9

Who Do You Turn To?

Things seemed to be going well with our family and the business through the early-to-middle 1980s. Christie and Rob liked living

The new Twin Engine Beechcraft Baron purchased in December 1983

in The Woodlands, and the pool was a big hit with them. The lifestyle in The Woodlands was ideal for raising a family. We started attending, then we joined First Baptist Church in The Woodlands. Both Rob and Christie accepted the Lord as their personal Savior at the same time and were baptized there.

As I had previously mentioned, I used some of the money that I had received from the cash-out of the Galveston store to purchase a new 1982 Beechcraft twin engine Baron. The Saratoga had been a great plane and could fly nonstop to Sarasota where Wellcraft was located, but it took almost six hours. Pat said this was too long to fly without a bathroom break. The Baron could make the trip in four hours, and I liked the added safety of the twin engine airplane. Since the aircraft business was hurting, I got a great deal and sold the

Saratoga for more than I paid for it. Everything just seemed to be working in our favor.

Just when the business seemed to be going really well, things were thrown into turmoil. At the time, our biggest line was Wellcraft Marine, and we were still working with the $300,000 worth of free financing that was part of the agreement to open the Houston store. Chaparral boats continued to be competitive, as well as Cobalt boats and Ranger Bass boats. Year after year, we were declared "The World's Largest Wellcraft Dealer", garnering lots of rewards. In spite of Wellcraft's success, Dick Genth was lured to Chris Craft by the head of Chris Craft Industries, Herb Seigel. Chris Craft Industries was a public holding corporation with interests in television broadcasting, plastics, and other manufacturing. This holding company had purchased Chris Craft boats in 1960 and renamed the company from Shields and Company NAFI to Chris Craft Industries in 1962. Chris Craft Industries had spent years in legal battles with Bangor Punta over the ownership of Piper Aircraft. The lawsuit went all the way to the Supreme Court, and the justices gave Chris Craft Industries and Bangor Punta thirty days to settle their differences because the judges could not determine which company had broken more laws to get control of Piper. Piper was doing well at the time, so Bangor Punta made a good offer to buy out Chris Craft's stock in Piper, and thus gain control of Piper Aircraft. At the time, Chris Craft was trying to get control of 20th Century Fox, and it needed a lot of cash.

Once the deal closed, Chris Craft Industries used most of the proceeds to gain a controlling interest in 20th Century Fox which had been ailing, because the big film that they had been counting on to rejuvenate them was way over budget. Chris Craft Industries was able to purchase a lot of the depressed stock in 20th Century Fox a few months before the big movie was released. That movie was *Star Wars*. Herb Seigel looked like the smartest guy on the planet. With his recent successes, Herb decided to rejuvenate its namesake, Chris Craft boats. At the time, Wellcraft was flying high in the boating world, and it was growing by leaps and bounds every year. It had obtained a large manufacturing facility in Sarasota, Florida, and was doing extremely well. Herb decided that Chris Craft needed Dick

Genth, the president of Wellcraft. They had been negotiating for months. While en route to Wellcraft's new west coast facility to oversee their west coast annual dealer meeting, Dick Genth had the corporate jet land in Houston, and he came to our North Houston store. I got a call from our Wellcraft representative, AW Heinze, telling me Dick was in town. I was visiting one of our other stores, so I made a

Wellcraft Dealer meeting during the 1980s

beeline to the North Houston store. When I got there, Dick was locked in an office on the phone. AW wouldn't tell me much except there was a really big deal going on. I don't think that AW knew any more than that.

When Dick came out of the office, he announced that Chris Craft had given him a $1,000,000 signing bonus (a lot of money in 1980), and he needed to get to the plane. AW was Dick's transportation to the airport, so I waited until AW returned to find out that Dick had just signed to take over Chris Craft. Dick went to the west coast, had the dealer meeting, returned to Sarasota, and announced that he was leaving for Chris Craft. All I was thinking about was my hand shake with Dick over the $300,000 deal and the Houston store.

It would take Dick years to get his team together at Chris Craft. The boats they were building were out-of-date, and there was a lot of work to do. In the meantime, Bob Long, the head of Wellcraft manufacturing took over the helm at Wellcraft. It was a short time later that he learned of my $300,000 deal with Dick Genth. Mac Spencer, the CFO, was the one to tell Bob about it. By that time, interest rates were soaring, and business had really slowed down except in the booming Houston area. Bob agreed to keep the $300,000 deal in place but said that he could not guarantee how long it might last. The next two years were really good for us, and Wellcraft really needed our business. Remember it would be 1982 when we would become the top dealership in the country for almost every line we handled. It will make sense later as to why I have devoted so much time to this story. Stay tuned!

There were some good times during this period. I have already mentioned the airplanes, the new home, our new church, the kids loving The Woodlands, but one story stands out that I would be remiss if I didn't pass on to the reader. During 1981, we were once again Wellcraft's largest dealer, and part of that honor was that we got to stay on the top floor of the Hyatt Regency Hotel in Sarasota during the dealer meeting. The honored guest that year was Michael Reagan, the adopted son of President Reagan, and his wife, Colleen. Michael had been racing one of Wellcraft's Scarab offshore race boats for charity that year. We had the guest room next to Michael and Colleen's on the top floor of the Hyatt Regency Hotel, and we enjoyed talking to them and visiting with the Secret Service agents. The Secret Service was particularly tight because President Reagan had been shot just a few months earlier. The good news is that the Secret Service eats well, and every morning, there was a table in the hall full of good things for all of us to eat. We could look down from our room and see the boats in the harbor where the dealers could inspect then and take them out for test rides. I mentioned to the Secret Service agents that the dealers were in shorts and knit shirts, and anyone could spot the agents since they all wore dark blazers, which looked totally out of place. The next day, they all showed up in matching blue and white casual outfits carrying small gym bags that I suppose held their weapons.

One day, Michael and Colleen asked Pat and me to lunch at the Boat House. The Boat House was a very nice, casual marina restaurant that extended over the water at the Hyatt House Marina. Since the weather was so nice, we had lunch out on the porch. Michael, Colleen, Pat, and I were at one table, and several Secret service agents were seated at a table near us. Michael was talking about how much each of them had been traveling, how they hadn't seen each other for a month, and how the dealer meeting was like a mini vacation for them. They said that they would take different paths right after our meeting. Michael would have to go to the west coast dealer meeting right after the east coast meeting, and Colleen had other business commitments. Pat and Michael exchanged kid pictures. They had one son, and Pat told him all about Rob and Christie, and she had a lot of pictures to show him. Colleen and I got in a big discussion about the recent revelation of "Who Shot JR". During the last episode of the TV series *Dallas*, JR (Larry Hagman's character) had been shot by a mysterious shooter, and everyone had been guessing who did it. The first episode of 1981 had revealed who did it, but we were wondering if they really knew who it was going to be when it originally aired. Anyone paying any attention to television at that time had been caught up in "Who Shot JR". Finally, Michael leaned over to Collen and me and said that we had to stop discussing "Who Shot JR" because every time we said it, the Secret Service agents jumped up a foot. They were a very nice couple, and we were glad to be able to spend some time with them.

Alas, all good things must come to an end, and the Houston economy started to suffer. When oil prices were high, Houston did well, and when oil prices went down, Houston suffered. It was that simple. Houston had gone through a boom for years when oil prices shot up after the 1979 oil embargo, and real estate had boomed in Houston for years after that. Any new business that opened was successful, and a lot of money was being made in Houston. In addition, a lot of people were going to Saudi Arabia on big contracts, coming back with piles of money, then buying everything in reach. Of course, the rest of the country was suffering from high oil prices and high interest rates. By 1983, oil prices began heading down and the boat business in the rest of the country started really improving. At the same time, our business started to fall off. Bob Long called me to Sarasota and said that we needed to discuss the deal that I had made with Dick Genth. He reminded me that Dick hadn't told the owners of Wellcraft about the deal and that he had held them off as long as possible. To make matters worse, Wellcraft had been sold to Irwin Jacobs' company named GENMAR. Bob Long proposed that they set up a special line of credit for the $300,000 with one of their lenders, Chrysler Credit. In turn, they would agree to pay the interest on the amount for up to ninety days after each boat was put on the account. That way, they wouldn't have $300,000 outstanding on their books, we would have the cash for the boats, and we wouldn't have to pay interest until after the boats were on the account for ninety days. This was a lot different than Dick's deal because in Dick's deal, when we sold the boat we could keep the money and then pay it off after the ninety days were up. That is how we obtained the cash flow to open the Houston store. I agreed to the deal, but Bob said that he would still have to get corporate to sign on the deal. It seemed to be a reasonable solution to the situation. What I didn't know was that as soon as the Wellcraft free interest part was over, Chrysler credit was going to stick us with high interest rates. Wellcraft had agreed to cosign the loan for the first ninety days, and Chrysler was free to hit us with high rates after that. This little detail had been buried in the fifteen pages of small print on the loan documents.

We started operating according to the new financial arrangement for about six months, when Wellcraft came back and said that corporate didn't want to keep doing it forever, and that they were going to stop the program after a year. Financially, this left us in a difficult situation just when business was slowing down. We were not happy with Wellcraft at all. Guess who resurfaced about that time—Dick Genth. I was sure that Dick had spies snooping around at Wellcraft. He admitted as much to me. He had moved Chris Craft from Pompano Beach, Florida, to five blocks from Wellcraft in Sarasota and was regularly stealing people from Wellcraft. In addition, Dick was signing up Wellcraft dealers left and right. The new Chris Craft sport boats looked like Wellcraft sport boats on steroids, the traditional cruisers had been redone, and prices had been dropped noticeably. If you asked someone at that time to name a boat line, they would have answered Chris Craft 80 percent of the time. Dick was pressing us to take on Chris Craft. He knew that if we as Wellcraft's largest dealer signed up, he could get a lot of other dealerships to sign up. Dealerships wouldn't drop Wellcraft, but rather add the Chris Craft line so they wouldn't have to deal with another dealership coming into their market area, nor deal with Dick trying to compete with Wellcraft. I kept putting Dick off, saying I didn't want to mess up the deal he had made while at Wellcraft. Dick jumped on the fact that Wellcraft was going back on his own deal and pushed hard for us to take on Chris Craft.

During a chance meeting in Florida, when we were coming back from South Seas Plantation, Bob Panneton, his wife Kathy, Pat, and I got to drive one of the new Chris Crafts. It was pretty nice. We really liked the new boats that Dick was building and didn't want to let the Chris Craft boats get away from us and into the hands of another dealership in Houston. I went to Wellcraft and told them that I wanted them to honor the deal that they previously made. Bob Long said it was out of his hands. I think Wellcraft was starting to have some financial problems at that time, and the corporate types just needed to get out of the deal. I do believe that it was out of his hands. This made it easier to take on Chris Craft and that is what we did. I explained to Bob Long in the telephone call that we were taking on Chris Craft. I explained that we would move Wellcraft out of the Houston store, since they didn't want to keep their bargain they had initially made for us to start the store. We would only put Chris Crafts in the store and rename the store Chris Craft of Houston. That would allow us to get additional space at the Houston Boat Show. It was a smart marketing move, since it leveraged Chris Craft's great name in the industry. Chaparral was happy, since they would stay in all stores including Chris Craft of Houston. It looked like there were two dealerships in Houston handling Chaparral. Dick made some concessions, and it really improved sales at that store. Chris Craft was a big hit in Houston. It also hit Wellcraft sales in the Houston area, but we remained either the number one or number two Wellcraft dealer in the country despite Chris Craft entering the scene.

The following year saw even more changes. When I was at the Wellcraft dealer meeting the following year, the Wellcraft people were trying to get more of our business. They knew we had taken on Chris Craft and said that we didn't need Chaparral since we had Wellcraft sport boats and Chris Craft sport boats. Sport boats are generally cruise and ski boats under twenty-five feet long. I resisted the move because I was very happy with where we were at the time. During the Wellcraft meeting, I got a message to call Jim Lane with

Chaparral boats. That struck me as very strange, since he knew that we were at the Wellcraft dealer meeting. I thought that he might have an even better deal, and I didn't want to order too many Wellcraft boats if there was a better deal coming from Chaparral. I called Jim Lane back, and to my surprise, he said that he just wanted to inform me, as a friend, (Jim and I both had the love of flying and would talk for hours about flying our airplanes and our various experiences) that they were not going to be able to offer the same type of discounts that they had offered in the past. I was shocked. He said that instead of the usual 13 percent discount off wholesale, we could only expect about 5 percent discount and maybe a little advertising coop help. He said that they weren't making enough money, so they had to make the adjustment. I told him that with that type of discount, the Wellcraft sport boats would sell for nearly 10 percent less than the Chaparral boats, and it would be hard to sell both on the same showroom floor with that much price difference. He continued talking about waiting to see the new models that were coming, and that there was room for both on the showroom floors of our stores. I couldn't believe what I was hearing. I called Pete Chadwick, our Chaparral representative, and he confirmed that they were doing that across the board. We weren't the only dealership being affected. The majority of the dealerships got about 5 to 7 percent off wholesale as volume incentives, but we bought a lot more than most dealerships. Pete told me that he thought there was something else going on that was driving Jim Lane's and Buck Pegg's decision.

I then had several meetings with Bob Long. I asked what he would do to make us want to drop Chaparral and only sell Wellcraft sport boats in the Wellcraft stores. He kept sweetening the deal until I couldn't say no. We were getting almost 17 percent off with the first load of boats. Of course, we ordered more boats than normal and wouldn't have to worry about anyone else getting Chaparral boats in Houston because of the huge price difference. When I got back to Houston, I called Jim Lane and told him what we had decided to do, and that I was very disappointed in being forced into making that decision. He said that he wasn't at liberty to tell me more, but I would understand in a few weeks why this was happening. Two weeks later, it was announced that Jim and Buck had sold Chaparral to a financial holding company. It seems that in their projections to the buyer they said that the maximum discount would be 5 percent off wholesale, and all their projections for profit were made on that basis. Since there were only about five or six dealerships in major markets that got the large discounts to make them competitive in their respective markets, the effect on the bottom line would not have been a lot, but it made a huge difference to us. The problem with those projections is that without the large dealerships, the volume wouldn't be there to sustain the profit margins. Buck and Jim planned to retire while they were on top, but much to their surprise, the buyer asked them to stay on and run the company for at least a year. They were offered a sweetheart deal to stay. The only problem was that they now had to make it all work out with the margins they had shown the buyer. Since the economy was improving and they were able to sign up new dealerships, they were able to pull it off by explaining that the lower margins first year were due to all the changes, plus the fact that the dealerships were being cautious about the change in ownership. I can't fault Jim, because he was just trying to help us and didn't mean us any harm. I really, really like those guys, and I just wish that whole deal had gone down a lot differently.

With the great new deal with Wellcraft, and our new Chris Craft boats, things were going well. The next few years were good ones for Houston, for our business, for Pat and me, and our family. Things seemed to be on an even keel. Our lease on the North Houston store was up, and we purchased the store out of our lease for 80 percent of its current value. Our lease deal really worked out well both for us and Charter Financial Group, who had made the deal in the first place. One day about a year after we purchased the North Houston store, Bill Penndel, the owner of the Mercedes dealership that was next to our North Houston store, showed up and said that he needed to purchase our store. He told us that he had a problem with his BMW franchise. He had taken on a new car line called Sterling (it was part of Austin Rover with help from Honda's Acura division) and wanted to put Sterling in with the BMW store that was to the north of the Mercedes dealership. It seems that BMW had given him an ultimatum that if he put Sterling in with BMW, he would lose his BMW franchise. Bill wanted to keep BMW happy, so he told them he would buy our dealership building and put Sterling in it, leaving BMW to itself. He would then have three dealerships side by side, and each would operate as a separate franchise. I told Bill that we were very happy where we were, since when people came and priced his Mercedes, our boats looked like a bargain. He laughed, saying that he would pay way too much for our building, and we could just build a new building. He was partially right: we had outgrown the building, and we didn't have any place to grow, so that sounded like it would work for us.

We worked toward a deal to sell the building to Intercontinental Motors (Bill's Company), and they would then lease it back to us for a year, giving us plenty of time to build a new store. We had already talked to Charter Financial, and they were ready to build a new store for us, sticking to a similar deal as we had done previously. We got $1,040,000 for the store, and we only owed about $600,000. Real estate was going through hard times due to the high interest rates, and we were in a position to get a good property at a very good price. We closed the deal with Bill in late 1984 and started looking for a new location. It turned out to be harder than one would expect, since so many pieces of property carried more debt than they were worth, and the owners couldn't afford to take a loss on selling their property to us. We knew we wanted to stay close to where we already were, since that was where our customers knew we were located. After several attempts to secure a property, we finally found a site a quarter of a mile up the freeway on the northbound side of Interstate 45; it would be twice as big as our current North Houston store. We secured the property, started the process of purchasing the property, and got bids on the building. We did everything through Charter Financial, and everything seemed to moving right along. We had taken longer to secure the property, but we seemed to have enough time to get everything done within our year. I talked to Bill Penndel and he said that if the building wasn't finished, we could go month to month until we were ready. BMW was happy now that Bill had purchased our location, and the Sterling cars hadn't even begun to arrive. In fact, the Sterling car was a total bust. The first car was based on an Acura Legend with a British interior. It didn't even arrive in the US until 1987. The brand only lasted a couple of years due to electrical problems, and the British currency made it very high-priced in the United States. As it turned out, Bill Penndel never took delivery of any Sterling cars.

It seemed very strange, but we kept experiencing delay after delay from Charter Financial over closing on the property and starting construction. This went on for months and months. Charter Financial finally admitted that they could not get financing. The fault didn't lie with us. It seems that Charter had gotten into a venture several years before when they financed the making of the movie, *The Buddy Holly Story*, starring Gary Busey. The movie came out in 1978, but they had been sued by a distributor, National Independent Theatre Exhibitors, Inc. (NITE) over the distribution of the movie. It seems that NITE had discussed the distribution of the film with Charter, but Charter decided that Columbia would distribute the film. NITE thought they had had a verbal agreement. A high profile lawsuit took place over the matter that would go on for years. It was finally settled on December 5, 1984, in the Eleventh Circuit of the United States Court of Appeals in Atlanta. Charter won the challenge, but the fight left them financially drained. Of course, we knew nothing about all of this. First, they couldn't get financing because of the ongoing lawsuit, and then their resources dried up after they won. Charter finally admitted that they could not honor their side of the deal. They explained that when they made the deal with us, they were confident that they would win their case, and it would not interfere with our deal. They didn't think that it would go to trial, but it did. Several high profile law firms were involved, and it cost a lot more than they anticipated. The people at Charter Financial were really good people. The only mistake they made with us was not telling us about what was going on. I suspect that if they had told me what they thought was going to happen, we would have gone on with them anyway. In the end, the principal that we worked with at Charter Financial, Jon Vogler, said, "I have to go out and get a real job." I have spoken to him several times over the years. He said that he opened a paint and body shop in North Houston. I guess we could have sued them, but they were already broke. As bad as it hurt us, I still have no ill feelings toward Jon or Charter Financial.

I should mention that if the reader remembers seeing *The Buddy Holly Story* in black and white, and also seeing it in color, the reason is that they had run out of money once the film was produced, and they decided to first show it in black and white, and if it was a success, rerelease it in color. It seems that it only cost about $150,000 to make the copies in black and white, and about $550,000 to print it in color, and they just didn't have enough money to make the copies in color. It was shot in color, so later when it the film was sold, and the new owner released it in color; then, it did much better. That is why if you see the movie on American Movie Classics, it will most likely be in black and white.

We were in quite a fix now. Most of our year was up, and we didn't have much to show for it. The good news is that a bank had repossessed the land we were purchasing, and with a glut of land for sale in Houston, they were content to wait on us to close the deal. We tried to get financing on our own, but we were having trouble getting a loan, because Houston was suffering a decline in real estate. The boom of the early 1980s had turned into a bust, but we had a white knight come to our rescue. Don Starnes, the president of Shoreline trailers, had been selling us trailers for years and wanted to sell us many more trailers. Don had been the vice president of AMF when it owned a lot of boat companies, and he had acquired Shoreline when AMF sold off all of its boat companies during hard times. AMF was famous for its Bowling Division, and AMF wanted to grow their bowling and pool table businesses. I respected Don because he was a great family man, a good Christian, and great mentor. Bob Panneton and I had the down payment money, and Don had the connections to get us financing. Don, Bob Panneton, and I secured the loan and closed on the property. The financing was provided by Houston Mortgage, and the owner used his own money to finance our building.

Finally, construction started, and everything seemed to be going well. It had been about fourteen months since we had made the initial deal with Bill Penndel, and he was happy for us to take another year, since the Sterling car franchise wasn't working work out for him, and our lease payments were covering his mortgage payments. We were paying month to month, and he didn't even know what he was going to do with the building once he got it. He said that he might put his used car department in our building. One day, we heard a rumor that something big was going down at Intercontinental Motors. The rumor was that Bill had been bought out and had left town. It seems that Bill had gotten into some financial trouble, and an auto group came in and purchased his Mercedes dealership, his BMW dealership, his home, and the location we were leasing month to month. Our lease with Bill stated that either of us could terminate the lease with a thirty-day notice, if either of us sold our business. Bill had told me he would never sell his dealership. It was only about a week later that a lawyer for the new owners came over and handed us our thirty-day notice. I told him we were being totally blindsided, and he said that he was sorry, but the Mercedes dealership had plans to sell a lot more used cars, and that they needed our location.

We decided to try and rent a facility for about three or four months, the amount of time it would take to complete our store. It was really hard to rent a building for that amount of time for a boat dealership on such short notice. We challenged our real estate man, Jack Butera, and he came up with an empty building about eight hundred feet behind our new store. The managers of the property had been trying to market it for three years in the down market, and they thought that if we moved in, someone would take notice, and then they would get to lease it to someone for a longer period. We signed a month-to-month lease and then had the task of moving a complete dealership in two weeks. It was very disruptive and our business dropped off. We had a large sign put on the new store property, saying that we were in temporary facilities right behind the store. We moved much of our inventory to our other stores and tried to keep going under very difficult circumstances.

Unfortunately, for us, the hope of the manager of that property came to pass. A new company called Universal Technical Institute (UTI) suddenly noticed our location and decided that they needed it. They told the managers that they would rent their entire building, which was about five times the space we were renting, if they could have it in thirty days. The management company agreed to relocate us to another one of their properties they were trying to lease, the Plains Machinery site, which was about a thousand feet north of our new store. They would pay the rent for the first two months, and then pay for us to move. By then, we had realized that we were being really hurt due to insufficient room for inventory at the temporary location. By contrast, the Plains Machinery building was the size of several football fields, so we agreed to the deal and moved a second time. This upheaval was catastrophic for business. UTI did move into the property and stayed there for years. Eventually, they built an extremely large complex near that original location. UTI is still there today. UTI now has eleven campuses all across the United States, and they helped a lot of people develop great technical skills. That is one positive result that came out of this mess.

Before all of this occurred, the North Houston store had become our largest and most profitable store, as it had been for the preceding four years. It was a high volume, low-cost store, located on a freeway that over 225,000 cars passed by every day. The multiple moves and ending up in a warehouse versus a storefront was a disaster, to say the least. Trying to run a business, build a store, and deal with ever changing manufacturers was a nightmare. One bright spot was that we were going to be one of the first dealerships to handle Bass Tracker boats. Prior to January 1986, Bass Tracker had only been sold through the Bass Tracker store in Springfield, Missouri, and through their Bass Pro Shops catalog. I had Billy Murray, the new Tracker rep, sitting in my office on January 28, 1986, signing us up to become a Bass Tracker dealer on the first day that he could sign up a dealer. They were only going to sign ten dealerships in the whole country on that day, and we had been selected to become a Tracker Dealership. I was in the middle of signing reams of paperwork when I got a phone call from Pat. She told me that the Space Shuttle Challenger had just blown up while it was being launched. I had a very small portable television in my office that someone had given me as a gift, and we watched what everyone else on the planet was watching. We saw the

Challenger lift off and then blow up, over and over again. I will never forget the faces of Christa McAuliffe's parents as they were watching the shuttle explode. It was a very sad day. Finally, Billy asked me if I was going to be able to sign the rest of the paperwork, and I said that as tragic as the Challenger accident was, I still needed to keep my end of our deal to sign up with Tracker. Johnny Morris and his people were, and still are wonderful people. At the time, we were in the early stages of building the new store, and Bill Penndel, who was buying the store, hadn't sold out yet. That would come soon enough.

We were within a couple of weeks of finishing the new store when something happened that to this day seems impossible to understand. It seems when Chrysler Credit came to do their monthly inventory check of the boats they had financed, they were shocked to see them in the old Plains Machinery building. They were supposed to do floor plan checks every month, but it had been several months since they had done a floor check, and they were worried about their inventory being located in a warehouse. They were at a point that their deal was about to end with Wellcraft, where Wellcraft would be responsible for any inventory losses if a dealer went out of business. It seems there was a provision in their deal with Wellcraft that the inventory couldn't be stored in a warehouse away from the dealership. They contacted Wellcraft and asked them to guarantee any losses from the boats in the warehouse (which wasn't really a warehouse but our current location). Chrysler Credit knew that Wellcraft wasn't going to use it anymore due to their high interest rates. They saw an opportunity to get out of their deal with Wellcraft. Wellcraft didn't want to be liable on the basis of a technicality, so they sent one of their people, that I considered a friend, to try and settle the issue with Chrysler Credit. He got into town late, and I showed him the new store and how it was close to being finished. I explained that since we had this huge building, we had moved a lot of our inventory from the other stores to there since fall was approaching, and the boats were kept out of the weather. Most of the boats financed through Chrysler Credit were at the Plains Machinery building. He asked me if he could have a key, so that he could take inventory himself and see exactly which boats were there. He said that he wanted to get out of town the following day, so if he could take the inventory that evening, he could make it out of town the next day once he contacted the Chrysler Credit people. I trusted him and told him to give the key to the guard at the building. Our insurance carrier required us to have a guard because it was a temporary facility, and we didn't know who else might have keys to the building. There were about thirty doors and about twenty-four overhead doors, and we didn't want to change all the locks.

I left him there at about 8:00 p.m. I got a call about 2:00 a.m. from the guard, saying that there were a bunch of trucks there picking up boats, and he wondered if it was okay since the guy I had introduced him to said it was okay. It seems that the only way that Chrysler Credit would keep Wellcraft from being liable was to have them pick up the boats, all of which had for the most part just arrived, and have Wellcraft sell them to other dealerships. When I got to the Plains building at about 2:30 a.m., they had left, and the building was a complete mess. There were empty beer bottles and trash everywhere, broken trailers, and paper all over the place. It was a nightmare. I still have the pictures from that night, and when I look at them, it seems unbelievable that anyone could have carried out so heinous an activity. Eventually, Wellcraft would be hurt more than anything they did to us. From that time on, they were in total decline, and I don't think they made any money ever again. Dealers had to ask themselves, if they could do such a thing to a dealership that had been one of their largest dealerships for so many years, what would Wellcraft do to them? I sent pictures of what happened to those that asked for them. I didn't go out of my way to call my fellow dealer friends, but it didn't take long for the word to get out.

Much to my surprise, the other lenders didn't know what had happened, so they got worried, and a feeding frenzy started. The next few days were the worst in our entire period as a boat dealer. I realized that we weren't going to be able to carry Wellcraft anymore, and we needed to downsize. I needed to get Wellcraft to negotiate so we could get rid of all our Wellcraft inventory. Our other suppliers could see that as well. Thank goodness for great friends like Don Starnes; we made it through the disaster. I prayed a lot, but I prayed the wrong prayer. I was asking the Lord to get me though these times, when I should have been giving the situation to Him, letting Him guide me though the mess. It became clear that we had to do something to bring Wellcraft and the other parties to the table. I had already contacted our attorney about suing Wellcraft, and he said it was out of his league. He referred me to H. Gray Burks who has become a friend for life. Gray was a business consultant and corporate attorney that dealt with these type of situations. Bob Panneton and I met with Gray and after looking at the raw facts (we were careful not to sugar coat anything, but tell Gray everything we knew). Gray said that we were no longer in control, and we had to regain control. He said that we needed to know who our friends were and who would support us through this mess. He said that our business needed to file a chapter 11 bankruptcy and start making deals. That way, we could end up with people that wanted to do business with us, and with our reputation, it shouldn't be very hard. We said that we didn't think we were bankrupt, and Gray said that if we didn't do it, we could surely go bankrupt. I think the key reason I didn't let my pride get in the way was that Gray had something on his desk with a cross on it and since both Bob Panneton and I were believers, we felt the strength of the Lord and the Holy Spirit leading us.

It turns out that everything Gray said came true. Since Wellcraft made up almost half of our business, we knew we were going to have to downsize. The Houston store had never made a lot of money because it was located in an expensive part of town. The ink was hardly dry on the chapter 11 filing when AW Heinze, the previous Wellcraft rep who had become our Chris Craft rep, was standing at our doorstep saying that Dick Genth had sent him to ask us what he needed to do to help us. Don Starnes jumped right in to help. The Bass Tracker representative liked the fact that they would not have as much competition. Our accessory suppliers said that they would take some of our accessory inventory back if we needed to downsize. It was a total blessing to see who our friends were when the chips are down. Gray was totally right. I am sure that the Lord put him in our path.

One thing I will always remember is that Gray said that whenever things get tough you should read the book of James. He said it was a short book, and we were going to have to read it a bunch of times to get through this mess. I can't remember how many times I have read the entire book of James. It only takes about an hour to read the entire book. I highly recommend it to anyone in business.

When the smoke settled, Chris Craft would become our premium line, Bass Tracker could become our volume line with bass boats and pontoon boats, and Cobalt would stay as our luxury line. Don Starnes's Shoreline trailers would provide the trailers that didn't come with the boats. We settled our lawsuit against Wellcraft, with them taking the rest of their boats without any expense to us, in return for us dropping our lawsuit against them and Chrysler Credit. Since these boats were technically classified as used, they had to be sold at a discount, so Wellcraft lost a lot more than the $300,000 they were worried about. Who knows how much business they lost because of the way they treated us. The chapter 11 allowed us to get out of the lease at the Houston store. We owned the Clear Lake store outside of the business, so we sold it. We had a buyer that had been wanting to purchase it for a long time. Unfortunately, his offer went down substantially because he knew we were in a hurry to move out and downsize. What I regret the most was that a lot of our employees lost their jobs when things weren't going very well in Houston.

It was amazing, but we closed on the new store, moved our total business in less than a month, and Chris Craft paid us to put beautiful neon Chris Craft signs on both sides of the store. Dick Genth loved to "stick it" to Wellcraft. Since Bob Panneton was still living in the Clear Lake area, and the one store couldn't support both of us, he decided to go back to work in the Aerospace industry, which was making a comeback in the Clear Lake area with the Space Shuttle flying regularly. One of the best people in our organization, Jay Barcello, bought out Bob Panneton's interest. I had bought out Bob Carlton and John Wegener when the mess with the North Houston store and the Mercedes dealer started, because I didn't want them to have to worry about all that was going on, and they lived a long way from the North Houston store where the growth of our business was now centered. I am so thankful that Bob Panneton, Bob Carlton, and John Wegener weren't caught up in this mess. I was also thankful that the Lord brought another good Christian man, Jay Barcello, to help us through these tough times. I am sure that the reader is wondering why anyone would ever want to go in business for themselves, in particular, the boat business. It is like Congress in terms of trying to get something done. Everyone was only looking out for themselves, and often they hurt the people they were trying to help. Pat says that I was naïve then, and still am now. I trusted people too much.

10

It is about Time!

Our grand opening of the new store was wonderful. It was great to have so many friends there to help us through hard times.

Life was much easier with only one store, located close to where we lived. We selected the best of the best employees from our other dealerships, though many of the people from the Clear Lake store did not want to move the forty miles between stores. One person whom I would be remiss in not mentioning is Charlotte McLemore. Charlotte was the person who did everything in the Clear Lake store. She managed the inventory between stores, kept track of when they were sold, and paid them off to the lenders. She was very upset about Chrysler Credit questioning us, since she took the inventory management very seriously. I would have loved to have her come with us to the new North Houston store, but she lived south of the Clear Lake store, and it would have been too far for her to drive. She is a wonderful person, and I am sorry that she had to spend so much time and effort helping us through those hard days. She was a jewel, and I will always be grateful for her support over the years.

The new store was a dream, and we started outgrowing it within a few months. We were a lot more efficient when we were quickly turning the inventory, and we started making money after the very first month. We were truly blessed. Although it didn't seem like it at the time, my prayers had been answered. I would have never, never guessed that what happened was just what our business needed. We stayed on our plan to pay off previous creditors other than the debt Wellcraft assumed due to their actions. Thankfully, we paid off our debt early. When we went to court to close our case, the judge said that she was about to retire, and that our case was the first one that she had taken to completion during her entire time as a judge. She said this would not have happened without a lot of people wanting to support our efforts, thus allowing us to prove ourselves.

The next few years were a lot less stressful, which allowed me to spend more time with my family. This was one of my best times in the boat business. Of course, the real problem with the boat business was the dependence on manufacturers, and when they have problems, the dealer has problems. At that time, our boat companies were doing well; therefore, we were doing well.

On January 18, 1989, I experienced what is best described as a "God Moment". We had just finished the Houston Boat Show the previous Sunday, and January 18 was my day off. I was delivering a large pontoon boat that had been sold at our boat show. The customer had asked us to deliver it to Lake Livingston, about fifty miles north of Houston. I offered to make the delivery so that the salesman could remain at the store and capitalize on post-boat show sales. I was supposed to meet the customer at the lake around 11:00 a.m. at the marina where he kept his boat. I got there, launched the boat, checked it out, put it in his slip, and waited for the customer to arrive. He never showed, and even though I had one of those large Panasonic cell phones (about the size of a desk phone), I had no coverage at Lake Livingston. I finally grew tired of waiting, then went to the marina office where they told me that the customer had called. He had gotten tied up with business and asked me to leave the keys with the marina manager. I gave the manager the keys and headed out with my Ford Bronco, pontoon trailer in tow. When I reached the road between I-45 and US 59, with my left blinker on for a left turn headed toward I-45, something totally amazing happened. I got what I could only describe as a command from the Lord. It was, "Turn right," and I said out loud, "What?" The command came again, "Turn right." I was pretty sure it was the Lord, since I've previously heard Him but never in this manner. Again, it was as though a command had been given, and I was receiving an instantaneous download. It was not like a booming voice, but I undoubtedly understood what He meant. I immediately turned right, even though I had no reason for what I did except the Lord commanded me. The trip would be about eight extra miles and thirty extra minutes. This was not at all a route that I would take to return to the dealership. During the whole trip back, I wondered why this had happened. I could only assume that the Lord was protecting me from something. I imagined explosions, car chases, etc., but I continued on. Just as I was arriving at the store, I heard on the radio that there had been a horrible car wreck on the road heading to I-45 from Lake Livingston. I thanked the Lord from my heart for protecting me. I could only imagine what would have happened to me with that short wheel base Bronco pulling a twenty-eight-foot trailer. I felt really blessed.

I was supposed to go home when I got to the store, but anyone that owns a business will naturally tell you that just doesn't happen. I got caught up with salesmen making deals and didn't get away from the store until about 6:00 p.m. Right after leaving the store, I was going north on I-45 when I saw several police cars in front of an ambulance, with two following behind and their lights flashing. I remember thinking that it was a very bad day for accidents, and I was so grateful that the Lord was there to protect me. That night, I told Pat what had happened, and she was amazed. We watched the ten o'clock news, and they told about a horrible accident near Lake Livingston where a man was hit head-on by a big truck being driven by a prisoner on work detail. At first, they thought the man was dead, but when they realized that he was still alive, they rushed him to Houston for treatment. I didn't put two and two together, but years later, the Lord would reveal what happened that day.

Fast forward to 2009 when I was teaching a Sunday school class at Southside Baptist Church in Richmond, Virginia. One of the class members recommended that the class read a book that she had just read, *90 Minutes in Heaven* by Don Piper. Over the next month, she would ask each week whether or not we had gotten the book. She said that she would loan her copy to us if we needed. A lady in the class took her up on it, and the next week, she started talking about it. The week after that, in the Lifeway bookstore, I saw the book on display, so I decided to buy a copy.

When I got home and started reading it, I learned that the author, Don Piper, was a pastor from Houston. One day, he was at Lake Livingston at a meeting, but he left early. His normal route was to take the road to US 59 and take it straight to where his church was located in Southwest Houston. When he got to the part where he said that he had his blinker on to make a left turn, the Lord spoke to him and commanded him to turn right to go west. The words Don spoke were the precise words that the Lord spoke to me at the same time, to turn right, which in my case was to head east. Don thought what I had thought at the time: it was a lot longer to go that way to his destination, and Don had never gone that way either before or since. I got chills up my spine. The date was January 18, 1989. Don tells in his book that he had suffered a horrible accident and died when he was hit by a dump truck driven by a prisoner on work duty. Don said that the medics came over and pronounced him dead. There was no pulse or sign of life. They said that they would cut him out of the car later.

Over an hour after that dreadful accident, another pastor from the same conference went to investigate why traffic was stopped. He found that the victim was his friend, Don Piper. He asked if he could pray for Don. The medics said it was too late, and that the car and the body were so mangled that nobody could get to the body. The pastor said that he would like to try. He climbed through what used to be the trunk to get inside the car and was able to put his hand on Don's shoulder. It was cold and still. He said that Don's arm was swung over his back, and blood was everywhere. He prayed for Don, and then started to sing a hymn. At about the second verse, he said that someone else started singing with him. It was Don Piper! The pastor crawled out of the car and told the medics that Don was still alive. The medics replied in disbelief that Don had been dead for over ninety minutes, and there was no chance that he was alive. They said that a body will twitch for hours sometimes. The pastor then asked if dead bodies also sang. The medic thought the pastor was crazy, and it was only after the pastor started making a scene that one of the policemen told the medic to humor the pastor and go check. The medic managed to reach into the car and discovered a pulse.

That was when they got the Jaws of Life and started tearing the car apart. It took over an hour to extract Don, then they immediately took him to a hospital in Livingston. Emergency room personnel stabilized Don but said that his injuries were too extensive for them to deal with there that they would have to send him to Houston. They said that a helicopter ride was too risky because of the extent of Don's injuries, so they decided to take him by ambulance instead.

In his book, Don says that he died and went to heaven, and he relates what happened there. At one point, he remembers hearing somebody singing, and he remembers singing with him. The next thing Don remembers is coming to in an ambulance with police cars chasing them, lots of red lights flashing, and the attendant telling him he was just entering Houston and would be getting some help soon. That was about the time I saw the caravan taking Don to the Houston Medical Center on I-45. They gave Don more pain medicine, and he didn't wake again for days.

I am not sure about the part I played that day, but I think the Lord wanted me to know just how real the events of that day were. I was there. The Lord spoke to me precisely like he did to Don Piper. I think seeing the ambulance coming down I-45 was a reminder that the Lord is always in control, no matter what. It just took me twenty years to learn exactly what happened that day. I am not sure whether the Lord was saving me, or just wanting me to not get in the way of what He had planned. I really believe that the He allowed me to be a part of this event so that I could share it with others and implore them to read Don Piper's book, *90 Minutes in Heaven*. Either way, I am truly blessed to have a God that loves me so much. I highly recommend that you get a copy of Don's book, if you haven't already read it, and realize that God gave Don a story to share with as many people as possible.

Back to the ongoing drama of the boat business! Dale Murray, along with Dick Genth as a minor partner, had purchased Chris Craft Boats from Chris Craft Industries during this time because Chris Craft Industries was in an all-out fight to get control of Twenty

Century Fox and needed as much money as they could get. During this time, things got even better at Chris Craft. They were coming out with new boats. They were expanding their production, and things looked really bright. Wellcraft had begun to slide, and I was grateful for the way things had worked out. Once again, just when things seem to be going well in the boat business, there was an upset. It seems that Dale Murray owned some other businesses that were struggling with financial problems, and Dale was taking money from Chris Craft to keep his other companies afloat (no pun intended). It got so bad that we were having to send cash to Chris Craft so they could build boats, which we had firm orders from customers. Here was our major line—in serious financial trouble that had nothing to do with the boat business. Of course, it all ended when Chris Craft filed bankruptcy. Our boats stopped coming, and we had boats that we had paid for that never came. We got hit on two fronts. In addition to boats we paid for, we also lost about $65,000 in unpaid warranties and bonus credits.

Eventually, OMC, Outboard Marine Corporation, purchased Chris Craft out of bankruptcy, and it became the premium line of their new boat division, which included about six lines of recently purchased boat companies. OMC knew nothing about building boats, and they were making mistake after mistake. They were reacting to the fact that Brunswick, the owner of Mercury Outboards and Mercruiser Stern Drives, had just bought SeaRay and Bayliner, the two largest boat companies at the time. OMC was quickly losing market share for their Johnson and Evinrude Outboards. Our Chris Craft business suffered through all of this.

In the middle of all of this, we got a notice that Interstate 45 in front of our store was going to be widened, and our store would lose sixty feet of frontage space. We were able to settle with the highway department, getting enough money to expand the store, and adding a lot of parking beside the store to make up for all the land we would lose out front.

Houston mortgage was great toward us, allowing us to purchase the property to the north of the store. We used the rest of the money to expand the store. It took a couple of years for the highway expansion to take place, so we had time to expand before the highway work started. The expansion of the property became a windfall for Don, Bob, and I, but turned out to be a significant hardship for the business. What the highway department originally told us regarding the time we would be impacted was a farce. It took much longer, and they really made a big mess. It cut our business by about 15 percent during the construction, and by the time they were finished, we were

Construction equipment isn't good for business.

being impacted by almost 25 percent. We were being hit from both sides because of OMC's and Chris Craft's problems.

We tightened our budgets and held on. It was time to sell the 1982 Baron, and I did so because as much as I enjoyed flying, it just wasn't feasible during the hard times we were facing. Sometimes, we just have to do what we have to do. It was the only airplane that I ever owned that I'd lost money on when I sold it, but it was time for both engine overhauls, and that would have cost $60,000. It all worked out, since I sold it for $30,000 less than I paid for it and got to enjoy it for almost ten years. The tax benefit when I had purchased it had been about $50,000 so I had come out ahead in the long run. I thank God for allowing me that wonderful experience. Flying made me feel really close to our Lord.

OMC was pouring lots of money into their new boat ventures, and losing money as fast as they were putting it in the businesses. We were really being hurt by all this, and Christie was about to start going to Georgia Tech the following next year, so I decided to stop fighting the boat business. I had been talking to one of my dealer friends, Ray Barber, who had a large dealership in Dallas, about selling the business rather than keep fighting the battles. Ray was the distributor for Ranger boats and had been after me for quite some time to sell our store to him. I was really worried that the business could fail while Christie was in college, and I would find myself in a serious dilemma. Ray was the Bayliner dealer in Dallas and wanted to be the Bayliner dealer in Houston. The dealer that had been handling Bayliner had just gone out of business, and Ray saw the opportunity to replace Chris Craft with Bayliner, reviving our business. I agreed to sell the business to Ray and become an employee of Ray's, managing the store for him. We would retain the name, Marine Products, and I would be the manager. All the employees would stay. This way, I would be assured to have a regular salary, being spared another winter where I put money in the business instead of taking a salary. Don Starnes, Bob Panneton, and I would still own the building and lease it to Ray Barber.

What happened next just goes to prove that what Pat always said about me was really true. Pat said that I was always too naive and trusted people too much. I always tried to do what I said and never deceived people on purpose. Once we completed the deal in September 1991, Ray announced that he wanted to close the store until the January 1992 Boat Show to give time for the Bayliner boats to come in. He said that the store would not make any money during that period, and he wanted to start fresh at the January Boat Show. I said that we had a written agreement about my salary, and Ray said that he would pay me what he owed me for those months, the week after the boat show. I suspect that Ray just didn't have the cash after buying the store to fund the offseason. I got very little cash out of the sale, so I was left hanging. Ray rationalized that this way, the employees and I could go on unemployment for three months and come back for the boat show. Not surprisingly, several left to work for other dealerships. I was the only one who would see guaranteed pay during this period.

I still don't know how Pat and I made it for those three months. I did finally decide to file for unemployment benefits, and got about $300 a week for those three months. That is $1,260 a month instead of the $5,000 plus bonuses I was promised. We were faithful and tithed, even on my unemployment money during this period and asked the Lord to help us through what was surely a difficult time. One thing after another happened, and each time that it seemed we would run out of money, we had someone who owed us money, or some account that had been closed from selling the business, just appear as a bill came due. To this date, neither Pat nor I can tell you how we made it through that time, but it was a time of cutting back and surviving without very much strain.

One thing happened that had to be the work of the Lord. Our property taxes on our home were due in early December of that year and they were about $2,800. In Texas, you pay for the whole year at one time. The money that we had set aside for that was used to pay bills during the off months. About three days before the taxes were due, we got a refund from some property that we owned. It came as a total surprise. We didn't even know that the refund was owed to us, and the amount was short by only a dollar from the exact amount that was owed for our home's property taxes. Talk about a blessing from heaven! God is great!

The January Boat Show was a huge success, and Ray reimbursed my back pay in two installments: 50 percent after the boat show and the rest in early February. The money came much slower than he had promised, but he eventually paid me what he owed me. I stopped my unemployment the first of January, on faith that Ray would honor his commitment.

There is a side to this story that needs to be told. I had made a deal with our daughter Christie that I would pay to send her to Texas A&M, which would have cost about $4,000 a year, but if she really, really wanted to go to Georgia Tech, like dear old dad did, she could go if she could get scholarships to pay for half of her first year's cost. Georgia Tech would cost about $7,500 a year because Christie would be an out-of-state student. Christie was determined to go to Georgia Tech just as I had, so she worked very hard and received about seven or eight scholarships. A lot were only $500, but she went after about eighteen to twenty scholarships. The largest was the Georgia Tech Houston Chapter of the Alumni Association, which was $2,500. Due to the oil business, the Houston Chapter had one of the best scholarships in the country. At that time, scholarships to Georgia

Tech were rare and even rarer for a female engineer. When we went to the Houston Alumni meeting for Christie to get her scholarship, everyone wanted to know how I got her to go to Georgia Tech, since none of them could get their children to go. I said it was quite simple: kids always do the opposite of what we want them to do. I had done everything I could to get her to go to Texas A&M, but Christie did the opposite and decided to attend to Georgia Tech.

Now, here is how God was planning for Christie to go to Georgia Tech and eventually meet her wonderful husband-to-be, Jimmy Sauers. When Ray paid me the three months of $5,000 a month that he owed me, I set aside the amount that I had gotten from unemployment, which was $1,260 a month for three months. I put the $3,780 into a college account for Christie. That amount was exactly what I would need for Christie's first year of college. Here is how this was so amazing. I didn't have a clue at the time as to how much I would need for Christie. We knew tuition was going up, and Christie didn't have any idea how many scholarships she would get. What I first thought was a huge negative—the fact that Ray wouldn't pay me per our agreement—turned into a huge blessing. Only the Lord could make something like this happen. He provided for us, and just as we were faithful to Him, He was faithful to us—we just didn't know it at the time. So many things in our life turned out this way. If we put our faith in the Lord, He will work things out for us, even though we don't always see it at the time. It is all about faith.

The next two years were a challenge, but I got to work steady hours without all the strain of owning the business. It was a perfect time for Christie to get started in college, as well as a time to start improving my relationship with the Lord. It became very clear at the end of the first year that the Lord had answered my prayers, just not the way I would have expected. He had answered them much better than I could have ever guessed. I am very thankful to this day.

Once again, the boat business was going through a lot of changes. Times were a lot harder than I would have hoped, but thank goodness I was now salaried and could plan my life without having to worry as much as before. I wanted to do a good job for Mr. Barber, since I knew how difficult the boat business could be. By the end of the second year, we were doing really well, and it was time to renew our lease. Don Starnes wanted to raise the rent, and Ray Barber wanted us to slash the rent. Ray sent me out to find a location for the store that would cost less. I was in a difficult situation. On one hand, I was working for Ray Barber, and my job depended on having a good location. On the other hand, if we moved, Don, Bob, and I would have to find someone to rent, or purchase, our store. I found an abandoned Nissan dealership where the owner would rent us part of the building including the showroom. We would only have limited parking right in front of the dealership, plus he would have the freedom to sell or rent the open lot beside the store. The rent for this location would be $8,000 and Ray was paying $10,000 a month for our store location. Don wanted us to go up to $11,000 a month, and Ray wanted us to go down to $8,500 a month. The $8,500 would barely cover the note. The Nissan location was a mess and would require a lot of work to make it work. Ray and Don didn't get along very well, since we had to work to get Ray to pay the rent on time, and Don didn't like it. Neither did I. Ray decided to move to the new location.

Don Starnes on an offshore fishing trip in one of our boats.

I worked hard for two months hiring contractors, getting the new store cleaned up, and arranging to move Ray's business to that location. It was about three miles closer to Houston than our current location. Businesses were moving out from downtown versus toward downtown. This turned out to be a very poor decision, but Ray was very stubborn. At the same time, Don was working on me to get back into the business. He rationalized that it must be really hard to work for Ray, which it was. Since business had really been picking up, he believed I could find a bunch of people who would really want to help us. Don was right. Word got out about Ray moving the store—I suspect that Don did a lot to put the news out—and the offers started coming in. We had taken on Regal Boats shortly before Ray bought the business to help replace the business we had lost because of Chris Craft's problems. Regal Boats was owned by the Kuck family, and they were wonderful Christians. Their business was in Orlando, Florida, and they had a very large impact on my Christian life. They led by example, and they will always be my friends. Seeing them pray before meetings, and in restaurants, helped me realize that by praying, we are witnessing for Christ. From that time on, our family has always prayed before any meal, and especially in any restaurant. We are respectful of others, but it is important to show others that we are not ashamed of our beliefs, rather, we want others to know how thankful we are for all that the Lord does for us each and every day. Ray really was a Bayliner guy and had only kept Regal because he knew I had such a strong relationship with them. I know Regal wanted me to keep them if I went into the business again, but I had to respect that Ray was the dealer now.

Starcraft was ready to jump in with their aluminum bass boats, pontoon, and fiberglass sport boats that had become very popular. Starcraft boats had broken off from the travel trailer and van conversion business and was trying to grow its business. One of our old friends from the OMC days, Bob Anderson, was the president of Celebrity Boats and needed our help. He had been trying to break into the Houston market for years and knew what we could do. One of my previous employees, Mike Iler, had started a business and copied our logo and had named his business Marine Sports instead of Marine Products. Since Mike had boat show space and Ray would keep our old boat show space, we decided to purchase his company since he had decided to move to Florida. This would give us good boat show space, which was very important.

The day after we successfully moved Ray Barber into his new Nissan store location and gotten all settled in, I told Ray that I was going back into the boat business at the old location. Two weeks after

I moved Ray out of the store, we reopened it as Marine Sports with about five employees from his old store. I don't think Ray had a clue that we were going to do that, since I had done such a good job of moving the store and seeing to it that everything was done properly. He immediately

The store as it opened as Marine Sports.

renamed his store Barber Boats Houston since he said the only reason that he kept the Marine Products name was because of the store's good reputation.

Ray kept Regal Boats to prevent us from getting the line, but only kept them for about another year. The one thing I really hated

about what happened was that I had to end my relationship with the Regal Boats people. They weathered the various storms in the boat business and continue to do well. We acquired Starcraft Boats and Celebrity Boats, then had a wonderful boat show and were off and running again. In the

Starcraft Boats became one of our main lines.

meantime, Christie had decided to switch to a co-op job after the first year at Georgia Tech. She would go to school for a quarter, work at an industry job for a quarter, and then keep rotating. I had tried to talk her out of it because I was afraid that she would not get a good job in her aerospace engineering field. I had known many fellow students, including my roommate, Jack Abbott, who were co-op students and didn't get jobs they liked. Christie was on a mission, and thank goodness that she didn't listen to me. Jobs were hard to find in aerospace engineering at that time, but Christie got a great co-op job at NASA's Johnson Space Center in Houston, where I had previously worked. There were only five co-op jobs, and Christie was number five. It was obvious that the Lord was at work again. I didn't even think about it, but I would only have to come up with the money for two quarters a year instead of three. Christie had landed the co-op job of a lifetime. What we didn't know was that NASA handles a co-op job as a hire, and when Christie went to school, she was treated as if she was merely on unpaid leave. That means her government start date came when she was nineteen years old. That means that Christie will be able to retire very early, if she wants, and is building seniority from the age of nineteen. Anyone who knows anything about the government knows just how important this is to one's career. On top of that, NASA paid her to travel to and from school, since they had her address listed as Georgia Tech. She got a travel allowance to travel to NASA and then return to school. Who would have guessed?

The business started well, and with its new lower overhead, we started growing and making money from the first boat show. Celebrity Boats was a great partner and started coming out with boats that we really needed. Starcraft had been purchased by

Brunswick Marine, the maker of Mercury Outboards several years before, and were trying to really grow Starcraft into a premium brand. They were investing a lot of money to make Starcraft a success. We were glad to have them as a partner.

Celebrity Boats was a great partner for us. Starcraft gave us aluminum bass boats, fiberglass sport boats, and pontoon boats. The next few years were probably the best we ever had in the boat business. We had two great lines that were doing everything they could to help both us and themselves succeed. Within a year we became Celebrity's largest dealer and were one of Starcraft's largest dealers. We needed a deck boat, and Starcraft came out with a really good deck boat that sold well. It looked like that we were back on track again. It must be obvious that it is very hard being in the boat business because when business is good, it is very good, and when it is bad, it is really bad. In addition to the swings of the boat business, we seemed to have a string of setbacks from outside the boat business.

The next few years were great. Our business was good and we were very focused. We had a lot of boat lines wanting us to take them on, but we resisted. We remembered who had been there when we needed them, and we were doing everything to create great partnerships with Celebrity Boats and Starcraft Boats. Christie was at Georgia Tech, and Rob was trying to decide where he wanted to go to college. Rob had quite a business going with building web pages for real estate agents. At that

Things were going really well again.

time, the internet was really new, and people didn't know how to build web sites. Rob had to build them in HTML, and then after he would build something, you would have to upload it (a really slow process), and then see what it looked like. "What you see is what you get" wasn't around yet. At first, he was earning up to $1,000 for a website. I told him that wouldn't last because someone would come up with an easier way to build web pages. The next year, Microsoft came out with Front Page, and for $150, anyone could learn to build web pages. I used it to build pages for the business. Rob did help me with one thing for the business. He built backgrounds for our web pages that had Starcraft and Celebrity printed hundreds of times on the background of each page. They were the same color so you couldn't see them when you viewed the site, but we immediately became the number one search site for each brand. We had no Google, and people used things like Webcrawler to find web sites. The problem was that Starcraft had been selling boats, travel trailers, and van conversions for decades, and we were swamped with phone calls for parts.

Celebrity's Firestar was a huge hit at the Houston Boat Show.

One of the things that we did for Celebrity boats was to help them build a new line of boats called Firestar. Pat was the one who came up with the name, and it was a huge success. Celebrity had a special meeting and flew all the dealers in to announce the new performance sport boat. The idea was to take the excitement of an offshore race boat and put it in a series of much smaller sport boats. Offshore race boats were about thirty-five to forty feet, and our Firestar boats would run from eighteen feet to twenty-two feet, but still have all the graphics and sportiness of the offshore race boats that cost five to six times as much. Firestar was a fantastic success. Our agreement for assisting Celebrity with designing the boats was for us to get the first twenty boats at a lower price and preferred delivery slots. They sold out the first year's production at that first meeting.

Celebrity had been under some financial pressure from their banks long before we had taken them on as a dealer. We did not know much about this, but after the success of the Firestar, Bob Anderson shared with us that he could finally get the banks off his back. It seems that he had been brought in to fix Celebrity, and the work that we had done together, particularly the Firestar, was just what Bob needed. It was a wonderful time for both of us. What we didn't know was things were going too well. The bank had taken Celebrity over from the previous owner, and its recent success was exactly what the bank needed to sell the company.

Starcraft had been doing really well also. We continued working with them, and they were coming out with new models like saltwater boats that we needed, as well as more sport and deck boats. They were growing, too, and the owners were very happy. With all this running around, I needed another airplane, so I purchased a demonstrator Mooney single engine airplane. I always said that it was like a Porsche—red, small, and fast. It was a great airplane that didn't cost nearly as much to operate as the Baron had. Things were going really well once again; our new boat company partners were growing with us, and we loved working with them. However, sometimes you can help a company too much. That is what happened with Celebrity Boats. We got a call from Bob Anderson one day, and he said that the company had gotten so profitable that the bank that owned it took an offer to sell it. Bob tried to get the bank to let the employees purchase the company, but the cash offer from Bombardier, the owner of SeaDoo, was tied to a quick sale, and before Bob could get a deal done, they sold Celebrity Boats to Bombardier. We met with the Bombardier people explaining that as their largest dealer (their boats being 40 percent of our sales), we had a very vested interest in Celebrity doing well. They reassured us that they were only going to grow the business and to please stick with them. Here I was, being naive again. Pat warned me, but since they were such a successful company, I felt that they would only help our business. During the next nine months, Celebrity slowed their production, and said they were developing a fresh line of boats that would take the boat business by storm. Celebrity boats were known as great riding, great performing boats that were real family boats.

Bombardier had a huge event to show off their new models. To our surprise, as they were announcing the new models, they informed us that all the old models that had been so successful for us were now being totally discontinued, including the ones we had on order. These would be replaced with the new Bombardier Celebrity boats. The boats were terrible. They were 20 percent slower than the old

My Mooney M20J was like a Porsche, red, small, and fast!

Celebrities, they didn't ride well, and handled worse than any boat we had ever tested. They were just plain ugly! To make matters worse, Bombardier wouldn't give us the prices of the boats.

The dealers were shocked and said that they didn't want any of the Bombardier boats. When at the end of the dealer meeting, they finally gave us the wholesale prices of the boats, prices had gone up 20 percent. I had a meeting with management at breakfast, and they said they needed to get us with Pierre Beaudoin, the current president of the SeaDoo divisions of Bombardier, at ten thirty that morning. We set up a meeting, and since we had a little time, we went to the airport to check on some service work the airport maintenance workers were doing on my Mooney. While we were there, I asked the people at the airport which plane the Bombardier people had come in on, since they also owned Lear Jet. They said that Mr. Beaudoin and his people had gotten there just before us and were taxiing for takeoff. It turned out that all the Bombardier people skipped town, including the two people who had set up our meeting with Mr. Beaudoin. I guess they didn't take rejection very well. We returned to the hotel and to the meeting place that they had set up, and no one showed up. There was no note, no phone call; they just cut and ran. Within six months, Celebrity boats was gone. Celebrity was to the boat business what Edsel was to the car business, only much, much worse. Years later, they came out with SeaDoo boats and built them in the empty Celebrity plant.

Now we had to start over and try to get a boat line that would replace Celebrity. This was a greater challenge than we had expected. Starcraft said we didn't need another line because they were coming up with a lot of new boats, and Brunswick was about to heavily to invest in growing Starcraft even more that it had already. That sounded good, but we were tired of putting too many eggs in one basket, so we continued to look. In the middle of this search, Brunswick decided to divest itself of Starcraft and several other brands. They put Starcraft up for sale. There is nothing worse for a line than to be put up for sale. Their strength had been built on Brunswick. It seems Brunswick had decided to try and revive their bowling division and needed the cash. This was like a one, two punch to the gut. Welcome to Boat Business 101.

I am sure that the reader now is wondering why anyone would ever want to go into the boat business, and I would say that hindsight is always 20/20. During the next couple of years, we soldiered on by taking on Chris Craft again. We elected to continue because OMC had found money in George Soros (yes, *that* George Soros!) and was trying to revive Chris Craft. They were building some really great boats and would be a great replacement for Celebrity. Of course, our business was hurt by all these changes, but we were recovering. Then, George Soros found out what boat manufacturing can be like and how fast he could burn money in the boat business. He stopped supporting Chris Craft and OMC filed for bankruptcy in 2000. We had taken on another OMC company, Logic Boats whose president was Bob Anderson, the former president of Celebrity Boats. That meant that two of our lines were in bankruptcy. If that wasn't bad enough, GENMAR Industries, run by Irwin Jacobs, purchased Chris Craft and Logic from OMC out of bankruptcy. GENMAR is the company that had purchased Wellcraft and done all those really bad things to us many years ago. GENMAR soon decided that Chris Craft was going to be too hard for them to recover, and sold it to a private group that wanted to take it another direction.

They wanted us to take on Glastron, which they had purchased a few years earlier, and Aquasport Boats, which they had purchased at about the same time. Aquasport boats were being built at the Wellcraft plant since Wellcraft was down to about a 20 percent production rate by then. They wanted us to take on Wellcraft, but there was *no way* we were going to do that. We did take on Glastron and

Aquasport along with several other lines, and that is where we were on September 11, 2001, when terrorists hit the United States. I had been praying for help with the boat business, but instead of giving the situation to the Lord, I was looking for the Lord to send more customers. I sold the Mooney airplane and tightened up again.

Christie's pet fish, Mr. Fish.

Business got really slow after 9/11. By then, I finally realized that I just couldn't work hard enough to overcome all the shortcomings of the boat business, nor did I possess the ability to deal with the crazy ups and downs of the business.

During this time, some great things had happened in our personal life, including Christie meeting her husband to be, Jimmy Sauers, while on a study abroad program one summer at Oxford University in Great Britain. Jimmy is a wonderful Christian and comes from a solid Christian family. Pat and I met Jimmy when Christie brought him home with her during one of her tours at NASA. Since she was going to be working at NASA for the next three months, she needed to bring her goldfish (Mr. Fish was his name) home. Jimmy agreed to hold the fish bowl with the fish the whole trip from Atlanta to Houston in his lap. We knew it must be true love for him to agree to do that! We are truly blessed to have Jimmy in our family. He proposed to Christie at the Georgia Tech Christian fellowship service on a Wednesday night in front of about three hundred people. I asked him if he ever considered what he would do if she said no. Jimmy said he knew she would say yes. They had a wonderful wedding at our church, First Baptist Church The Woodlands, shortly after they both graduated from Georgia Tech. Jimmy found a job in Houston, and Christie had been hired full time at NASA at the Johnson Space Center in Houston. We were doubly blessed.

Rob had tried a stint at the University of Texas, but it wasn't for him. He decided to join the Air Force and received his training in secure communications. Because of his rank in basic training, he got his selection of duties and chose the Pentagon. He spent his entire time in the Air Force learning computer engineering and science on the Air Force's dime. He really enjoyed his time at the Pentagon and made some life-long friends. Rob was working with teams of contractors that were overseeing the rebuilding of the Pentagon with modern and secure communications equipment. When Rob came to Christie's and Jimmy's wedding, we knew that he wasn't well. When he got back to Washington, the Air Force did some testing and found that Rob had a rare immune system illness called primary sclerosing cholangitis (PSC). PSC occurs when, due to previous illness, there is scar tissue in the liver, and the immune system, thinking it is a foreign tissue, attacks it until the liver fails.

The Air Force gave Rob a medical discharge even though he didn't want one. We tried to fight it, but their mind was made up. We went to San Antonio to support Rob's efforts not to be discharged, but the Air Force was determined. Rob had said that the EPA would have passed out if they could see how horrible the environmental conditions were in the basement of the Pentagon. It was there that we think Rob's problems got started. We realized that PSC is a genetic condition, but if he had never gotten sick while working at the Pentagon, there would have never been anything to start the PSC. He was not "worldwide deployable," they said, because he must remain close to a hospital. Rob landed a good job in Austin, Texas, in the IT field, received good medical care from the Air Force, and seemed happy even though he didn't know where his PSC would lead.

It was hard to believe, but in 1999, NASA was celebrating the thirtieth anniversary of Apollo 11 and the other Apollo moon landings. There was a whole weekend of events scheduled, and I needed that kind of diversion with all the issues going on in our lives. There were receptions, picnics, and a big dinner on Saturday night. About 250 flight operation people and crew support people attended the banquet dinner on July 23, 1999. When we came in the door, there were four mounted photographs taken during the mission, and all the members from the Apollo 11 Flight Control and Flight Operations were asked to sign each mount. I signed all four. John Young was there and gave a great speech, and that was rare because John is normally fairly quiet as I have mentioned earlier. Bob Carlton, John Wegener, Chris Kraft, and all the higher-ups were there as well as a lot of crew members. We had a great time, and toward the end of the evening, Bob Legler, one of my Lunar Module systems branch people, started announcing some door prizes. Winners received space pens, desk items, and the like. At the end, Bob Legler asked if we remembered that

During the 30th anniversary reunion of Apollo 11, John Young is addressing attendees. Chris Kraft is at the left. Bob Carlton and John Wegener are seated on the right.

when we came in that we were asked to sign four mounted photographs from Apollo 11. Of course, we did. Bob announced that three would go to the crew (Neil Armstrong, Buzz Aldrin, and Michael Collins), and the fourth was the grand door prize. As he was about to pull the ticket for the super prize, I lowered my head and said a little prayer. I promised God that I would never ask for any luck the rest of my life if the Lord could let me win the photograph prize. To my astonishment as Bob Legler pulled the ticket with the winner's name on it, he said, "Oh, it is one of our own, Bob Nance." I couldn't believe it, but I won the super door prize! Before I got up, I thanked the Lord for answering my prayer. I was so blessed. After the dinner, a gentleman came up and talked to me about the photograph that I had just won with everyone's signature around it. The photograph is of the two astronauts opening the flag on the lunar surface as taken from the camera on the Lunar Module. The gentleman said that his part of the mission was to design a spring that would be popped out from the flag pole to make the flag look like it was flying. He said that about two months before Apollo 11 took off, somebody realized that the flag would just lay limp beside the flag pole, since there is no air or wind on the moon. This gentleman was given the task of designing something that would make the flag look like it was flying in the wind. He was very proud of his contribution to the space program. This was just another example of how many people contributed to make Apollo 11 a success.

In April, 2002, NASA repeated the celebration for Apollo 16, which was John Young's and Charlie Duke's landing mission. I also attended it since I owed so much to John, and I had been the propulsion flight controller for his landing, just like on Apollo 11. I must admit that the Apollo 16 mission was a lot less stressful because we landed with almost 6 percent of the propellant remaining. The banquet was very similar with the four photographs for everyone to sign. There weren't quite as many people at the Apollo 16 banquet, but it was fun just as well. The flight control troops were all there; it was the headquarters types that weren't there. When it came time to do the door prizes, it went just about the same, and Bob Legler was the master of ceremonies just like at the Apollo 11 celebration. As he was about to draw the name for the photograph he said, "Well, we know who isn't going to win the photograph, after Bob Nance won the Apollo 11 one." In fact, he said that he was going to get a waitress to draw the ticket to be sure everyone knew it was fair. I had not the slightest anticipation that I would get it, since I had already used up my favor with the Lord. To everyone's surprise, and particularly Bob Legler, I won the Apollo 16 signed photograph, too. I offered to let someone else draw for it, but the crowd insisted that I won it fair and square, so I now have both the Apollo 11 and Apollo 16 signed photographs. Many of the people who signed them have since passed away, since I was one of the youngest people on the mission. These signed photos are priceless to me. I can't believe the Lord loves me so much that this happened. The odds are astronomical that I would win the two photographs for the two missions on which I was the Lunar Module Powered Descent flight controller.

Between the two Apollo reunions were the events of September 11, 2001, in New York, the Pentagon, and in a field in Pennsylvania.

It was horrible. I was at home watching the events unfold on the TV when I got a phone call from someone at work, and they asked me if I knew what was going on. It was my day off that week, but I was planning to go to work later in the day. We were talking on the phone, and I was watching TV when the first World Trade Center Tower (Tower 2) completely fell. At first, I thought just the top part collapsed, but then I realized that the entire tower fell, just like a building being demolished. I really don't think the terrorists were smart enough to realize that the weight of the building would collapse the entire building. It was catastrophic. I never made it to work that day. The country was in total shock, in fact, the world was in total shock. It was just unbelievable that human beings could commit such a travesty against innocent people. What kind of god would want its people to do such a horrible thing? It was clearly Satan at work.

Obviously, the boat business really suffered. People started cancelling their boats that were on order. People felt that the economy was going to take a nose dive. Air traffic had been totally stopped for days, and the stock markets had been closed for days. The world was in turmoil, and a new boat was the last thing on people's minds. It seemed like every time things started to get better, there would be another upset, and this time it was a huge upset. People just can't plan for this kind of thing. We just have to deal with it the best we can.

Pat and I dealt with all this stress in our lives by becoming more active in our church. We started attending Bible study regularly and continued seeking the Lord. The only problem was that we were praying for the Lord to help us fix our problems. Things hadn't gotten bad enough for us give our problems to Him.

By the fall of 2002, I was ready to give up on the boat business. I owned about 70 percent of the business, and Bobby Prade, who came over from Barber Boats, owned the other 30 percent of the business. I told Bobby that it was time for us to get out while we were ahead. During the summer, we made a lot of money in the boat business, and then we would lose a lot in the winter months. I wanted to sell off the inventory and close the business. Bobby had entered the boat business with dreams of making a lot of money, and we had had a lot of great years, but every time things started going good, we would have a huge upset from outside. It is one thing to make a mistake and then take responsibility for our mistakes, but we were constantly trying to make up for other companies' problems, and it was time to get out. Bobby begged me to hang in there; he was sure things were going to get better. I really didn't think that we could make it through the winter, but I agreed to try.

Pat and I started a Bible study that fall based on Rick Warren's book, *The Purpose Driven Life*. It was as if Rick had written it for us. As we went through the study, we could see that even though we thought we were being good Christians and bringing up our children in a Christian home, we were not giving our problems to the Lord. We were working to protect what we had, not working to forward His Kingdom.

About that time, Pat's mom was having a lot of difficult medical issues in Richmond, Virginia, and now we were trying to deal with this from Houston, in addition to the boat business issues, Rob's illness, and growing money issues. *Purpose Driven Life* showed us that we were living for the wrong things and not giving our issues to the Lord; instead, we were asking the Lord to solve our problems. What we didn't realize was the Lord was using these issues to mold us. A few weeks after we completed our study, the Lord changed all that. One evening, as I was becoming more and more overwhelmed/discouraged by all the issues, I got on my knees. I confessed to God that I was sorry that I had tried to fix things on my own, instead of giving my problems to Him and trusting Him. I asked forgiveness for not trusting Him, always trying to do things on my own and always asking God to support me in my folly. I remember from Rick Warren's book that we shouldn't tell the Creator of the Universe how things should go in our lives. We are saying that we know more than God, and He just needs to help us with our plans. My prayer was a confession: I *finally* got it—God didn't want me to limit His power but to give our problems to Him because we had total faith in Him! Does this sound familiar? Remember back in chapter 1 over forty years earlier, when I finally realized I would never come up with a message to the church on my own until I gave it to God. Some of us are really, really slow learners.

I was crying and rambling in my prayer because the more I prayed, the more I realized the folly of how I had been living my life. At that moment, the Lord spoke again just like back when I was a teenager. The message was simple and direct—Move back to Virginia and take care of our parents! It didn't come across as a command; rather, the message was full of grace. Once again, beyond the words, it came with instant understanding. The Lord wanted us to put Him first and forget the boat business. He had been waiting a long time to hear me give that problem to Him. I had been very slow to surrender our problems to Him, and this had brought a lot of stress and hardship to our family along the way. I pondered all of this and realized I had to talk with Pat about it. The next morning, I told Pat that I needed to discuss something with her that was very important. To my surprise, she said that she had to discuss something with me, too. It seems that she had prayed to the Lord the previous night, and He had given her the same instructions. In forty-five seconds, we told each other that we needed to pick up, move back to Virginia and take care of our parents, leaving the boat business behind. Our lives changed that quickly. We were going to sell the boat business and move to Virginia without jobs and with no idea where we would live, but we knew it was God's will and that He would take care of us.

I sold my 70 percent of the business to Bobby Prade for next to nothing and took a second mortgage on our home, loaned $75,000 to the business, and also loaned half of my profit sharing (retirement money) to the business, so Bobby would have a fighting chance to save the business. Since I had personally guaranteed the financing of the inventory of boats, I needed Bobby to be a success so I could get my name off those notes after a period of time. Pat and I started looking for jobs and started planning our move to Virginia. We could have never in a million years pulled this off without the Lord. He gave us strength that we didn't even know we had. Rob, who was living and working in Austin, said he couldn't believe that we were leaving with him fighting PSC. We told him that the Lord was going to take care of things, and we just had faith in Him, knowing He would work things out. The Lord did more than we could have even imagined.

11

What a Blessing!

The next chapter of our life should be titled—If you trust in the Lord, there is nothing, absolutely nothing that He cannot do! We learned that it is all about faith. The Lord wants us to have faith in Him.

Paul said in his letter to Philippians, "Forgetting what is behind and straining toward what is ahead, I press on toward the goal to win the prize for which God has called me Heavenward in Christ Jesus" (Phil. 3:13). Paul got it. The Lord had to transform Paul to get him to understand his real mission in life. Sometimes, the Lord has to show us what life without trusting in Him looks like, so that we learn to trust Him.

We decided to have faith in God, and He has blessed us beyond belief. I only wonder what my life would have been like, if before I started in the boat business, I had given my plan to the Lord, before I even made that decision on my own. That doesn't matter now. What *does* matter is this: What is going to be is based on faith in the Lord Jesus Christ!

Pat and I both started looking for jobs in the Richmond, Virginia area. Pat started applying for teaching jobs with various school systems in the region. We thought we might be able to live in Northern Virginia and commute. I applied with NASA and several other engineering firms. I was not getting very much response from my applications, probably because I had been out of engineering for so long.

One day, I asked Pat what she thought I could do other than engineering. Pat said that I really loved the selling part of the boat business, working with customers, and helping people. The fact was, running and managing the business kept me away from what I liked the most. Pat suggested that I should take a sales job in an auto dealership working with customers without all the headaches of owning the business. I had always loved the engineering that went into the BMWs, and I could see myself selling BMWs. I had given Pat a BMW Z-3 in 1998 for her birthday, and she really loved it, and I did, too, when she let me drive it.

I called my parents in Richmond and asked if there was a BMW dealership in Richmond. My dad said that there was one on the west end of Richmond, but he thought there was another one opening up soon,

Pat loved sporting around in her BMW Z-3

within a mile of their home. He said that there was a sign on the property, and he would go and check it out. He gave me a call the next day and said it was a new BMW dealership, and they were opening in July, just a couple of months away. Dad said that they were going to have to really work hard to open in July, since it was May and they weren't too far along on construction. He gave me the phone number that was on the sign. When I followed up with a phone call, I discovered that the dealership was owned by Crown Automotive out of Greensboro, North Carolina. I was able to talk directly to the head of Human Resources (which later I would come to realize was a miracle unto itself—she was very hard to get on the phone). I told her my background and explained that I wanted a job doing what I loved for the last ten years before retirement. I explained that I had been doing sales training for thirty years and loved working with the luxury market. After we finished talking, she said that she wanted me to come to Richmond for an interview; she felt sure that they would want to hire me. She explained that they also owned the other BMW dealership in Richmond, and they would be doing the hiring for the new dealership. She said that she would call and set up a meeting for me. I told her that I could come up in a week. I got a phone call back the next day saying that they were anxious to meet me, and we set up an appointment for me to be interviewed by the general manager at the existing dealership, Richmond BMW.

Pat was still teaching when I made the trip to Richmond. I stayed with my parents while I was in Richmond. My interview went great, and after talking to several people, they came back and asked if I could be ready to start about the middle of July at the new store. I told them that I would let them know the next day, after I discussed it with Pat that evening. I couldn't call her during the day since she was teaching. They told me that they had not started hiring for the store yet, and if I accepted, I would be employee number 1. I called Pat that night and gave her the good news, and she said that she really thought I would enjoy the job. I told Pat I wanted to sleep on it and would let them know the next day. My dad was a car guy and he really liked the idea that I might be selling BMWs. All this being said, I still wanted to hold out for the possible NASA job.

The next morning, my mom was fixing breakfast at the stove when dad and I noticed that she seemed dazed. Before we realized it, as she passed out, she put both of her hands on the stove to try and catch herself; then she fell straight back. Luckily, we were both close enough that we caught her before she hit her head on the floor. Her hands were badly burnt, and she was out for almost a minute, which is a long time. We called 911, and the EMS people were really quick in getting there. She was awake by then but extremely shaky. She kept wanting to get up, but we wouldn't let her.

Once they got her to the hospital, they determined that her blood pressure had dropped and since she was standing more than normal on account of my visit, she had just run out of blood to her head. The body just shuts down in that situation with the person automatically falling down so normal blood pressure could be restored. Mom's regular doctor was not working that day, so one of the other doctors in his office attended to her. His name was Dr. Bob Cohen. He asked her what happened, and she explained that her son was in town doing a job interview, and she was standing at the stove making breakfast when she fainted. She said she did not remember putting her hands on the stove and burning them. Dr. Cohen said that he was going to adjust her medications and advised that we go to Denny's the next time we wanted breakfast.

Dr. Cohen then asked me what type of job I was interviewing for, and I told him that I was interviewing for the new BMW dealership. Dr. Cohen then identified himself as a long-time BMW owner, said he loved BMWs, and he couldn't wait for the new BMW dealership to open. He went on and on about how great the people were at the current BMW dealership, and that I couldn't pick a better place to work. He said that he would be my first customer and gave me his name and phone number. After he left, I called the general manager of Richmond BMW and accepted the job at the new Richmond BMW of Midlothian. That night, I created my database for prospects for BMW, and Dr. Bob Cohen was my very first prospect. I am sure that the Lord was all over my decision to take the job.

To this day, when people who wonder why bad things happen to good people, I remind them that the Lord may be using them, as His Good and Faithful Servants, to help someone else. We too often think that everything is about us. Sometimes, the Lord uses circumstances to move things to help someone else. It would be much later that I would realize that the Lord could not have put a better person in front of me than Dr. Cohen to help me make my decision to take the job at Richmond BMW Midlothian. In my mind at that time, I really wanted to hold out for the job at NASA, which would never come. The Lord knew what I needed when I surely didn't.

I spent the rest of the trip looking at schools and areas around town, so we would have some idea of good various areas in which to live when Pat got a job offer. We now knew where I would be working, so now it was easier to plan. When I got back home, we started planning for when we would move and how we would work things out. I would rent a trailer and tow it to Virginia with my Ford Expedition, about the fourteenth of July 2003, and live with my parents at first until I could find a place to live. Pat would stay in Texas and teach summer school since we needed the money, and she had already committed to doing that long before we decided to move. She was running a computer lab to help students recover lost credits due to failures and attendance issues. I was going to continue to draw a salary from the boat dealership for doing consulting work through the end of June. We would spend the month of June packing and making arrangements to sell our home in The Woodlands.

By the time I left, we had gotten the house in Houston ready to show, and in addition to everything else she had to do, Pat had to keep the house totally clean. Those were hard times. We were executing our plan step by step and trusting in the Lord the whole way. I can honestly say that we did ask the Lord for strength lots of times as we went through this process. I got to Richmond without incident and moved into my parents' guest room.

When I reported to work about the nineteenth of July, I learned that the new Midlothian store on the southwest side of town was not ready, so I was told to report to Richmond BMW for training. For the next month, I would be selling at Richmond BMW alongside the current sales staff. In addition, they had already hired about three other salesmen for the new store, who would be there, also. Most of the existing salesmen weren't too excited about all the additional salesmen on the floor, but it turns out that July 2003 ended up being the best month they had ever had, and then they beat that record in August. I sold eight cars that first month, and it would be the fewest I would ever sell during my time at both stores.

Our biggest concern at that time was that Pat hadn't gotten any job offers. We kept asking if she could get an interview, and since they had plenty of applicants, no one would offer an interview to someone that was still in Texas. My day off was Wednesday, so every Wednesday, I would go to the Chesterfield County School HR department and sit there, waiting to speak to someone on behalf of my wife. By the third Wednesday in a row, I think that they were tired of looking at me for three or four hours at a time. They said that the head of hiring was new that year, and she was extremely busy, but the gentleman who had just retired from that job after many years was still working in the office in IT (seems that his last year before official retirement was to oversee the installation of a new computer system), and he would see me. I think it was to try to get rid of me. He was extremely nice, and I told him that Pat had just been named the Teacher of the Year the previous year for the large school district outside of Houston. I also told him about all her other awards, and he thanked me for being so diligent in trying to see someone in HR. He asked me to wait a few minutes, and he went and talked to the new head of HR, then came back and asked how soon Pat could come in for an interview. By the time Pat got there a few days later, she had three job offers from Chesterfield County Schools. After a

The entrance to Braxton in Richmond, VA

brief interview, she spent the day going to each school, and each of the schools tried to sell her on why she should teach at their school. In the end, Pat chose Bird High School near the Chesterfield County government complex.

In the final days before Pat had to return to Texas, we looked at areas we might like to live. We did look at some houses, but we were surprised by the high prices in Richmond compared to Texas. The cost of living is much cheaper in Texas than it is in Virginia; people are just used to paying more on the East Coast from Virginia through the Northeast. I worked to identify neighborhoods in Richmond where we could live. I drew a circle with a ten-mile radius around my BMW store. I then drew a five-mile radius around Pat's school and determined that we would live within the area common to both circles. That is the way engineers do things. The football-shaped area was where we concentrated our home search. At the top of the area was a fifty-five and up development called Braxton, and it was the first area we looked at. There were several houses that appealed to us. We liked the hardwood floors, the double pane windows, and the fact that all the maintenance was included. One home was open, and we just walked in and picked up a flyer, but said even though we loved the home, it seemed too expensive. We must have looked at dozens of homes during those few days, and the more we looked, the more confused we got. We did come to understand that we were going to have to pay a lot more than we hoped.

Pat went back to Texas, and I went back to work. The dealership didn't mind my taking off, because they had too many salesmen at the Richmond BMW store with the new store still unfinished. The next week, I took Tuesday off, and that day was August 12, 2003. This was our anniversary, but Pat was in Texas and I was in Richmond. We had talked and decided that the very first house we had looked at in Braxton was the one we liked the best, so I drove to Bird High School and then drove the route Pat would have to take to drive from the school to Braxton. It only took about seven or eight minutes and was just about the five miles that we expected. The house we liked was still open, and I looked it over again. It was perfect for us. It had far fewer rooms than our home in Houston, but the rooms were large, and the craftsmanship was the quality that we liked in a home. I liked the huge garage that would help us with all the stuff we would be bringing from Houston. When I came out of the house, a pickup truck drove up and the gentleman asked if he could help me. I told him that we were interested in this particular home, and he said that his father, W. S. Carnes, was the builder and that the development was the site of their family farm when he was growing up. Their old family home had been fixed up and served as the club house. There was even a lake stocked with fish.

He called his sister, Teri Carnes Pruitt, and made an appointment for me to meet her that afternoon at the house. She was handling the sales of the subdivision along with a larger development that she and her older brother were building in another part of Chesterfield County. The appointment was set for 2:00 p.m. I got to the home a little early and went inside the home to look it over again. I had come to the realization that it was going to be almost impossible for us to get the home while we still owned a home in Texas, and Pat and I both starting new jobs. Our credit was good, but we also had to show that we could afford to pay for the loan while carrying a mortgage on the home in Houston. I stood at a particular part of the kitchen, and with my hands on the counter, prayed to God that I knew He had brought us a long way, that He had blessed us by giving both of us good jobs, and I didn't really know whether getting this house was what He wanted us to do. I told Him that whatever He wanted for us would be fine. He had already blessed us so much.

A few minutes later, Teri arrived, and I told her our story starting with the study of Rick Warren's book *Purpose Driven Life*, and how the Lord had provided great jobs for us. I told her we really wanted this house, but we really didn't see how we could get it until we sold our home in Texas. I offered to give her $10,000 to hold the house until we sold our home in Texas. That was the extra money we had put aside as part of the down payment for the new home. The rest would come when we sold the home in Houston. Much to my surprise, Teri said that she had four similar homes that had been built as spec homes, and she felt that if she could sell one of them, she could sell the others quickly. She said that she had a lot of people looking at them, and once the first one was sold, the rest would follow. She said that she would be willing to take $5,000 down on the home and rent it to us for $1,000 a month until the home in Houston sold. Once our home in Houston was sold, we could close on the new home and the $5,000 we paid and each of the $1,000 a month in rent would go toward the sale of the home to us. We could take delivery as soon as the paperwork could be drawn up, and the rent would start the first of September. I couldn't believe what I was hearing. It was truly a huge blessing from the Lord. I tried to call Pat, but she was teaching in the middle of a class, so I just left a message. I told Teri that I would call her back as soon as I talked to Pat, then thanked Teri about ten times. She knew that I was in sales, so she suggested I just help her sell the rest of the houses on that block.

I started driving to the next house on my list, which was at the opposite end of my chosen area. It was about a half hour later that Pat called back. I was still driving, and I told her to hold on while I found a place to park so I could talk to her. I was in the small town of

Chester and pulled off the main road, went down a side street, made a turn, and pulled up in front of a small flower shop that wasn't very busy. While parked there, I told Pat everything that had happened, and she was delighted. She wanted the house but had convinced herself that there was no way we could get it. We decided to take Teri up on her offer. There was no reason to look at any other homes because the Lord had provided for us in a mighty way. Pat asked if there were any churches nearby. I told her that that I had seen a Baptist Church about a quarter of a mile to the south of the entrance to Braxton. I had only seen it because I decided to test the drive time from Pat's new school to Braxton. She said for me to check it out.

I called Teri and said that we were "good to go" on her generous offer. She said that she was still in the area, and we would meet at the house to draw up a temporary agreement, so she would then have something to give to her attorney to use in drawing up the final agreement. I drove back to the house and met Teri. She had a form already filled out with the particulars, and they were exactly as we had agreed. She asked if while renting, would it be okay for us to pay the monthly fee for trash, lawn service, etc., that all homeowners paid. She said she had discussed her offer with her dad, and he wanted to know who was going to pay that fee. It was $125 a month, and I told her that we had expected to pay that fee anyway. Only then did she add it to the contract. She left, and I stood at that same spot in the kitchen, praising the Lord for His faithfulness. To this day, I pray every morning at that very spot in the kitchen. It is a huge reminder of how faithful our God is to us, if we are faithful to Him. By the way, Teri is a fine Christian, and she sold all the homes on our street before the end of the year. I helped her by producing a three-page foldout brochure to pass out to prospects.

As I left Braxton, I drove the couple thousand feet to Southside Baptist Church, and I got out and peeked in the door. I was met by Pastor Dennis Tucker. I explained that we were moving into the area and were looking for a church home. Dennis asked me to come visit with him. I told him the whole story, how we started with *Purpose Driven Life*, and how God had provided great jobs, and now blessed us by giving us a deal of a lifetime on our home in Braxton. Dennis encouraged us to try Southside Baptist Church. I told him I had been attending my parents' church but would come to visit the first Sunday after Pat arrived at the end of the month. I told Pastor Tucker that his church seemed like the ideal church for us, one where we could take an active part in praising our Lord. I told him we had prayed that the Lord would bring us to just the right church. I will never forget what Dennis said next. He said that he had been praying that the Lord would send to Southside Baptist Church someone from Braxton, since Southside had such a nice subdivision so close and no members from there. We were the answer to Dennis' prayer! We worship a wonderful and powerful God.

Southside Baptist Church.

The opening date for Richmond BMW of Midlothian was finally shaping up to be late August. That happened exactly when we were planning to move a large part of our belongings from Texas, along with Pat making the trip. Our family came to the rescue, with Jimmy and Rob offering to drive the Penske Rental truck from Houston to Richmond for us. I flew back to Houston the week before the move, helped pack, and helped figure out what we should take and what we should leave, so the house wouldn't look totally empty. Because the dealership was about to open, I had to fly back to Richmond, and Jimmy, Rob, and Pat made the trip, along will our trusty dog, Bandit. We rented the largest Penske truck that we could rent, a twenty-six-footer, and they were to leave Houston about the same time I was driving the first car into the parking lot of Richmond BMW of Midlothian on August 26. Pat drove her Z-4, following the Penske moving truck. The morning of August 26 when they were to leave, they discovered that the battery was dead in the truck. They jumped the truck, got it started, and took it along with our belongings to Penske to get the truck checked out. They replaced the battery and they said that they were good to go. They lost several hours but were on the way by noon. Everything seemed to be going fine until they got to Louisiana and the alternator light came on. They were afraid to turn the truck off, so they located the nearest Penske truck center, which wasn't very far out of their way. They shut the truck down when they got out of the truck, and when the Penske people tried to start it again, the battery did not start the truck. They had said they could fix it when Jimmy had called ahead, but in fact, they did not have a new alternator. They just put a new battery in the truck and said that the truck center in Mobile, Alabama, had an alternator that they could put in when the guys got there. The crew decided that they would not want to drive and then take a chance shutting the truck off, so they found a place to stay and got up the next morning to head to Mobile. The battery was on its last leg when they got to Mobile, but they made it. The Penske people in Mobile installed a new alternator and another fresh battery, and they were off again. The rest of the trip was without incident except for Bandit. Bandit hated riding in a car much less a big truck. He spent the whole trip under the passenger's feet in the truck, shaking when he wasn't asleep. The Lord once again let us know that things in life aren't always going to be easy, but if we trust in Him, He will take care of us.

I was busy getting ready for the store to open on Friday the twenty-ninth, and Pat needed to get to Richmond because she was supposed to be at a meeting at her new school on the same day. Rob, Jimmy, and Pat got to our new home about 7:00 p.m. on August 28, and I got home about ten minutes after them. My brother had come down from Roanoke to help unload, along with my dad. We unloaded the truck in about two hours, and I took the truck back that night. We were in Richmond! Dad took Jimmy and Rob to the airport on Friday for their flight back to Texas (with us paying their airfare), and Pat made it to her meeting on Friday. I made it to work at the new store, and we were off and running. School would not start until the following Tuesday, since Monday was Labor Day. This gave Pat some time to rest a little and start unpacking. We had been very careful to label each box as to what room it would go in, so we at least had the right boxes in the right rooms. I had to work Friday, Saturday, and Monday, but thankfully, I was in Richmond versus driving from Texas.

I sold and delivered the first car from the new store that weekend while Pat played catchup, since she had missed some meetings by getting to Richmond so late. Everything worked out, and by the end of the first week, we were settling into a routine. What had just taken place seemed like a blur and a miracle at the same time. We had come so very far in just a few months. We could not see how all of this could happen, but our Lord is all-powerful and there is nothing that He cannot do.

I had told Pat about meeting Pastor Tucker, and we decided to go to Southside Baptist Church that next Sunday. Since I had been in Richmond for six weeks at that point, we had not gone to Sunday school and church together in a long time. I had asked Dennis what class we should attend, and he recommended Connie Early's couples class, which sounded a lot like the class we had just left in Texas. Connie was a gifted teacher, and we felt at home from the minute we got there. Connie talked to us after the class and made sure we were attending the service afterward. She made us feel so welcomed. The worship service was great, and we saw Connie singing in the choir. They wore beautiful robes and looked like angels sitting in the choir loft. Dennis gave a great sermon that seemed to be meant for us. Maybe it was, since we had told him we were coming. It was about having faith to let God lead your life. Many of the people there came by and made us feel welcomed.

After the service, we were walking along the rather long sidewalk to the parking area, and we were discussing what had just happened and how instantly we felt at home. I was just saying that it was as though God planned for us to be at Southside Baptist Church, when we heard a voice shout out—"Pat and Bob". It was Connie Early running down the sidewalk with her choir robe flowing around her, and she really did look like an angel descending on us. Connie was running to thank us for coming and invited us back the next Sunday. We had planned to visit several churches, but Connie's expression of love told us we found our church home.

We attended the following Sunday and joined Southside Baptist Church on the third Sunday. One of the things that we had worried about the most was the fact that we had felt so plugged in at our church in The Woodlands, we wondered if we would find a church home in Richmond. I remembered what my fraternity brother, Tommy Burson, who had gotten me to join Delta Upsilon in the first place had said, "Sometimes it is better to be a big fish in a small pond, than be a small fish in a big pond." Southside Baptist would allow me to develop my spiritual gifts much quicker, since Southside Baptist Church was about a third the size of our church in The Woodlands. Pat and I would have lots of opportunity to develop our spiritual skills at Southside over the next few years.

The Choir at Southside Baptist Church near our home

We need to jump forward a couple of years to something that happened related to our move to Richmond. Connie and her husband, Joe, became great mentors to Pat and myself. Joe was a truck driver for a local trucking company and Connie owned a flower shop in Chester, VA. We didn't know much about it, but one day Connie said that she had decided to close her shop because it was just a lot of work for only a little gain. She was spending a lot of time taking care of older parents, and the shop was just taking too much of her time. She invited the Sunday school class to come down one evening to see if there was anything we wanted to get before she had a big close-out sale. She said she would give us some great deals, and she wanted us to have first choice on the things she was going to sell. As I said, we didn't know much about the shop, but we got the directions and went to her shop one day after Pat finished work. I was off that day, so we went together, about ten miles from our home. As we drove down Iron Bridge Road into Chester, I started noticing something familiar about the area. After following the directions with several turns, we pulled up in front of Connie's shop, which was a combination florist and gift shop. I was shocked. I had to catch my breath. Connie's shop was the very shop that I had pulled in front of when I initially talked to Pat about the house in Braxton. Teri had made an unbeatable offer for us on this house, and it was in front of this shop that Pat and I decided to buy the house. I call it God's exclamation point! My message is this: As long as you put your faith in the Lord, He will be in control of your life and get you through any circumstance, no matter how long it takes. We only have to be patient.

During that first year in Richmond, we had a lot of adjustments to make. Each of us were both making a lot less money now, and the only way we managed to make ends meet was through the deal that I had made with Teri Pruitt. Back in Texas, our house was not selling, and the only offer we had received was a low-ball offer, and the people needed to sell their house in order to purchase ours. We told them to get back to us when they sold their house, and we would talk. Unfortunately, we were paying for things like a pool service that we had never paid for in the twenty years we had lived in the house in Houston, as well as utilities. I didn't hear much from Bobby, so I didn't know how things were going in the boat business. Pat was enjoying teaching at her new school in Richmond, but there are always a lot of things to get used to when changing school districts. This is especially the case when teachers move to another state. Pat was surprised to learn that she was making almost $9,000 less a year in Virginia compared to Texas. On the other hand, my car sales were growing beyond my expectations, mostly due to excellent follow-up with my customers. In 2003, most of the car dealerships had the mindset that when a person walked in the door, they needed to sell them a car right away or they would never see the customer again. I had a different opinion. I had learned from the boat business that luxury buyers do research before making this kind of decision. I began sending thank you cards the same day that customers visited with me. I got their email addresses so I could follow up with them, when we held specials or other events. I even created my own website for my customers, with helpful tips and information. Today, most car dealerships have learned to improve their follow-up procedures. The problem today is that many dealerships hire someone else to do it for them, which makes follow-up an impersonal act versus personal. People spending $50,000 or more on a car want personal attention, not a lot of phone calls from agents that aren't even at the dealership. I had a huge advantage in this regard. I was the top salesman most months in the three years that I worked the floor. If I wasn't number one, I was number two. I was selling almost half of all the new cars that were being sold by the entire dealership. My follow-up system did not work as well on used cars, however. In the used car market, cars sold more quickly, so my follow-up was less effective. I didn't sell as many used cars, but I was selling the normal number of used cars, and double or triple the number of new cars compared to the other salesmen. I loved to help the new salesmen learn good sales techniques, and several of them are now general managers of their own dealerships.

Pat was so glad that she could be close to her parents and help them. Pat's mother had fallen and broken her hip, so she had to spend time in a rehab facility. In addition, Pat's dad had developed macular degeneration of the retina, and he had lost his driver's license. We had gotten to Richmond just as all this was happening. The Lord knew before we did that we were going to have to be here for them. Although the city would provide transportation for them to go to doctor's appointments, they said that they didn't want to bother anyone. Thank goodness we were there to help. Pat would go after school and help them get groceries and prescriptions and take them to doctors' appointments. Pat's dad could still do things like cut the grass and help around the home. They were living in the same home that Pat had grown up in, just a few blocks from Jahnke Road Baptist Church where Pat and I were married. It was a real blessing that we were now in Richmond for them. They were great parents and devoted Christians. Jimmy had been a deacon at Jahnke Road Baptist for a long time.

That first year was a struggle with Pat's mom being in the hospital so much. Pat had to take her dad to see her, as well as take care of him. Pat's dad had some medical issues and ended up going to the hospital himself. Her dad went to an assisted living facility for his own safety once he got out of the hospital. We told him that he only had to be there for a little while, but we suspected that it could be a lot longer. Pat's mom had to be moved to several facilities during that year, and she ended up in a nursing facility. While there, she contracted MRSA, a staph infection that is hard to get rid of because it has become resistant to antibiotics. We finally got her out of the hospital and into the assisted living facility with Pat's dad. While Pat's dad loved all the activities and the regular meals, Pat's mom did not like it at all. She would just sit in their room while Jimmy went to various activities. They even had church services at the assisted living facility, which Pat's dad called Hymn sings. Pat's mother did attend those. Morningside of Bellgrade was a beautiful, caring, and well-run facility. Unfortunately, Pat's mom got sick again and she went back to the hospital. She died exactly one year, to the day of when Pat had arrived back in Richmond with Jimmy and Rob. Yet one more of God's exclamation points! We were at her bedside with Pat's dad and sister singing hymns when she died.

During that first year in Richmond while Pat was dealing with her parents' issues, I was struggling with an issue of my own. The post-9-11 times had been hard on the boat business, and Bobby was not able to make things work. That winter, Bobby decided to close the boat business. I think he tried to make it work without putting in the money that he had previously agreed he would put in, but I am not sure that would have made a difference. I had guaranteed the floor plan notes, and our agreement was I would be removed from the notes if Bobby was able to stay in business for a year. I now had new financial pressures. Not only did I have guarantee issues, but there wouldn't be anyone in the store which Bob Panneton, Don Starnes, and I still owned. I made a few trips to Houston and with my parents and Don Starnes' help, I was able to work out a deal with the lenders. In this deal, I would give them my equity in the property, and they would use that as a settlement for my guarantees. Pat and I had paid off most of our credit cards and other debts before we moved to Richmond. We could afford making less, but we still had two house payments. Removing all debt except for the old home in Houston was a blessing. This was a stressful time but by the spring of 2004, we were able to sell the store to Bass Pro Shops' Tracker Marine and close out that chapter of our lives by the spring of 2004. We did have some smaller debts to pay out over time. The boat store remains one of the Bass Pro Shops Tracker Marine stores, and I hope they are doing well.

I talk to Don Starnes every so often, and he has done well. He had sold Shoreline trailers years before and the new owners failed before they totally paid him, so he had a lot of experience in these types of circumstances. He started a consulting business to help companies that are going through difficult times to survive. Bob Panneton had gone to work for NASA, and Bob recently retired. Both Don and Bob got their equity out of the building, which was substantial, and I am very glad that someone made some money from the boat business. We had some great years along with a lot of heartache. I will say that the boat business taught me a lot about whether or not to trust your suppliers. They are only going to look out for themselves, and when the chips are down, they will simply ask, "What have you done for me lately?" As I write this, one thing comes to mind. A.W. Heinz, the former Wellcraft and Chris Craft rep had once shown me a book of his, entitled *How to Make a Million Dollars in the Boat Business.* Inside the book lay the answer: "Start with two million dollars." In retrospect, I think this is really true.

The huge recession of 2007 through 2010 was horrible for the boat business. Most of the lines we handled had gone through multiple bankruptcies, or closed, or just disappeared. The boat business went down 80 percent, and it has only moderately recovered. Chaparral Boats was one of the few businesses to survive. Cobalt Boats also survived, but names like Johnson Outboard Motors, Mariner, Celebrity, Monark, Wahoo, Maxum, Proline, and SeaPro have all disappeared. I thank the Lord every day that He got us out of the boat business. If I had stayed in the boat business, our lives would have been a complete mess, and I would have never been able to retire. Thank goodness that we gave our situation to the Lord when we did. I only wish we had done it a lot sooner.

We finally sold the house in The Woodlands in July 2004 to the very people who had made us an offer back in September 2003. It took them that long to sell their house. They came up a little on their offer, and it would just cover our mortgage, plus the second mortgage that I had taken out to keep the boat business afloat. All we got from this sale was escrow for taxes and insurance, but at least that chapter of our life was now over, and we gladly accepted it. We wouldn't have to pay $125 a month for a pool service, nor the utility bills. In the Texas summer heat, even our vacant house ran us $300 to $400 a month for electricity. We felt like our move to Richmond, and resetting our lives, was now complete.

The second and third years in Richmond were filled with Pat continuing to help her dad who was doing well at Morningside. I must say that we were pleasantly surprised. He kept himself very busy with all the activities, and Pat or I would visit him at least every other day. Pat and I felt that we needed to sell his house on Jahnke Road, but we didn't want to say anything until he was ready. Pat and her sister, Dorothy, were trying to keep the house up, and I assisted with paying the bills and taking care of related matters. In the summer-time, the sisters would go over, cut the grass, and plant a few things in the garden. Mr. Dameron had always kept a wonderful garden, and the girls cherished those memories. Eventually, Mr. Dameron said that if Pat didn't have the house to worry about, she could come visit him more often. Pat said that was very true since many days she would do something at the house and then come see him for a short time. It was about a year after he had been in Morningside that he said that it was time to sell the house. He realized that he would never be able to go back. It was a blessing that he mentioned it without us having to say anything to him. It took a lot to get the house ready to show, but we sold it in less than two months, feeling that we got a very good price for the home. With Mr. Dameron's savings, the money for the house, and his Social Security checks, he would have enough money to stay in Morningside for at least fifteen years. We thanked God that Mr. Dameron was so well provided for.

I was doing well at the BMW dealership, and I was starting to make more money than some of the managers were. I had a business within a business. Even though the other salesmen could see me writing thank you notes and sending emails, they just sat by the door waiting for more people to walk in. By the end of the third year, most of my customers were either referrals or previous customers who were buying a second BMW for a family member or a new one for themselves. I had some great customers. One of the things I would do while on my test drives with customers was to ask questions about them and their families. These times often ended up with them asking me about my story. I would use the time to tell them that I grew up in Richmond and moved to Houston to work at NASA after college. I would tell them that after the glory days at NASA, I had started a boat business. Many years later while going through the *Purpose Driven Life* book by Rick Warren with our church, my wife and I realized it was time to return to Richmond and help our parents. I would tell them that at my wife's suggestion, I decided to sell BMWs for the last ten years before I retired. I would tell them that I was having a ball selling BMWs—driving cool cars, meeting really nice customers, and helping people fulfill their dreams of owning a BMW. It was a great way to witness to all the people that I came in contact with while working at Richmond BMW of Midlothian.

One day, I got a call from one of the people that I had taken on a test drive. He said that he would like to have lunch with me at a nice restaurant and have me meet someone. I agreed, and we met with Buddy Childress, the executive director of Needle's Eye Ministries. They are a Christian organization that serves as a spiritual connection between business professionals and matters of faith. Needle's Eye Ministries is a network of professional men and women who want to see the business culture changed by Jesus Christ, where CEOs become servant leaders, board members are no longer driven by the bottom line, and those experiencing career transition find their identity in the Lord. There are several programs to accomplish their goals. The principle event is a monthly lunch meeting held at three different places around Richmond where they host a fellowship and a speaker. Buddy wanted to learn more about my experiences at NASA, the boat business, and how we ended up back in Richmond. By the end of the lunch meeting, Buddy asked me to be the guest speaker to open their first series of meetings for the next year. We decided that my topic should be "Life Is Full of Choices." I would talk about how we had to make difficult choices at NASA, particularly

Life is full of Choices

Scripture: Proverbs 3: 5-6 NIV *Trust in the Lord with all your heart and lean not on your own understanding. In all your ways acknowledge him, and he will make your paths straight.*

❖ There are many Choices Made in Life – School, job
❖ As a Rocket Scientist for NASA, I was part of a group that had to make many choices that involved life or death.
❖ As an owner of a Boat Dealership I made decisions that affected many people
❖ We decided to move back to Richmond from Houston because our parents had health issues.

The first slide in my Power Point Presentation that I made at the Needle's Eye Ministries opening session.

during Apollo 13, and how often we had prayed for guidance during that mission. I would talk about how things turned out when I didn't ask for the Lord's guidance during the boat business years. I would then talk about how when I finally gave my problems to the Lord, He orchestrated a series of events that if we wrote a movie script about it and turned it in, it would be rejected as totally not believable.

Our general manager at the time, Joe Chapman, agreed to let me take the time off for the three luncheon meetings and I started preparing. I did a Powerpoint presentation including NASA and boat business pictures. I asked the Holy Spirit to guide me so I would not make it about myself, but rather, tell these businessmen that they needed to put their faith in the Creator of the Universe, not in men. The three meetings took place over a two-week period, and they kept me very busy. What surprised me was how many people were coming to the meetings. The first meeting had about 75 people, the second meeting had about 80 people, and the last meeting saw around 150 people. What a blessing to have such a great group of businessmen to witness to—to tell my story. Something amazing happened in the second meeting, which was held at the country club in the western part of Richmond. After the luncheon and presentation was over, a gentleman came up and introduced himself to me. He was Teri Pruitt's husband. I had told the whole story of how God had sent an angel, through Teri Pruitt, to allow us to get our home when all seemed impossible. Teri's husband was a major real estate developer in Richmond and had just opened a large upscale mall called Short Pump in the west end of Richmond. He thanked me for my nice comments about Teri and said that he would pass them on to her. Still another exclamation point in my life!

Sinner's Prayer

"Dear Lord Jesus, I know I am a sinner, and I ask for your forgiveness.

I believe you died for my sins and rose from the dead.

I trust and follow you as my Lord and Savior. Guide my life and help me to do your will.

In your name, Amen."

This simple prayer is all that it takes to accept Jesus Christ as your Savior.

What happened at the third and final luncheon was even more amazing. As I said, it was by far the largest group, held at the Omni Hotel in the business district of Richmond. At the end of each talk, Buddy would say that there were cards at each table, and if anyone wanted to become a Christian, or would like to learn more about Jesus, or would just want us to pray for them, all they had to do was simply fill out the card. Buddy would pray at the end of the meeting and said if they wanted to become a Christian, all they had to do was pray the Sinner's Prayer with Buddy and accept Jesus Christ as their Savior. We had received a lot of cards during the sessions asking for more information, and Buddy had told me about them. They called me the next day and told me that there had been two professions of faith at the last session. I can't tell you how grateful I was that I could have been a small part in that. To this day, one of my favorite sayings is that if every Christian could help two people in their lifetime accept Jesus Christ, the whole world would be saved in less than one hundred years. Jesus did not say we are responsible to make a person a Christian. The Holy Spirit will do that. We are to simply advance the message, and the Holy Spirit will do the rest.

Pat's dad had done well for a long time, but his health was starting to fail. He finally had to move to a facility where he could get more medical attention. He was having a hard time eating, and this was the start of his decline. He had enjoyed almost three years of great living, and he had met new friends during those years. He was finally put in hospice, and they told us exactly what was going to happen. Once again, Pat, her sister, and I were with Mr. Dameron until the end. Just as hospice had told us, he awoke from the near-sleep state that he had been in for a few days to speak. We each got to talk to him, but his voice was very shallow. When it was my turn to sit next to him, he motioned for me to come closer. He told me that he loved to fish, and the fishing trip that I had taken him on while he was in Houston was the best fishing trip he had ever had. He did love to fish. He thanked me. It was a moment I will never forget. He slipped away several hours later. He never spoke again. I can't wait until we get to heaven and start reliving fishing stories. I wonder if it is okay to exaggerate in heaven.

By 2006, I was making more money as the store's top salesman than the used car manager. I started talking to the general manager about getting an assistant, so I could sell more cars. In the end, he decided to make me the new car sales manager instead. He said that I might not make as much money, but I wouldn't have to work the long hours I was working either. I could truly take a day off instead of meeting customers on those days. It sounded like a great deal, and I took it. I remained the new car sales manager until I retired in 2013, exactly ten years after I started. This was my plan from the very beginning. I don't think the dealership thought I would actually retire. They had never had anyone retire from that dealership before.

Pat and I had become very active in Southside Baptist Church. I had become a deacon, and by 2007 would become chairman of the deacons. We changed the way they operated. A deacon is supposed to be the spiritual leader of the church, not a board member to run the church. When I became a deacon, I did not like the way the deacons met, as though they were in a board meeting discussing things like the need for repairs or who would or would not get a raise. As soon as I became the chairman of the deacons, we started meeting in the deacons' homes, discussing ways to reach people spiritually, and praying for people's needs. The deacons took to the new program like ducks to water. I thought it might be difficult, but they made it easy. They were a great group of Christians. We left building and personnel issues to the appropriate committees. Pat and I began teaching a Sunday school class that was called the Contemporary Class. We wanted to answer "How does the Bible say I should handle this situation?" We were using the Bible as our "Owner's Manual" to see how to live our everyday lives. I must admit that the class opened our eyes to see that many people are hurting and need help. After starting that class, Pat and I felt like we had been sheltered all our lives from the type of problems people are going through daily. We were trying to answer questions like, "What should I do when my ex-husband gets out of jail and wants me to come live with him again?" People are in trouble and they need to know the Lord Jesus Christ, or they will never get through life without major disasters. We wonder why so many bad things happen each day, but there are people right in our churches seeking help.

We continued to grow our walk with the Lord. We met some missionaries, Stew and Lissa Roberson, going out into the field to China and have made some life-long friends. Pat and I were the unofficial missionary teachers at the annual Vacation Bible School as we reported each summer on the work and progress of our missionaries in China. We would have well over 200 attend Vacation Bible School when we only had 180 attending worship on Sunday. It was an awesome experience.

My parents suffered several health issues during this time, but they have pulled through and continue to do well. They are still living on their own, and both still drive at ninety-two and ninety-one years old. They recently celebrated their seventy second wedding anniversary. We took them to see *Moses* at Sight and Sound Theatre near Lancaster, Pennsylvania. Mom and dad were married in Lancaster, and they had a grand time exploring the old neighborhoods. The presentation of *Moses* was spectacular and we all enjoyed it. They worried about leaving home, but everything went extremely well and we all had a wonderful time together. Pat and I made the reservations and purchased the tickets months in advance, then left it up to the Lord to move them to take the trip from Richmond. I think Pat and I enjoyed it just as much as they did. Seeing their faces light up as they relived their early years and seeing how far they had come was a great blessing for us. They have been great Christian role models for our entire family.

Myself, Pat, Christie and Jimmy on a mountain top in Colorado during our visit to Boulder.

Christie continued her job at NASA, and Jimmy stayed in the engineering and computer field. NASA sent Christie to get her master's degree at the University of Colorado in Boulder, Colorado. NASA paid her tuition, travel, and salary while they were in Boulder. Jimmy quit his job and worked part time while they were in Boulder. What an awesome husband he is! They made a lot of friends at their church in Boulder and try to get back every year to visit friends and to ski. We visited them during their year that they were in Boulder. During the first visit, we went skiing, and best of all, Christie gave me a snowmobile trail ride for my birthday. Was I ever surprised. We went with a guide who took us up to 12,000 feet, which was above the tree line. Everything was great until we got off the snowmobiles and tried to walk. There isn't much air at 12,000 feet, and you get tired very quickly. We had never done anything like that before, and it was a most memorable experience. The views were wonderful. The Lord just continued to show us His majesty, over and over.

Once Christie and Jimmy got back to Texas, they started having babies (better known as grandchildren). Allie Sauers was born in 2005, Annabel Sauers in 2007, and Amie Sauers in 2009. They are terrific grandchildren. Christie and Jimmy have been wonderful Christian parents, and they make us very proud. They come to visit often, and we get the grandchildren every summer for a couple weeks. We always have a precious time together, yet another gift from God.

The year 2009 was a phenomenal year for us. BMW had a program to send sales managers to the European delivery facility in Munich, Germany. Each manager would take delivery of a car and

We enjoyed seeing some of Europe

drive it around Europe so the manager could tell his customers about European delivery. Joe asked me if we wanted to go. I said yes, immediately. I didn't even have to call Pat. There was a cost savings when taking European delivery, so BMW had agreed to give that money to the dealership. That amount was based on the car that the dealership selected, and came in the form of a credit that could be applied toward an offset of travel expenses. I picked a 750Li BMW that had a credit of almost $6,500. We only spent a few hundred dollars over our $6,500 credit, and we loved every minute of the trip. We took it during Pat's spring break plus a few days of personal leave. The trip was nine days in total. We flew into Munich, did some sightseeing, then took delivery of the new 7 series. We drove to

Baden-Baden and then on to Paris. We dropped the car at Charles De Gaulle Airport and took a cab into Paris, near the Louvre. I can honestly say that the cab ride from the airport to our hotel must have been the most exciting part of the trip. It took place during the evening rush hour, and I have never heard so much horn blowing and shouting in my life. Pat knows French, and said she couldn't repeat most of what our driver said.

We had a fabulous time in Paris. One highlight was lunch in the Eiffel Tower at the Jules Verne Restaurant. The experience was wonderful. I had a customer call me while on vacation from there a month before, checking on his car that was due in when he got back. He told us that we had to go there when we went to Paris, so we did. We rode the Chunnel Train to London, and we attended church services that Sunday, Easter Sunday, at Westminster Abbey. We arrived early, got great seats, and thoroughly enjoyed the service. Pat got to see where many of the famous poets were buried in the wing of Westminster Abbey. We toured the new Globe Theatre and toured London. Except for the opportunity at Needles Eye Ministries, this was the best thing that happened to me during my time at BMW. It was the first and only time BMW has done this. They had set this up just before the economic fall in 2008, and when we got there, virtually nobody was taking delivery of new BMWs. The month of our trip was the month that the Economic Stimulus was being passed in the United States. Since Pat and I had planned our trip so early, we were one of the few people that got to go, the only ones from the entire Crown Organization. BMW cut the program back after the economy fell. Once again the Lord blessed us more than I could have ever imagined.

If the trip to Europe wasn't enough, we were invited in 2009 to attend the fortieth reunion of the Apollo 11 Mission in 2009. It was held in Washington DC, only a hundred miles from Richmond. NASA sent an email to the Apollo 11 flight controllers asking if anyone would like to attend the event. Since most of them still lived in Texas or other parts of the country, not many attended. Pat and I got a special invitation to attend the press conference, sitting right there with the CNN reporters. Jim Lovell, Tom Stafford, Charlie Duke, and several other astronauts were the ones holding the press confer-

ence. While listening to the astronauts tell stories and talk about the future, I leaned over to Pat and said that I had not only helped them with their missions, but I had sold a boat to most of them. Pat said, "That is nothing, I had most of them in my office, trying to get them to help their children straighten

While at the 40ᵗʰ year reunion of Apollo 11, I bumped into Gene Kranz, and we had our own reunion.

out in school". Since most of these astronauts had seventh grade kids while they were flying Apollo missions, Pat was right on. At the time, some astronaut kids were known to be a fairly rowdy bunch.

That night, we were invited to a big dinner at the Smithsonian Air and Space Museum. We had toured the museum during the day, and museum employees said that it would be closing for a big VIP party that evening. By the time we returned in the evening, the entire building had been transformed. Things were moved aside to create an eating area and a large seating area. There was a mock-up of the Lunar Module, which brought back memories. This version of the Lunar Module was a very up-to-date version; we had made a lot of changes from mission to mission by adding vents along with ports for the slosh baffles. The crew was there, along with many non-NASA celebrities. Neil Degrasse Tyson served as the master of ceremonies. The highlight of my evening was when I ran into Gene Kranz and Charlie Duke. I will never forget what Gene said to me. He said, "Hell, you know it is a great party when Nance is here." He made my evening. Gene never gave you a lot of praise to your face because he knew he would expect even more from you later. Gene Kranz and Chris Kraft were the heart and soul of the Apollo program, and it was a pleasure to have known them. John Young was there, but I didn't get to speak to him.

During this time, we were living on the income that we were planning to use when we were both retired and saving the rest through 401k's and teacher retirement plans. If we had stayed in the boat business, I would have never been able to retire. We had come to Virginia with very little in savings, plus I had given half of my retirement to the boat business to try and save it. Needless to say, it was almost unbelievable that we could save 30 percent of our income. The Lord was teaching us the rewards of our faithfulness and teaching us budgeting at the same time. We were now able to enjoy great trips and time with family: things that the boat business had never allowed.

In 2010, we did something that I think surprised both Pat and me. We went to the February Richmond Boat Show, primarily to visit some old friends from the boat business. We found ourselves remembering just how much we loved to boat. Pat and I also loved to fish, plus we loved the area around the Middlesex area of Virginia and the Chesapeake Bay. The boat business was on its knees from the recession, so we were able to get a new 2010 Triton Saltwater boat built

Pat and Bob enjoy boating much more than they ever did when they were in the boat business!

exactly the way we wanted it at a huge discount. At long last, we could enjoy boating without the hassle of the boat business. We discovered that there are "Boatels" here in Virginia where you store your boat on a rack inside a large building. All you have to do is to call ahead, and they will place your boat in the water at the dock by the time you get there. Call it "Boating Made Easy". We both looked forward to Wednesday, my day off, when we would head out to the

Chesapeake Bay. We have boated more now than we had ever done when we were in the boat business. It clearly set the stage for my upcoming retirement in 2013.

The Lord continues to bless our family, and we are so very grateful. I know this sounds like a broken record, but it is true. Just read Malachi 3:10, "Bring the whole tithe into the store house (read, show your faith in the Lord), that there may be food in my house. Test me in this," says the Lord Almighty, "and see if I will not throw open the floodgates of heaven and pour out so much blessing that you will not have room enough for it." This is what the Lord has taught me during my life: If I learn to seek Him first; I let Him direct my life instead of insisting that I direct it; then He will lead me into the Way of Blessing that I could have never created nor envisioned for myself. To God be the Glory, Amen!

12

Miracles Do Happen

During the period of 2005 to 2012, Christie and Jimmy had been growing their family and growing in their faith and service to the Lord. Christie worked on several projects at NASA, but she truly found her element when she was given the task of building the mock up for the new Orion spacecraft. Orion was designed to send man out of earth's orbit and eventually on to Mars. Christie really enjoyed the challenge, and she got to work on the design with everyone from the contractor, Lockheed, to the astronauts. I must say that I enjoyed seeing the progress when we visited Houston over the years. During this time, Jimmy was working for Reliant Energy, a large power company in Texas. Reliant has morphed several times, each time growing bigger and bigger, eventually reaching out into other fields. Jimmy has always been supportive of Christie's work, and he works his hours around both her schedule and the needs of their daughters. There is no way for us to thank the Lord enough for sending Jimmy into our family's lives. Jimmy is our son just as much as Rob is.

After they graduated from Georgia Tech, Jimmy and Christie moved to Houston and began going to a new church in the Clear Creek area, Clear Creek Community Church. Back then, the church was meeting in Clear Creek High School, and now the church has over 7,500 members attending multiple campuses. Many of Clear Creek's members are new Christians who came to faith principally through small groups. People need to find answers as to how to live their daily lives based on scripture, so what better way than to study the Bible and be mentored by others that have gone through similar circumstances.

One thing that Christie has done throughout her NASA career is never to forget how she got to NASA. Christie has mentored co-op students since the time she first got to NASA, and she has had a very

Christie got to make a bunch of zero G flights in the "Vomit Comet" to test space gear for the International Space Station.

positive impact on a lot of young people's lives. When Christie was a co-op, Gene Kranz came to a co-op meeting and talked to them about finding a career at NASA. Christie identified herself as my daughter, and she asked Gene how I could have carried so much responsibility at such a young age. I was twenty-four when we landed on the moon. Gene answered that everyone was young because it was my generation that knew something about computers. Gene said that he was the old man in the room, and although he was relatively young, he didn't know anything at all about these newfangled computers. It is important to remember that when we landed on the moon, hand-held calculators hadn't even been invented. Desktop computers were twenty years away, and the internet was twenty-five to thirty years in the future. As Christie and Jimmy provided mentoring to the co-ops, they could see a need for helping them find a place to live while at NASA. The students would work a semester, go to school a semester, and rotate between the two.

Eventually, Jimmy and Christie moved to the Seabrook area, near NASA, moving into a home with five bedrooms. Daughters Allie and Annabel insisted on sharing a bedroom and Amie had one to herself, which means Jimmy and Christie had several extra bedrooms. A few years ago, they invited one of the co-ops, Sarah, to move in with them while she was on co-op duty. It was a great success. Sarah was a strong Christian, and they all got along great. They had a waiting list of people wanting to stay with them. After a lot of prayer and the economy pushing home prices down, Jimmy and Christie decided to purchase a home for the co-ops where they could stay when they were at NASA. They would call it the *Lighthouse*, and Sarah would be the first manager of the home. They opened the house in the fall, and some of the parents of the students that would move into the house came and helped fix up the house so it would work well for four students. One parent came and installed a door to help with access to a second-floor bath. There was lots of painting, yard work, and things to be done do to make the *Lighthouse* a home for the students. The home even had a nice patio that would be great for entertaining. I am sure that not only did the students feel super blessed, but their parents felt blessed that their children had found such a great Christian environment to live in while on co-op. They only charged between $400 and $500 a month depending on the need. You can't find the smallest apartment in the area for that kind of money. It is a beautiful house, just a few blocks from where Jimmy and Christie live.

The *Lighthouse* holds regular prayer and other small group meetings and is truly a *Lighthouse* to the girls they are helping. As time went on, Jimmy and Christie reached out and helped others who were just starting to work at NASA or for a contractor, or had now become full time once they graduated from college. I am not sure who has been blessed more, the students or Jimmy and Christie. We have met many of the students on several occasions, and they love the *Lighthouse*.

They did have one problem. The male co-ops started asking what about them. The *Lighthouse* was a girl's-only residence, and the guys wanted a place, too. After much praying, Jimmy and Christie decided to purchase a second home, this one for the guys. They instantly had a waiting list, and it has been "pretty much" full ever since it opened. It is located a little further away, but only about a mile, and it is only about three blocks from where astronaut John Young and his wife currently live. They named this house the *Anchor*. The *Anchor* has a garden in the backyard, and some of the students came from a farming background, so they have a nice garden, plus Jimmy and Christie get some free vegetables from the guys. The residents have had work days and have done a full front yard makeover with Jimmy and Christie providing the plants and supplies, and the guys providing some of the labor. What a blessing for everyone! Again, they are charging the guys about $400 to $500 a month, and everyone is happy. Jimmy and Christie are covering their expenses for the most part, and they are providing a Christian environment for these students. They are changing these students' lives. We came to Houston right after I retired and took the grandgirls "trick or treating" (a lot of trick or treating) and then we all met up at the *Lighthouse*. There the guys had come over from the *Anchor*, and together they held a block party for the neighbors of the *Lighthouse*. They were giving away hamburgers and hot dogs with all the fixings. It was great after walking about three miles of "trick or treating." They played games and even had a Corn Hole tournament. It was a wonderful time. Just think about how that impacts our three grandchildren when they see what their parents are doing to help others. Everyone is blessed. I know we are.

The CO-OP students from the "Lighthouse" and "Anchor" host a Halloween block party at the "Lighthouse"

We have another story of blessing that is equally amazing, and it is truly a story of a lifetime. Our son Rob, you remember, was diagnosed with a rare liver disease a couple of years before we left Texas to come back to Virginia. It is an autoimmune disease in which the immune system thinks the liver is bad, so it attacks the liver. There is no cure for it except a liver replacement. Also, there is no guarantee that the disease won't come back, except that drugs can suppress the immune system. When Rob got the disease, he was in the Air Force at the Pentagon. Rob had come to Jimmy and Christie's wedding from Washington, and he looked really pale. We took him to the hospital, and they said he was just recovering from being sick and gave him some medicine. Rob was a groomsman and almost fainted during the wedding. He had to sit down rather than faint. He just wanted to get back to Washington and go to see his doctors there. He was too sick to travel alone, so my parents arranged to go on the same flight as Rob back to Virginia. When they changed planes in Charlotte, North Carolina, he looked so sick that they almost didn't let Rob board the plane. If my parents hadn't been with them, they wouldn't have let him on the plane. He got back to DC and went to the hospital there. They transferred him to Walter Reed, where they had some good specialists to help Rob. They were the ones who realized that Rob probably had primary sclerosing cholangitis (PSC), so they scheduled a biopsy. We went to Walter Reed to visit Rob and meet with his doctors. They said that they were fairly certain Rob had PSC, but they would have to do some more work to confirm that he had PSC. It is a rare disease and generally only shows up in developed countries. It seems that the immune system in undeveloped countries is so busy fighting other diseases that it doesn't have time to worry about PSC. At that time, the only cure was a liver transplant, and those were fairly new at the time. They told us that they would try to delay the full onset of the disease for years. Rob was extremely sick because he suffered from ulcerative colitis (ulcers of the colon) that had caused bleeding of the colon, and that is why Rob was so weak. Almost all cases of PSC start as ulcerative colitis, and if the patient never gets ulcerative colitis, he could live his whole life and never develop PSC. It just depends on how the immune system accepts the scar tissue that is created in the liver from the ulcerative colitis.

Once they treated Rob for the ulcerative colitis, his symptoms disappeared. The doctors explained that he would have recurrences of the ulcerative colitis for the rest of his life, plus the PSC would slowly degrade his liver until he got to the point where his liver was below about 30 percent efficiency, and that is when he would have to have the liver transplant. The idea was to see how long he could put that off so that medicine would have time to address the disease more fully. Rob really enjoyed the Air Force, and he wanted to stay in for as long as possible. Rob was receiving state-of-art training that he couldn't get from school. Rob said that the military in the Pentagon got the very latest equipment and training, while colleges were typically years behind.

Rob had told us stories about the Pentagon being in horrible shape, since it was constructed in only nine months during World War II, and it looked like it. He said that if the EPA ever went into the basement of the Pentagon, they would have a heart attack because of the horrible smell, mold, bad wiring, and unsafe living conditions. The Pentagon was going through a total renovation to fix it, and that was the area in which Rob was working. He would have to supervise work crews because of the top-secret nature of his work. The Air Force was responsible for its portion of the Pentagon, and they first had to remove the old wiring before they could rewire the building. He got to work in several different disciplines, and it was good training. The Air Force wouldn't take responsibility for Rob getting sick from his work and wanted him to take a medical discharge. We helped Rob fight it, but they just didn't want him to get any sicker on their watch. The good news is that he would qualify for good medical care and eventual disability. He didn't want to leave the Air Force, but they forced him out, saying that he was not "worldwide deployable."

Remember that I keep mentioning if you give your situation to the Lord, He will help you in ways that you cannot even imagine. Rob got out of the Air Force in early summer of 2001. When the passenger airliner hit the Pentagon on September 11, 2001, he was desperately trying to get in contact with his friends at the Pentagon. It seems the area that the plane hit was the very area where Rob and his friends had been working. When Rob finally got in contact with his friends, they were all safe, but everyone knew coworkers who had been lost, ones who were still working there. His team was at a meeting that morning in another part of the Pentagon. They were on the way back to that area when the terrorist attack took place. If Rob had been there, the dynamics might have been different. All we know is that Rob wasn't there that morning to see that horrible terrorist attack and he was safe. Praise the Lord!

Rob had loved his time in Austin while he was at the University of Texas, so he felt good when he got out of the Air Force, and quickly got a job with an IT company in Austin. He loved the work and loved Austin. He seemed to be settling into Austin when we told him that we were going to move back to Virginia to help take care of the grandparents and get away from the boat business with all its challenges. He was dismayed, but we told him that we would be there for him, that getting away from the boat business would give me more time to help when the time came if he ever had to get a liver transplant. We told him that we were only hours away by plane. The Lord was at work again even though we wouldn't realize it for years.

His doctors were in Houston since that is where the transplant team was for that area of Texas, and that is where they wanted Rob to go for evaluation. He had good doctors in Austin, but he had to come to Houston every so often for a full evaluation of his current status. I had been reading online about some drugs that had been helping delay PSC, and during one of the visits, I mentioned to Rob's doctors that I had read about a particular medication that was normally used to prevent itching as the liver failed. In higher doses, this was show-ing signs of slowing down PSC. The article came out in December 2002, and we met with the doctors the following month. The doctor said that he had read the article, and he turned to his nurse and asked what dose Rob was taking of that particular medicine. When she said 100 mg, I will never forget what he said. He said, "That is a baby dose; change him to 1500 mg." That was just the first step in years of slowing the PSC and delaying the need for a liver transplant.

When we moved to Richmond in 2003, Rob seemed to be doing well in Austin. He had had several girlfriends, but then he met the one! Christy Wright was attending the University of Austin to get her masters in Social Work. Her mother was a social worker in Wrightsville Beach, North Carolina, and Christy wanted to follow in her footsteps. She and Rob seemed to hit it off right from the start. We could tell from Rob's emails that he was in love, and we felt that he was so blessed to find someone that was willing to overlook possible future health issues and just love Rob for who he was. Now, that is a huge blessing! When we met Christy, we could see she was everything that Rob had said she was. We loved her from the start. We went to Christy's graduation and were thrilled to learn that they were planning to move to the Raleigh area, since there were so many opportunities in social work for Christy to find a job there and lots of IT businesses for Rob to find a job. Before the move, they had a bigger event to plan for—their wedding. It would be held at Wrightsville Beach, North Carolina, which was a lot closer than Texas. We were quick to point out to Rob that the Lord knew, long before any of us, that he would end up in North Carolina and even closer to us than if we were still in Texas.

They got married in March 2005 in Wrightsville Beach, and it was a wonderful wedding. It took place at a marina on the scenic

Jimmy, Christie, Rob, Christy, Pat, & myself at Rob and Christy's wedding. Christie was pregnant with Allie.

Intracoastal Waterway in a beautiful setting. Christie and Jimmy and most of the family attended. My parents got sick at the last moment, and they didn't make it, but Pat's dad did make it. Christie was pregnant with Allie, who would be born at the end of May. When we had made the decision to move to Richmond, leaving Rob in Texas was our biggest concern, and now the Lord had not only taken care of that, but also had given Rob a beautiful bride who would be at his side as future events would unfold. We had come such a long way since leaving Houston. We were about to become grandparents, Rob was looking so much better, and he had just married a wonderful Christian girl who would be there for Rob through thick and thin. As a bonus, the Lord threw in that they would soon move close to us, just because He can. We are so very blessed. Praise the Lord!

Over the next two years, Rob and Christy would secure jobs in the Raleigh area and find a home in Clayton, North Carolina, in a development called Flowers Plantation, southeast of Raleigh. Rob got the job in IT that he was looking for, and Christy found a job working with dialysis patients at a local clinic. Rob obtained good health insurance with his company, which was very important. Rob was able to transfer his medical information to University of North Carolina Medical Center in Chapel Hill. It was an hour from their home, much better than the drive from Austin to Houston, which was about three hours. Doctors were seeing a slow deterioration of his liver, but it still seemed that a transplant would be years away. From time to time, Rob would have a bout of ulcerative colitis, but other than that seemed to be in good health. Rob and Christy did a lot of the things that young married people do while building a life together. There was a lot of yard work and planting to do at their new house. Rob got to experience grass cutting and even built his own "shed" to match their house—to house his riding mower. They have a lovely home, and it is a lot bigger than our first home. That is what everyone wants for their children.

The next few years would see life being as normal as it could be for Rob and Christy. Christy's mom and dad were starting to retire, and Rob and Christy only had a little over two hours either way to visit each set of parents. Rob eventually moved to a better job, following his boss at his previous job. It was good, but Rob's old company, Pack Rat (one of the two main companies that sell storage containers to people for moving and storage), was missing Rob, so they had Rob doing business on the side, since the people they hired were having problems keeping up while the company expanded. Eventually, Pack Rat would sign on to let Rob's new company handle their IT work, and Rob helped with the transfer. They were going national at the time and needed a computer system to handle it, to track a storage container from Raleigh to California, for example. Rob was doing so well health-wise, that he was having trouble getting the Air Force to pay any disability.

About the spring of 2011, things started to deteriorate for Rob. Even though his liver was still well enough that he didn't require a transplant, he developed a condition called pulmonary hypertension. It seems that all the meds that Rob had been taking over the years had an effect on his body's ability to transfer blood from the heart to the lungs. The arteries to the lungs were showing higher pressures than were safe. The condition is generally caused by medication for other conditions, which was exactly what was happening to Rob. The problem was that once the pulmonary hypertension levels get too high, the patient is no longer allowed to get a liver transplant because of the high risk of a heart attack, thus potentially "wasting" a liver that could have gone to someone else.

Rob went to see a specialist, Dr. Ford, who prescribed medicine and consulted with the transplant team to adjust Rob's meds. They wanted to keep Rob well enough to get on the transplant list. Previously, before a point system that was established, several famous people received liver transplants ahead of other patients. The majority of people that suffer liver failure tend to abuse alcohol. Mickey Mantle was one of the people that first got a liver transplant, but he did not survive long. He had a history of alcohol abuse, as did Larry Hagman of *I Dream of Jeannie* and *Dallas'* J.R. Ewing fame. This all happened in the 1995 time frame when liver transplants were very new. Larry obviously did well to go on to star in the TV series *Dallas*. Shortly after Mickey and Larry received their transplants, a system called the MELD score was devised. Now, patients are evaluated based on various factors to determine who gets a liver first. In 2011, Rob had a MELD score in the high teens, and most people were getting a liver if it became available when they had a MELD score around 35.

The doctors had to get the pulmonary hypertension under control without allowing the liver to fail too soon. It was a delicate balance. Rob's MELD score started to rise as the meds were adjusted; they kept experimenting with the medicine for pulmonary hypertension, and Rob was plagued with headaches. We didn't know it at the time, but Rob and Christy were trying to have a baby and were going through in-vitro fertilization. They wanted to try to have a baby before the transplant, because the antirejection drugs after the transplant would probably make Rob sterile. They told Rob that the drugs for the pulmonary hypertension might make him sterile anyway. Rob delayed the meds for a month or two, and it turned out to be a bad decision. In December 2011, Rob became really sick and things went from bad to worse. Rob ended up in the hospital at UNC in Chapel Hill; the MELD score was rising, and the pulmonary hypertension was out of control. He had started taking the medicine the month before, but it was too late. He was in rough shape. Rob was extremely sick.

What happened next was almost worse than the illness. We were on our way to see them, and Christy was with Rob at the hospital when one of the doctors, who was doing his rounds with a group of med students, had stopped outside of Rob's room. He announced to the med students that in this room, there was a patient who didn't take his meds as he should, who would probably be unable to recover from the pulmonary hypertension enough to ever get a liver transplant. The doctor said this loud enough for both Rob and Christy to hear. We got there right after it happened; Christy was crying, and Rob was upset. I was furious! We were able to talk to Rob's transplant team doctor, Dr. Hayashi, and told him what had happened. He was upset, as well. We all agreed that what had happened was a mistake, and we needed to go forward from there, getting Rob well enough to get on a strong regimen to control his pulmonary hypertension and getting him where he could get on the transplant list yet again. The doctor agreed, and it took several weeks to get things somewhat under control for Rob to be well enough to get out of the hospital.

Something happened a few days later that disgusted us all. I hadn't mentioned it, but when we got to the hospital, Rob's complexion was yellow from head to toe because the liver wasn't functioning as it should. He was not just a little yellow but extremely yellow. The week after he got out of the hospital, Rob and Christy were at the drugstore getting some medicine that the doctors had prescribed for him. Suddenly, somebody ran up to Rob and took his picture, saying something to the effect of he had never seen a yellow man before.

I guess it ended up on someone's Facebook page. Some people just have no sense and are just plain crude.

What happened next was that we discovered that the transplant team had set Rob up with an appointment to see Dr. Ford at the very end of February, which was over two months away. Rob needed to get going on his treatment. He left all sorts of messages and was getting nowhere. He needed to see Dr. Ford sooner, so he could get a plan for a more aggressive attack on the pulmonary hypertension. It seems as if they had written Rob off. Thankfully, I had a BMW customer who just happened to be on the liver transplant team at MCV Hospital in Richmond, the premier hospital for liver transplants in Virginia. His name is Dr. Bob Hope, and he had been following Rob's case for years. Both he and his wife had BMWs, and he stopped in, often, always asking me about how Rob was doing. As soon as we heard the news about Rob's inability to see Dr. Ford, I talked to Dr. Hope and filled him in on what was going on. He said that he didn't want to judge another doctor, but it just didn't sound right. He said that he would talk to the head of their liver transplant team and see what he said. The next day, I got a call from Dr. Hope. He said that the head of their team assured him that Rob's transplant team was top-notch, and Rob had a great doctor, but at the same time, he agreed that they needed to get Rob on meds to get the pulmonary hypertension under control and quickly. They agreed to consult and give Rob a second opinion. It was the middle of the week, and an appointment was set for the following Monday. They said that Rob would have to call both Dr. Ford and Rob's transplant doctor and have them release their records to the MCV team.

I think we all wanted the same thing, and that is exactly what happened. Within twenty-four hours, Rob had an appointment with Dr. Ford for that week, and his transplant doctor asked that they reevaluate Rob's condition before getting a second opinion. The good news is that the MCV team had reassured us that Rob's team was very good and just needed a push to get them going. We were finally making some progress.

Now, all this time we were praying for Rob's tests to be good, and for him to get well enough so that he didn't need a transplant at that time. We were good at *giving the Lord instructions* on just how He needed to help Rob. Even though we knew better, when it is your child, you try too hard sometimes.

It was sometime in February of 2012 that we finally realized we had been making a mistake trying to tell God how to help Rob. I think it was a Sunday school lesson that Pat and I were teaching at Southside Baptist Church that helped us realize we needed to turn Rob over to the Lord and stop trying to tell the Lord what we wanted Him to do. We remembered how things had turned out when we were in Houston and decided to give our situation to the Lord. He had guided and directed us to move to Richmond and things had worked out way better than we could have imagined. We encouraged Rob and Christy to do the same thing. We reminded them how everyone thought we were crazy to leave Texas, and yet the Lord had worked this out for us. Why wouldn't we trust Him with Rob's life?

At the same time, we were encouraging Rob and Christy that they needed a church home. They needed a support system in place, and they needed the Lord to get through these tough times. Dr. Ford prescribed some medicine that seemed to be working. Rob was starting to get his pulmonary hypertension under control, but it still was not good enough to get approved for the transplant. Still, things were starting to move in the right direction. Rob was having some side effects from the meds but was able to work for the most part. He had a lot of doctors' visits and had to go to UNC a lot because that was where the transplant team was located.

Month after month, we were continuing to see improvement in Rob's numbers, and we continued to pray to the Lord. We were giving Rob's situation to Him, and we had faith that the Lord would do what was best. Finally, about the end of June, Rob's pulmonary hypertension was under control enough to put him on the transplant list. Rob was still yellow in color due to the failing liver, but he looked a lot better than he had while in the hospital. There had to be a review by a special panel to determine what Rob's MELD score should be based on the pulmonary hypertension. At the same time, Rob and Christy told us that they had found a church and were really being helped by the church family. Rob had decided to be baptized again, since he felt that he didn't totally understand what it was all about when he was baptized as a boy. I can't describe how we as parents felt after that phone call. We were elated as we realized that our prayers were being answered.

By August, we had gone to Raleigh and seen Rob baptized. Rob's new church family was awesome. They were so nice to us and our visit there was a truly wonderful experience. Rob carried a beeper around with him because he was on the transplant list. Not only was Rob on the transplant list, his MELD score was very high because the evaluation team gave Rob about ten extra points on account of his pulmonary hypertension. The team knew that if his pulmonary hypertension numbers dropped, he would probably never be able to get a transplant. Rob had a MELD score of about 37 by then, which meant he was above the average score for people who got transplants. He was feeling better and was looking good. When Rob met with the transplant team in September, they told him that based on average wait times (though there is nothing normal about all this), he could expect a liver to become available in about ninety days. They told him that he was at the very top of the list for that area of the country. We continued to pray for the Lord's will to be done. We were starting to see just how the Lord was working things out. Thank goodness He didn't listen to us. The pulmonary hypertension was actually going to be the thing that put Rob *on the top* of the list.

Roll forward to Monday, October 8. I was driving to work and Pat was at home, since she had retired from teaching in 2010. I quite often pray when I am driving—with my eyes open. This time is good "alone" time with the Lord. I can tell you exactly where I was on Midlothian Turnpike, just about to pass the McDonalds at the Arboretum, praying to the Lord about blessing various people that I know needed prayers, when suddenly the Lord spoke to me midsentence in my prayer. I wasn't even praying about Rob yet, but just like before, it came as download. Not only did I hear the words as though I was remembering something that had already been said, but I totally knew what it meant. The Holy Spirit said, "Today is the day" and I asked, "What?" and the Holy Spirit said again, "Today is the day." Luckily, I didn't slam on my brakes. I knew exactly what He meant but couldn't believe that the Creator of the Universe had just spoken to me through the Holy Spirit. The Lord's words came with understanding, and I didn't know if I was going crazy or should jump for joy. I was tingling all over. I gathered myself, finished my prayer, and thanked the Lord for sharing such good news with me. What I started wondering was why the Lord had chosen to share this with me. I must say that I was both confused and happy at the same time. I remember the exact time and place when this happened. It was 8:50 a.m., and I was about three miles from work.

The managers went into a meeting every morning with Joe, the general manager. I was sitting across from Joe, with Troy, the back-up finance manager, and Austin, the used car manager, at the end of the desk. We were reviewing what had happened over the weekend, and we were deciding which cars should be delivered that day. Austin was talking when I got a phone call from Pat. I normally wouldn't take her call during the meeting, but I was thinking that it might be related to Rob. I told Joe that I needed to take it, since Pat almost never called me at work and it might be important. Pat said that Christy had called to say she was on her way home to pick up Rob. He was on the way to work when he got a call that a liver was available and he should get to UNC Hospital ASAP. Rob was getting his things ready, and Christy was going to take him to the hospital. I told Pat I would meet her at the house in about thirty minutes, and together we would go to UNC Chapel Hill. The guys' eyes were big, since they knew of Rob's condition and realized this it sounded like good news.

What happened next, as I hung up, must have really surprised them. I exhaled and remembered sinking about a foot down in my seat. I said that the Lord had told me on the way in to work that today was the day, and I didn't know if I was more excited about Rob or the fact that the Lord had chosen to tell me about it in advance. I made a beeline for home, and we were off to UNC Chapel Hill.

The whole way down Pat was reminding me that we had been told there had to be a match of blood type, but I answered that they wouldn't have called Rob if there wasn't a match. She reminded me that they said that on average, you had to go in about three times before you actually got a liver because everything had to be perfect. She reminded me that three people would be called in, and the one who got the liver was determined by different factors. Pat reminded me that the doctor said Rob's pulmonary hypertension numbers had to be within limits on that day in order for him to get the liver. Each time I would tell her that Rob was going to get his liver transplant that day. At the time, I didn't tell her that I had "inside information". I started realizing that one of the reasons the Lord chose to tell me was to let me help Pat to not be so anxious. I can't remember the number of times during that trip that I said a silent prayer thanking the Lord for being so faithful. I knew that the Lord was in control and that His will would be done. I can't tell you how much I was at peace. I was to be the rock that day.

When we got to the hospital, Rob was already in a room and people were buzzing around everywhere. We learned that the donor had been killed in a car accident that morning, and the team that was on the way to harvest the organs just happened to be Rob's liver transplant team. We didn't know until that day that the various transplant teams take turns going to harvest the organs from the donor, at the hospital where the victim was when they died. They told us that the organs were coming from a seventeen-year-old who had died in a car accident; it would take the doctors about an hour to get to the hospital; about two hours to harvest the organs, and then another hour to return. They told us that two other patients were called in for the possible liver, but Rob was first on the list if his numbers checked out. Rob was about to go through a battery of tests to see if he could meet the criteria, and if he couldn't, the next person who was going through all the same tests would move up. If they passed their tests, they would get the liver, and so on to the third patient.

Pat and Christy were nervous, but I told them that things would be fine. I reminded them that Rob had been tested just a week before. Of course, I had a better reason to know that everything was going to be fine. Still, the wait for the tests and results seemed interminable. They finished the tests around three thirty that afternoon, and then there was more waiting. The key was the pulmonary hypertension number as it indicated the efficiency of the blood from Rob's heart to his lungs. A lot of people were coming and going, but there was one nurse who was obviously the coordinator of all that was going on. She told us that the tests were good and even though the pulmonary hypertension number was close, it was within limits. She told us that Rob's transplant team was still on its way back from the harvesting of the organs from the donor. It hit us just then how the parents of the donor must be struggling, and we asked if we could get any information on the donor. The coordinating nurse told us that this information would always be kept private. She told us that after about six months, Rob could send a letter through their office to the donor's family. Of course, as soon as she left the room, a quick search on my iPhone showed that a high school student had been killed in a car crash on the way to school that morning about an hour away from the hospital. Our prayers were out for the family of the victim, and we realized how much suffering they were going through at that time.

Once the liver transplant doctor got to the hospital and got things in motion, he came in and told Rob it just so happened that it was his team's day to harvest the organs. He said that the liver was in perfect shape and Rob had passed all the tests. The doctor said that they were making arrangements for both the operating room and the staff to perform the transplant. He told us that there would be quite a few other transplants going on from the same donor, so the hospital was going to be very busy. We were relieved, and all Rob could say was, "Let's get on with it!" The doctor had said that the liver transplant would be the longest of all the transplants because the liver transplant required connecting so many blood vessels. He said it would take about nine to ten hours, and not to worry. He said that the next time he would see us would be after the operation, likely early the next morning. He told us that the coordination nurse would show us where to go to wait, and that we should try and get some sleep. He said that he would wake us up if we were asleep. Pat and Christy said, "Don't worry, we will be awake." I told the doctor that I would be the one who was awake, and I would wake them as soon as he found us. It had been a long day so far, but it was to be an even longer evening.

The coordinating nurse came back in right after the doctor left, and she told us that there would be about an hour of prep before Rob left his room for the operating room. When that time came, she would have someone take us to the special waiting room for family members of transplant patients, where there would be refreshments and lounge chairs for resting. There was a lot of activity and lots and lots of IVs and monitors hooked up on Rob. You got the sense that "this is really getting ready to happen." We couldn't help but feel that this had been a twelve-year journey, and it was surreal that the transplant day had arrived. What a journey it had been! When the time came to take Rob into the surgery, we all stopped and said prayers with Rob, thanking the Lord for bringing Rob this far and giving all the praise to the Lord. We asked the Lord to bless the doctors, and we also prayed for the donor and their family. Rob's pastor and some of the church members had come by and prayed with Rob, as well.

Right after Rob was wheeled out, the coordinating nurse came back in and said that Rob was actually in the best shape of anybody that she had seen get a liver transplant. She said that the increased MELD score for the pulmonary hypertension is what advanced him so quickly. It was at that moment that it really hit us just how the Lord had taken Rob on a journey that would allow this day to happen. We had once prayed for the transplant to be delayed as long as possible. Then Rob got sick, and the whole episode in the hospital ended up with Rob receiving more aggressive treatment for his pulmonary hypertension. We realized that the Lord knew what to do without instructions from us. When we gave Rob's situation to the Lord, amazing things happened: Rob grew closer than ever to the Lord, he got baptized for the second time, he found a great new church family, and the transplant board gave him a huge bump in MELD score because of his pulmonary hypertension. In addition, Rob's health had improved, he got the call five weeks after receiving the higher MELD score that a liver might be available, the donor was a healthy person (not a small thing since sometimes the donor can be an older person that might not be too healthy), the Lord told me that "today is the day", the transplant team just happened to be the team that harvested the organs, Rob passed all the tests to make him number one for the transplant, and then the nurse told us that Rob was the healthiest patient that she had ever seen get a liver. Whew! We discussed all that the Lord had done in Rob's life and acknowledged how truly blessed we were. We prayed again, adding just how grateful we were that the Lord had sent Christy to our family to be there for Rob. Christy is just as much our daughter as our daughter Christie. In case you didn't notice it, Christ is in both of their names!

Then the long wait began. Christy got to see Rob one last time just outside of the operating room, and then we settled into the special waiting room. We tried to keep the family informed, but in Rob's original room, cell phones didn't work. Now that we were in the family waiting room, we didn't want to leave for more than a moment, because we were waiting for any news. The nurse told me where to go for cell phone coverage, and I passed on to the family all that had taken place. We asked them to not only pray for Rob, but also for the family of the donor.

What we didn't realize until then was that there were groups of families in the waiting room, waiting for news of their loved ones who were getting transplants. Over the next couple of hours, we would come to realize that not only were we being blessed through that young organ donor, each of the other families were sharing our same experience. Two were in for kidney transplants, one for a heart, and several others, but we never could hear what type of transplant they were getting. As each doctor came in to tell about their loved one's transplant, we realized that they were from the same donor. One by one, each family received the news, then left to go home and get some sleep. They would come back the following morning to be there when their loved one woke up. At one point, there had been about twenty family members in the large waiting room. We learned that most of the transplants only took about five hours; most of the doctors came out before midnight. One family seemed to be waiting a lot longer than the others. From overhearing their discussions, their family member was getting a kidney transplant. Finally, about 1:00 a.m., the doctor came out and told them that the kidney transplant had taken place, but there had been some complications. The operation took a lot longer than normal, and they were still monitoring the patient. The doctor said that there had been a lot of bleeding, and they might have to go back in if it didn't stop. It reminded me that getting a transplant didn't necessarily mean that everything would automatically turn out fine.

Pat and Christy had stayed awake until then, but I told them that they needed some rest and should try and get a little. Christy lounged back in one of the chairs and said that she would try to get a little sleep but to wake her if anything happened. Pat wouldn't get in one of the lounge chairs because she and I both knew that if she did that, she would be out like a light. Instead, she fell asleep sitting up in her chair. I propped her head up with a pillow, and she got a little sleep. Pat and Christy kept waking up every time anybody moved just a little bit. Since I can "power nap," I did manage a little rest.

About 3:15 a.m., I was seated facing the door with Pat and Christy resting to my left when I spotted the doctor. I had expected to see a nurse first, but there aren't a whole lot of staff at that time of the morning. We made eye contact, I tapped Pat on the shoulder, and I remember wiggling Christy's toe and saying the doctor had come. I walked to him, and before I could say anything, he said that the transplant had gone well. He said that Rob's liver was in worse shape than he had thought, but the new liver was in place and successfully transplanted. He said that it would be several days before we knew if it was going to function properly, but there was no reason to believe that it wouldn't. He told us to go and get some rest, that Rob was in good hands, and that they would keep him medicated for a day or two to allow his body to start recovering from the surgery. What a relief. Praise the Lord!

I had made reservations the previous evening at the nearby Marriott Courtyard Hotel for Christy and Pat and me, so we headed to check in. I didn't suspect that they have many people check in at 4:00 a.m., and I can honestly say that I don't remember hitting the bed. Once the alarm clock was set, I remember collapsing on the bed, and I think I fell asleep about halfway down. It wasn't that we were that sleepy, rather, it was the overwhelming sense of relief that overtook us.

We had packed our bags quickly before we left Richmond, but Christy wanted to get Rob to the hospital ASAP and didn't have time to pack a bag. We suggested that she go home the next morning before coming to the hospital. We told her that we could go directly to the hospital and report to her by cell phone once we learned anything. We got to the hospital at about 10:30 a.m. the following morning. Rob was in a special transplant ICU unit, and we had very limited access to him. They told us that Rob was still sedated and would probably be medicated for the rest of the day, but everything was going well. They let us see him for a few moments. He had tubes and monitors running everywhere. He had twice as many things hooked up to him than when we had last seen him, and we only thought back then that he had a lot hooked up to him! The staff seemed to really know what they were doing, so we felt good. We got a lesson from one of the nurses about how important it would be to put on the booties and gowns before we visited Rob. Germs are the enemy of any transplant recipient, since the patient is given very strong immune system degraders to prevent rejection. We called Christy and told her to take her time and not to rush. We were holding down the fort, and if anything came up, we would call. We had sent texts to everyone but my parents the previous night. My parents don't text, so we called them and told them about Rob's condition. We texted everyone else and sent a picture of Rob that I took from outside of his room.

The next few days were marked by concern over organs starting to work again and waiting for the liver to start working. After about three or four days, everything started working including the liver. Once the liver started working, it just kept working better and better. It had a lot of work to do. Rob had turned yellowish again, and every day that the new liver worked, Rob's color improved. It was amazing to behold. More blessings. My parents came down the next Sunday, and we were all able to visit Rob in his room. We would visit Rob in shifts. The transplant team just didn't want too many people in his room at once.

What I remember the most from that time was sitting on the side of the bed with Rob on the first day that he could sit up and telling him that the Lord had blessed him by giving him a testimony—one that very few people could ever have. Rob could use his experience to help encourage others to be faithful and give their problems to the Lord. Rob could help others know that the Lord would get them through their problems in ways they could never imagine. I remember telling Rob that if we wrote a book about the process that led to his getting a transplant and gave it to an editor, they would reject it as totally unbelievable. That is the strength of our Lord. He can do the impossible. All we have to do is give our problems to Him and have patience.

Rob had an amazing recovery. His doctors told him that he might be able to go back to work in about six months. Within two months, Rob was doing work from home, and he met the family in southern Virginia over Christmas so that everyone could see him. The attached picture was taken on the day after Christmas, and it shows just how great Rob looked. The liver was functioning perfectly and his yellow color had totally disappeared. Another surprise was that his pulmonary hypertension was going away, since it had been caused by the drugs they had been giving Rob to delay the transplant. I can't tell you just how blessed we were that Christmas. Rob went to work forty hours a week the first of January, one week shy of three months after his transplant. He was going to doctor check-ups about twice a month, and by February his appointments were changed to once a month. His doctors were amazed at Rob's recovery.

Pat, Christie, my Dad, my Mom, Annabel, Allie, Jimmy, Amie, Christy, and Rob - 6 weeks after the transplant when they came to Virginia.

I don't want to give the impression that everything was easy during Rob's recovery. The doctors had to do some adjusting of Rob's post-transplant meds, mainly because Rob continued to do *better* than they had anticipated. Some of the meds did give Rob headaches and other side effects, but as the doses were reduced, Rob felt better and better. Rob will have to take medication for the rest of his life, but now is taking only a third of what he was taking at first. The new liver has not given Rob any issues. He has to be very careful with his immune system, which has been suppressed to help prevent rejection, but that is a small price to pay for the ability to work sixty to seventy hours a week, do yard work, and even do some boating and fishing with us.

There is no doubting it—Rob's story is a story of biblical proportions! Think about all the things that had to happen to get Rob his transplant. This is an amazing story, and one that only the Lord could make happen. It is a story that has to be told just as the Lord commanded us. It is a story of faith and love.

13

Sharing Is What It Is All About

The Lord keeps blessing our family. In 2012, we joined Bon Air Baptist Church because of their emphasis on missions and small groups. We realized that with all the blessings the Lord was giving us, we needed to serve Him in new and different ways. Bon Air is a much larger church than Southside Baptist and offers a lot of outreach opportunities that we felt we needed. We found a great adult Bible study class, and I am now one of the teachers in that class. We have been active on many fronts. I became a deacon and am now the chairman of the deacons. The deacons have started a ministry called Serve like Jesus that is where the deacons join with laity to serve members in our church family in need. Pat has become even more active than she was while serving as director of Women's Ministry at Southside Baptist. Pat has become a team leader in member mobilization to help new members and new Christians get "plugged in". I am sure that the Lord knew we needed to grow more in our walk with Him if we were going to be able to properly serve Him. We have been in several small groups, and it was during one of those small groups that I realized that if I was to serve the Lord, I needed to write this book in hopes that others might be helped in their walk with the Lord. The Lord used Betty Tibbs to give me the final push. Pat had been trying to get me to write this ever since Rob got his transplant. It is amazing how the Lord uses others to help us on our walk with Him. We have done things that we would have never thought that we would do—we call it "stepping out of our comfort zone", and we have been blessed by it. We have travelled with church friends, hosted small groups in our home, and held events in our home for church members, all the while sharing our testimony with others.

We continued to be blessed by family and our church. Pat and I have been able to travel and learn more about the beautiful country that the Lord has given us to enjoy.

In the fall of 2013, soon after I retired, we took a trip through New England to experience the beauty of the trees changing color for fall. As we drove through Vermont, our eyes were captivated by the brilliant reds and yellows of autumn. It was amazing to see all the beauty that the Lord had made for us to enjoy. It makes no sense for trees to turn into all these beautiful colors. There is seemingly no advantage to the trees to produce beautiful leaves. They exist to show God's glory, and He clearly put them here for us to enjoy. Because we spend so much time thinking about material things, we can miss all the divinely created beauty that surrounds us.

I have enjoyed being an amateur astronomer since retirement. The Lord clearly didn't limit beauty to our planet; it is revealed throughout the cosmos. We seem to be discovering more and more beauty all over the universe thanks to all the new telescopes that are now in space. There is nothing more exciting than looking through a telescope to experience the Lord's hand in the Universe. Using advanced processing techniques and stacking that wasn't available a decade ago, I can make pictures of planets that are as good as any earth

Photos I have taken and processed using my telescope showing Saturn, Orion Nebula, Jupiter, and the Moon.

bound-telescope preceding the Hubble Space Telescope. To me, that is very exciting. The more I study the heavens, the easier it is to see that God has a plan for us as well. Every time we think we have everything figured out, we realize that we don't have a clue. Just a few years ago, everyone "knew" that we came from "The Big Bang" and the universe was expanding. Now we "know" that we can only see 5 percent of what is out there, the universe isn't expanding anything like what we thought, and there is both dark matter and dark energy that we don't know anything about. I am so glad that our God has a sense of humor. He is in control, and we just need to keep our eyes open and take in all that He has put before us.

Pat and I also spent three weeks out west touring nine states, and once again we were in awe of all the beauty that the Lord has given us to enjoy. How could anyone ever consider that all this came from a bunch of rocks bumping together, and that for some strange reason this collision created all the beauty that our world holds for us? It is clearly the work of our Lord.

In 2014, our small group of church members made a trip to Nags Head, which is a quaint little beach town in North Carolina, and we enjoyed some of the best Bible study and prayer times that I have ever experienced in my life. One of the couples in our group had been missionaries, and they brought a totally new perspective into our walk with the Lord. Their names are Paul and Sally Cline. I had mentioned before that ever since my days with the Regal Boat people, we have given thanks for meals even when we are out in public at a restaurant. Paul Cline taught us to tell the waiter or waitress that we are Christians, that we are about to give thanks for our food, and then to ask if the waiter or waitress would mind if we prayed for them. If they said yes,

Our small group on our trip to Nags Head – Phil and Betty Tibbs, Paul and Sally Cline, Mac and Cindy Canada, and Pat and I.

we would ask if there is anything that they would like us to pray for. I can't begin to explain how it blessed us to have waiters and waitresses ask us to pray for them. Some were extremely open, sharing issues that they needed help for. We had one young girl say that she was good and didn't need to be prayed for, but about ten seconds later, she came back and said that she did have a need. We asked if she would mind us asking about her need. She said that her boyfriend, who had moved to Atlanta, was wanting her to quit her job in Nags Head and go live with him. She stayed while we prayed, and we included her in our prayers. Afterward, she asked what we thought she should do. We told her to tell her boyfriend that if he was ready to get married, she was ready to come to Atlanta. She seemed to like that solution. I still pray for her. As a Christian, the Lord wants us to pray for all people who have needs.

The Lord has continued to bless us in ways we would have not ever imagined. I can't fathom what our life would have been like had we not submitted our situation to the Lord back in Texas, when the Lord told us to move back to Virginia. As human beings, we try to fix things ourselves. It is only once we have totally messed things up that we realize we need to turn to the Lord. Imagine how much easier it would be if we turn to the Lord *first*, instead of when we are mired in trouble.

When we do finally turn to the Lord, we tend to tell the Lord how to help us. We are saying that the Creator of the Universe needs instructions from us. What I have learned is that the Lord will allow our problems to pile up until we realize that we need Him. Once we reach that point, the Lord wants us to turn our problems over to Him. Remember that I would pray to the Lord to help the boat business—I was thinking the Lord just needed to send some more customers. Looking back, that sounds so misguided. The Lord wants us to realize that we need Him, and then turn Him loose without instructions from us.

Once we turn our problems over to the Lord, He starts getting us on the right path. He is always ready to turn back the clock if we regress. He wants us to witness to others so they don't have to go through the same heartaches that we have gone through. The Lord has a lot of lives to choreograph. Think of the story about Don Piper. For twenty years, I didn't even realize what the Lord had done for me to be able to witness to others about Don Piper's story. This means that the Lord plans years, decades, even centuries in advance. Maybe we have trouble just in planning from one hour to the next! The Lord blessed me with being part of Don's story in order to help others. One of the things I have realized over time is that the person doing the witnessing is generally more blessed than the person receiving the witness. The whole story of how we got our home in Richmond and meeting the Needles Eye group for the opportunity to witness to others was a huge blessing.

The Lord has taught me that things happening in my life might not be "about me" at all. Maybe the Lord feels that you are so ready to witness for Him, that He will insert a difficulty into your life. This is not to punish you, but rather, to give you the opportunity to witness to someone else. Those who you witness to need to see the strength of your faith so that you can help them in their walk with the Lord. Over the years, I have been able to witness to others in many ways using the talents that the Lord gave me. I presented a study that I did entitled "How Great Is our God," where I showed the magnificence of the universe: its galaxies, stars, and planets in all their beauty, put into place for us to discover. I have had the opportunity to share this story with many groups, and it spurred my interest in astronomy. The Lord knows how much I love to discover mysteries that He has created for us. Too many people miss the beauty that the Lord puts right in front of them. Try just sitting out in a park, looking at a tree and the small animals going about their business. The simplest things that God has given us are the most enchanting. Think of flowers, snow, ocean waves, and green grass. There is nothing like them in the universe. The Lord blesses us each day, and most of the time, we totally miss it.

With the Lord's blessing comes responsibility. The Lord wants us to share our testimony with others. Christ will come again when everyone has had the opportunity to learn about Him. We are not responsible to convert others, but we *are* responsible to share our faith and testimony. The Holy Spirit will do the rest. Being a Christian isn't about going to church at a particular time. It is about prayer, studying the Word, and sharing our testimony. It is a lifetime assignment. Tithing is about faith, it isn't about money. The Lord wants us to cultivate a daily relationship with Him, not just a once-a-week relationship. The way we live our lives is a testimony to the Lord, and it can be either a positive or a negative testimony. If we choose not to follow the Lord, we give Satan room to enter our lives and then control our lives.

A Christian can't go to church on Sunday and live a different life the rest of the week. How do you think that will go when the Book of Life is opened? Even if you live a righteous life the rest of the week, are you doing what the Lord wants you to do if you don't share your blessings with someone else? Your testimony is the most important thing that you own.

I would like to review what I have learned during my time here on this earth and in my walk with the Lord. I am clearly a work in progress. I think my biggest failure is pride. It is the reason that it took me so long to turn my life over to the Lord. Below are twelve things I have learned in my life travels. Sharing them with you, the reader, is my blessing to you.

1. Trust in the Lord with all your heart and all your soul and you will be blessed more than you can imagine.

2. God created us to have a loving relationship with Him, the Creator of the Universe.

3. The Lord wants us to trust Him and give our problems to Him without instructions from us.

4. We cannot overcome Satan without help from our Lord. Satan is of this world and won't be defeated until Jesus comes again.

5. God does not punish us for our sins. Our punishment will be that we will be absent from our Lord for eternity if we don't accept Him and ask forgiveness for our sins. When Jesus died on the Cross, he took on our sins: past sins, current sins, and future sins.

6. We must be patient. The Lord is the all-powerful and all-knowing Creator of the Universe. He has a lot of lives to blend together so that His will is done. He is always faithful to us, just not always on our time table.

7. When bad things happen, we wonder where God is. We always assume that when something bad happens, it is all about us. The Lord may just have enough faith in us to believe that we can be a good witness to someone else that needs to see our faith in times of difficulty. When bad things happen, ask yourself: how can I show my faith so that someone can be helped by this situation? If you find yourself in the hospital, wondering why this is happening to you, it might not be about you at all. Maybe a nurse or doctor had been praying for help in their life and the Lord has sent you to be their angel. If you only focus on yourself, you just might miss the opportunity to help someone else.

8. God created this beautiful universe for us to enjoy. I love the way scientists keep saying they have the universe figured out, only to find out that they don't have a clue. I think God planned it that way, from the farthest star to the smallest particle. We should revel every day in things that God created for us to enjoy. The beauty of fall and the wonder of spring didn't just happen from a couple of rocks hitting together.

9. There is nothing more important in your life than your relationship with the Lord. The Lord loves to hear from us often. It is called prayer. We can pray anywhere, anytime. We have a direct hotline to our Lord.

10. He wants us in His Word—the *Bible*—often. It is our handbook for life.

11. The Lord wants us to share His love with everyone we come in contact with a simple "God bless you" at the checkout counter, giving thanks for our meal in a restaurant, a meal for a person who's down but not out, showing the Lord that we have faith in Him by tithing when we

don't have the money, and showing how important it is to share His message by sharing our testimony so that others will come to know Him. We are not responsible for leading a person to Christ—we just need to help move the bar a little and then let the Holy Spirit do the rest.

12. God sent His one and only Son to take the form of a man and die on the cross so that we could have eternal life in heaven with the Father. It is the most wonderful gift there has ever been—all we must do is to accept it.

May you take these words to heart and experience your own joy-filled journey, with the Lord at the helm of your life. He will never lead you astray, but instead, will guide you into a future that will fulfill you beyond your wildest imagination.

ABOUT THE AUTHOR

Robert Nance

Bob Nance helped land Neil Armstrong and Buzz Aldrin on the moon and helped get the Apollo 13 astronauts safely back to earth. Thanks to his work on getting the Apollo 13 astronauts back, Bob received the Presidential Medal of Freedom as part of the Apollo 13 Mission Operations Team. Bob entered the business world after his NASA days and ran a pleasure boat business that served as the largest dealer for several boat lines. As a "fun" job during the last ten years before retirement, Bob served as Sales Manager for a BMW dealership in Richmond, Virginia.

Bob has had many obstacles in his life from not seeing a plan on how to get to NASA, from major business ups and downs, to those involving his son needing a liver transplant when he was so sick he couldn't get on the transplant list.

A church small group encouraged Bob to share how the Lord has achieved miraculous things in his life. Bob was led to share his failures and how no matter how many times the Lord blessed him, he was slow to give his difficulties to the Lord. Today, Bob shares his love of the Lord through writing and serving the Lord at his church in Richmond, Virginia.

CPSIA information can be obtained
at www.ICGtesting.com
Printed in the USA
LVHW110529101219
640002LV00004B/531/P